SUCCESS STRATEGIES FOR INVESTMENT REAL ESTATE

Second Edition

SUCCESS STRATEGIES FOR INVESTMENT REAL ESTATE

The Professional's Guide to Better Service and Increased Commissions

by

Jerry D. Anderson, CCIM

PRENTICE HALL CCIM

PRENTICE-HALL, INC., Englewood Cliffs, New Jersey 07632

COMMERCIAL-INVESTMENT REAL ESTATE COUNCIL™
of the REALTORS NATIONAL MARKETING INSTITUTE®
of the NATIONAL ASSOCIATION OF REALTORS®
Chicago, Illinois

Library of Congress Catalog Card Number: 82-061402

 This 1987 edition published by PRENTICE-HALL, Inc., A Division of Simon & Schuster, Englewood Cliffs, New Jersey 07632

Printed in the United States of America

10 9 8 7 6 5 4 3 2 1

ISBN 0-13-859257-8 001

Prentice-Hall International (UK) Limited, *London*
Prentice-Hall of Australia Pty. Limited, *Sydney*
Prentice-Hall Canada Inc., *Toronto*
Prentice-Hall Hispanoamericana, S.A., *Mexico*
Prentice-Hall of India Private Limited, *New Delhi*
Prentice-Hall of Japan, Inc., *Tokyo*
Prentice-Hall of Southeast Asia Pte. Ltd., *Singapore*
Editora Prentice-Hall do Brasil, Ltda., *Rio de Janeiro*

PREFACE

This text is for those who are bored with the algebraic formulas detailed in investment and finance textbooks and yet still want more than *"118 ways to get rich overnight without risking any of your own cash."*

Although *Success Strategies* will address the problems, frustrations and obstructions faced by the investment professional in today's real estate market, the concepts and strategies exposed here can be applied by anyone who spends or intends to spend their precious working hours selling or investing in assets of the investment marketplace.

When I started selling commercial-investment real estate, I searched for books, courses and companies to assist me in my training. I quickly realized there were only two roads available. The Commercial-Investment Courses of REALTORS NATIONAL MARKETING INSTITUTE trained me to calculate IRR, FMRR and show my clients an effective detailed cash flow analysis. The local book store told me how to turn a *Few Dollars Into Thousands* and *Wake Up a Little Financial Genius Inside My Head*, but nowhere could I find a text or a company to give me both the technical background and the practical knowledge I needed to get started in the investment real estate field. I was plenty motivated, yes—knowledgeable, no.

This book is intended to fill this gap for both the student intending to enter the investment marketplace and the seasoned professional with investment knowledge and sales skills who would like to "pull it all together." Practical applications will be stressed in addition to the conceptual understanding of a detailed after tax analysis which must be grasped in order to relate to the sophisticated investment community so active in today's marketplace.

In this book, I can offer you practical education and plead for professionalism, but ultimately you will need more than that in your arsenal of selling skills. The following modern parable by James Cahill says it best:

THE SALESMAN

> And in those days, behold there came through the gates of the city a salesman from afar off, and it came to pass as the day went by he sold plenty.
>
> And in that city were they that were the order takers and they

spent their days in adding to the alibi sheets. Mightily were they astonished. They said one to the other, "What the hell; how doth he getteth away with it?" And it came to pass that many were gathered in the back office and a soothsayer came among them. And he was one wise guy. And they spoke and questioned him, saying, "How is it that this stranger accomplished the impossible?"

Whereupon the soothsayer made answer: "He of whom you speak is one hustler. He ariseth very early in the morning and goeth forth full of pep. He complaineth not, neither doth he know despair. He is arrayed in purple and fine linen, while ye go forth with pants unpressed.

While ye gather here and say one to the other, 'Verily this is a terrible day to work,' he is already abroad. And when the eleventh hour cometh, he needeth no alibis. He knoweth his line and they that would stave him off, they give him orders. Men say unto him, 'nay' when he cometh in, yet when he goeth forth he hath their names on the line that is dotted.

He taketh with him the two angels, 'inspiration' and 'perspiration', and worketh to beat hell.

Verily I say unto you, go and do likewise."

Confidence

Found on the back of an envelope after the death in a plane crash of former Atomic Energy Commission Chairman Gordon Dean:

> "The greatest builder of confidence is the ability to do something—almost anything—well. When that confidence comes, strive for humility; you aren't as good as all that."

Note

The examples in this book reflect recent changes in tax and depreciation regulations. However, some interest rates, rental terms, mortgage terms and other numbers may not be compatible with lending policies or market conditions in all parts of the country at all times during the life of this book. Such deviations should not distract the reader from the principles involved nor diminish the value of the processes used in the examples.

ACKNOWLEDGMENTS

This book is the result of years of experience in the real estate business. The knowledge and experiences expressed are the culmination of my frustrations and successes thus far in my career. My thanks go out to all the professionals in the business who have helped me through the times when my patience and ideas ran thin.

I offer my special thanks to my wife Jody and son Jeffrey who encouraged me to start the book and provided support and understanding throughout the publishing process.

Acknowledgments are in order for Lou Thomas, the president of Coldwell-Banker/T. K. Harris, who relieved me of my office management responsibilities so that I could write *Success Strategies for Investment Real Estate*. Robert Conner and Galen Oakes permitted their properties to be used in the section on packaging property.

The review team of William Fitzpatrick, Sandy Petersen, Kay McIntyre and Jay Levine provided expertise and suggestions throughout the writing of this book.

Eleanor Sciacca must be acknowledged for her many long hours spent typing the manuscript. A thanks also to Roger Fox for his creative illustrations, constantly done under publishing deadlines.

Thanks are in order to Barbara Gamez of RNMI for her interest and fortitude throughout the publishing process. And finally, special thanks to Helene Berlin of RNMI, who prodded me many a time to complete the next chapter. A professional in her own field, Helene possesses a keen sense for taking confusing written material and turning it into a polished product. Without her knowledge and expertise, this publication would never have come to print.

Many thanks to these individuals and the many others who were instrumental in the production of this book. Finally, the clients I have been fortunate enough to have served over the years must be acknowledged because without them the strategies and ideas expressed here would be pure academic exercises.

Jerry D. Anderson, CCIM

ABOUT THE AUTHOR

Jerry D. Anderson, an investment specialist with Coldwell Banker of Boca Raton, Florida, holds the Certified Commercial-Investment Member (CCIM) designation of the REALTORS NATIONAL MARKETING INSTITUTE®. He has been in the real estate business since 1970, primarily in commercial-investment sales.

Anderson is active in investment sales both nationwide and on a local level. In addition, he is a frequent lecturer at both state and national real estate conventions.

The author of numerous journal articles on investment real estate, Anderson also writes an investment column for two newspapers. He is a senior instructor in the commercial-investment courses (leading to the CCIM designation) of the Marketing Institute and also serves the Marketing Institute as chairman of several committees.

CONTENTS

Section III Practical Application

Section I
OVERVIEW

Chapter 1

Investments

What do investors expect from their investments? What variables are common to all investments? What are some alternatives to real estate? Exactly how do stocks, bonds, mutual funds, commodities, gold, silver, art, gems, oil, gas, cattle, equipment leasing, and savings accounts perform as investment vehicles? How can real estate compete?

Chapter 2

Real Estate as an Investment

What does real estate have to offer as an investment? What benefits does real estate yield? What advantages and disadvantages does real estate hold for an investor? Is real estate ownership all that it's cracked up to be?

Chapter 3

The Financial Picture of Real Estate

How do the financial benefits of real estate fit together? What is CFBT? What's all this about tax shelter? What language does the IRS speak anyhow? Didn't the tax laws change depreciation? How much tax is due if the property is sold? Isn't there an easy way to figure all this? How about some tips to help explain all this to a client who only wants the bottom line? What does a client mean by "soft costs" and "split funding"? What's the most important thing for me to know about taxes?

Chapter 4

Types of Properties

Aren't all investment properties essentially the same? I'm in residential real estate. How about an investment program of single family homes? What are the income and expense variables of land, apartments, office buildings, shopping centers, industrial space, self-service storage units (miniwarehouses), net leased restaurants, and condominium conversion projects? Are special use investment properties like miniwarehouses or racquetball clubs worth my time, money and effort?

1 INVESTMENTS

Over the years the investment real estate broker will many times ask the following question: "Disregarding the type of investment entity, what do you expect from your investment portfolio?" The answer it seems always includes two concerns, clouded by other issues:

> "I expect my investments to give me a good return on my money and some long-term growth."
>
> "I hope my investments can provide me with cash to use later in my life when my ability to earn money is less than it is today."
>
> "My investments provide me protection against tomorrow's inflation and give me some cash in the meantime."
>
> "I hope my portfolio saves me taxes, provides an attractive return and gives me an opportunity for future growth."
>
> "My investments give me security for the future plus a limited amount of cash flow and tax benefits as the years go by."
>
> "Since I cannot spend all the money I currently produce, my investments give me a chance to save some cash for a later date."

The two common elements heard over and over again are periodic return on the initial investment plus protection and growth for the entire amount invested.

As one can see from the above comments, investment expectations are unique to the individual and thus difficult to explain in the form of a definition. The real estate broker's role becomes one of discovering clients' expectations and then finding investments which best serve their needs by providing a product that meets their goals and objectives.

Investment Variables

With these items in mind one has to consider the economic variables at work on all investments.

Leverage

Some investment opportunities utilize borrowed funds which might increase the yield or return to the investor. This also gives the investor an opportunity to control the investment vehicle without paying the total cash or cost of the entity. In most circumstances the ability to control the investment with less than a total cash position works out to serve the investor positively. Investors refer to this as leverage.

An example of extreme lack of leverage would be a savings account or a fund in which all cash is required as an outlay. The other end of the spectrum would be a piece of real estate on which it is possible to borrow more than is needed for the investment; i.e., finance the property with 100 percent or more debt. Most leverage situations fall somewhere between these two extreme examples.

Management

A certain amount of management is required in any investment. Even though a certificate of deposit might require minimum effort, one must still seek the highest rate available and move funds about as rates change. The constant concern and "hovering" needed to manage a cash outlay in the commodities market is an example of a highly management intensive investment. Stocks, metals and real estate rate fairly high in management requirements.

Marketability or Liquidity

The dictionary defines liquidity as the ability to turn assets into cash quickly. Investments which can be marketed readily are more liquid than those which are difficult to market. Marketability is certainly affected by economic supply and demand factors, but practically speaking liquidity simply means the ease at which the investment can be turned into cash. Actively traded stocks can be bought or sold in minutes on the Stock Exchange, while a large complicated real estate transaction might take eight to ten months to complete. Although a 1957 Thunderbird may be an attractive investment to some, there may be a limited market for the asset when cash is needed.

Appreciation or Inflation Protection

Fixed return investments such as bonds, savings accounts and preferred stock have basically limited protection or appreciation because of their fixed rate and dollar return. Stocks, on the other hand, have the capacity to change value drastically overnight depending on the industry, a merger or the economic position of the company. Along with this tremendous potential goes the possibility of a stock going down in value as rapidly as it went up.

All investments carry some potential for change in value. As mentioned, many times change is locked in at a preferred rate, but this change in value plays an important role in the protection of the dollar's purchasing power at the time of liquidation of the investment. Probably no investment vehicle has been affected more by the variables of appreciation and inflation than real estate.

Tax Benefits

A number of investments available in the marketplace, including real estate, offer tax relief or tax savings in the form of deductions via capital cost recovery (depreciation). Some investments have the capacity to defer tax liability to a later date if the investment is earmarked for individual retirement. Research and development benefits for certain industries and oil and gas drilling costs are other examples of the tax benefits of investment ownership.

Tax shelter is a popular term which essentially denotes tax savings because of the investment in the asset. Upon a sale, any long-term gain is given favorable treatment under the current tax laws; this helps spur economic investment and also yields tax savings.

Relative Yield

Investments throw off some combination of cash benefits. These cash benefits, when measured against the initial cost, produce a percentage yield which can be used as a measurement tool against other investments or against the rate of inflation. The cash flows can be annual or can be in the form of a lump sum return at the time of liquidation.

An example of yield would be the 5¼ percent interest paid on a regular passbook savings account or the percentage rate paid on a money market fund.

Risk

There are several specific risks involved in investing.

The loss of purchasing power is one risk, as opposed to the financial and business risk involved in the investment of dollars. The main risk concern of investors is usually related to the return *of* the invested capital more than the expected return or profit *from* the investment. It is an accepted principle of investment that the degree of risk will probably increase when the expected return moves upward. Conversely, a low return might indicate a minimal amount of risk. At some point of risk-taking, investment ceases to be investment and becomes speculation. At some point speculation becomes gambling; indeed some Las Vegas gamblers refer to their gaming activities as investment activity.

Quality, Quantity and Durability

It has been said that the risk of any investment is made up of component parts as they relate to the quality of the expected income. For example, a certificate of deposit guaranteed by the U.S. government would be an investment of higher quality than one without government backing.

Figure 1–1
Investment Variables

The quantity of the income becomes of prime importance when considering risk. A stock which doubles in value might entail more risk than one which increases at a slow, steady rate.

The durability of the income also comes into play as one views risk. The opportunity to invest in a lease might not be as desirable if the lease is short term as opposed to a 10 or 15-year income schedule.

Planning

With so many variables constantly at work in the investment arena, it becomes apparent that the full knowledge of an investment vehicle is imperative if we are to meet our own or our client's objectives. Careful planning is necessary if we are to minimize risk and take advantage of all the potential benefits a chosen investment has to offer.

An individual's overall investment program should consist of what many investment counselors refer to as the investment pyramid (see Figure 1-2). Every individual, regardless of his financial situation, should give first priority to "foundation" investments—that is, adequate insurance, savings earmarked for specific purposes and sufficient liquid funds for family emergencies. Such investments should involve a minimum of risk.

For those who have these adequate "foundation" investments, a second tier on the pyramid might best be termed "growth" investments. Included in this category are such investments as strong common stock or real estate which, in addition to a chance for appreciation, produce a regular and reasonably predictable income.

These investments involve somewhat greater risks. Stocks can go down as well as up. Real estate is subject to a variety of both physical and economic hazards and can be nonliquid. Nevertheless, these opportunities offer a somewhat greater reward potential than do lesser risk investments. For this reason, second-tier "growth" investments are designed to provide at least a partial hedge against continued inflation. These investments usually embody the principle of leverage.

The top of the investment pyramid is made up of a "speculative" tier. This is thc level best summed up by saying: "Never speculate money you cannot afford to lose." This is not to say that this tier does not play an important role in the investment portfolio, however.

The key to structuring investment portfolios is not only placing investments at the right level but also keeping the tiers in proportion to the goals and objectives of the investor.

Figure 1–2
Planning

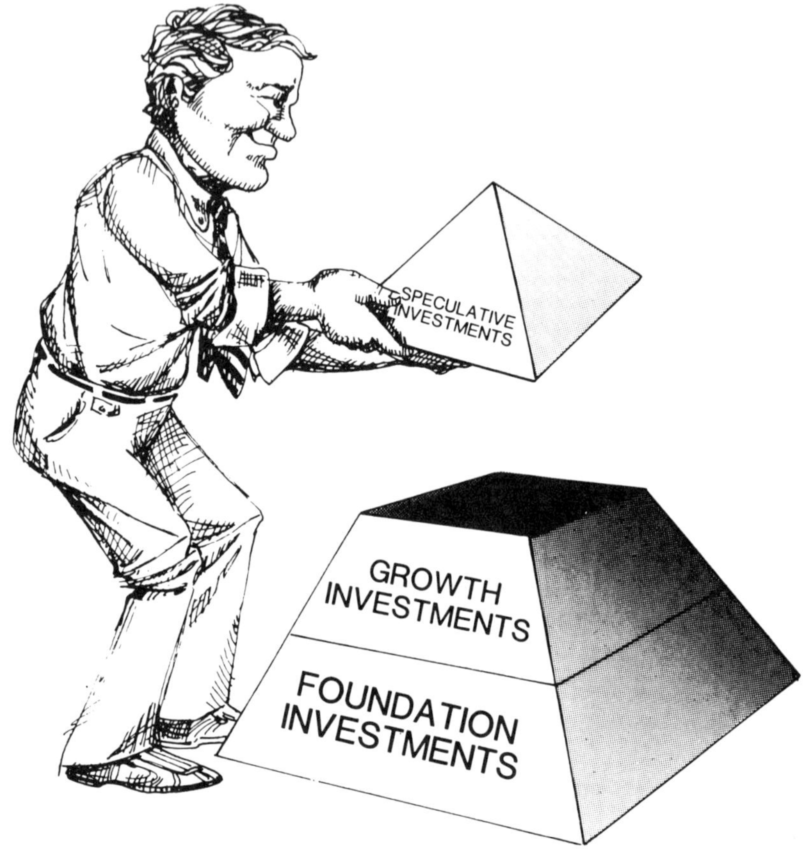

The Investment Community

The investment community is made up of people, and people make investment decisions. If one is to be successful in the commercial-investment brokerage business he must take his head out of the real estate sand and look at some other alternatives potential investors may investigate. (Later in this book we will explore the many "people" benefits that we as real estate brokers have to offer.) The following by no means comprises the only investment options available. The alternatives are offered as a general overview of alternatives which compete for the investor's dollars in a competitive investment community. Expanded knowledge in these areas can do nothing but help us understand in greater depth the product we call "real estate."

Bonds

Often the keystone of investment portfolios, corporate bonds pay a competitively attractive rate of interest on specific dates, mature at full face value at a predetermined date, have strong liquidity and are backed by the credit strength of some of the country's largest corporations.

Although corporate bonds are usually considered "income" investments, many bonds can be purchased at a discount which can then provide a predictable appreciation factor if held to maturity. Other more speculative bonds have higher appreciation potential for investors willing to assume more risk.

Municipal bonds are debt issues of state, county and local governments and are frequently considered second in quality only to U.S. government securities. They provide regular income which is exempt from federal taxes and many times are free from state or local income taxes as well. For investors in moderately high tax brackets, municipal bonds can represent a greater after-tax return than might be achieved in investments which generate taxable income.

Stock Market

The stock market is a very complicated investment arena. Many investors spend their lives studying trends and stock movement. Here we will attempt only to define and characterize the various kinds of stock investments available.

Common stocks are common shares of public or utility companies and some industrial corporations. They provide income through dividends which often approach the rates available on corporate bonds. These shares offer appreciation potential should their dividend rates be increased or should prices rise as a reflection of the company's earnings growth.

Many common stocks, especially those of small companies, newer business ventures or established companies whose business prospects are unclear, carry both a higher degree of risk and the opportunity for substantial price gains.

Blue chip stocks are considered to be quality stocks and usually provide good income. *Growth stocks* hold the potential for long appreciation. *Volatile issues* can offer faster profits but with commensurately higher risks.

Over-the-counter stocks are usually unlisted shares of corporations which trade over the counter and typically represent smaller, lesser-known companies. They offer excellent oportunity for substantial capital gains but at a much greater risk than common stock. It has been said that some of these vehicles may even classify as speculation which many stock brokerage firms define as taking above-average risks for the chance to make above-average profits.

One has to have the nerve—the emotional attitude—to accept rapid price fluctuations. Investors are generally cautioned by professionals to avoid risking money they can't afford to lose.

Preferred stocks offer a fixed and usually generous amount of income from their dividends. These stocks are superior in position to a corporation's common stock and consequently are of better quality.

The term *convertible issues* simply refers to offerings which corporations make available as corporate bonds or preferred stock. These vehicles can be converted at a later date to common stock in the firm. The fixed dividend is higher and yet long-term appreciation may still be available.

When an investor buys shares in a company he is really buying ownership in that company. Management has the responsibility of running the company and pleasing the shareholders. The management structure is geared to increase earnings, thus increasing dividends. When a company is successful it pays out part of the money it earns as dividends. Many small and rapidly growing companies are less prone to pay out large dividends as they reinvest their profits in the company to maintain growth.

A company's stock is priced either according to the dividend amount or what the prospects of future dividends appear to be. Stock shares grow in value because investors in the marketplace think an increase of earnings currently can be translated into healthy, growing dividends. Most profits in the stock market come from increased value in shares. Since stocks are capital assets, capital gains treatment is available for any long-term gain, thus helping increase the yield on an after-tax basis.

The price or value of a stock is quoted daily on the financial page of many newspapers. Companies listed on the New York Stock Exchange generally have several million or more shares issued. If a stock has five million shares outstanding and the quoted price is $5 per share, it means the *market* is valuing the company at $25 million.

This market which determines the value is made up of buyers and sellers who deal in the market daily. They react to sales, earnings, dividends, prospects, marketing techniques, merger possibilities and general economic factors with ongoing buying and selling activity which in turn establishes market value.

Price/Earning Ratio A measurement concept utilized in the stock market is the price/earning ratio. This concept is important to the active investment real estate broker because many investors will try to carry the technique into evaluating real estate investments. Any investment broker or salesperson who has ever talked real estate to a stock market investor has probably encountered the price/earning ratio as the investor tries to determine the value of the real estate.

A company's earnings—past, present and, most importantly, future—are the key elements to its price movement. If earnings appear to be falling, the price of the stock will slump. Conversely, if earnings seem to be improving the stock will generally increase in price.

If a company has five million shares outstanding and earned after taxes $5 million, the *earnings per share* is $1 per share that particular year. If the next year the same company were to earn $10 million after tax, the *earnings per share* would increase to $2 per share. This increase would probably spark favorable market activity.

If we look at this company, which is earning $2 per share, and find that the stock exchange listings show that the shares are selling for $10 per share, the price/earning ratio (P/E) is 5: $10 per share price divided by $2 per share earnings.

This widely used price/earning ratio has much historical significance. In strong economic times a sound average of all price/earning ratios on the New York Stock Exchange might be around 10. In more speculative times the average price/earning ratio may climb to 18 or so, while during a depression it may dip to around 6. The daily listings in the *Wall Street Journal* provide an excellent perspective on the P/E of all stocks listed on the New York Stock Exchange.

Some strong individual stocks may sell for as high as 30 or 40 times annual earnings, based on potential for earnings growth. At the same time some "stodgy" blue chips may sell for as low as four or five times earnings. Many people think good buying opportunities exist on stocks which sell for less than ten times their annual earnings.

Market Indicators The market's price movement is measured by a variety of indicators and averages, but the most famous is the "Dow Jones industrial average." The daily price movement of these 30 stocks is the principal measure of all stock movement. Broader stock indexes such as the New York Stock Exchange indicator and the Standard and Poor's indicator give a wider depiction of price movement because more stocks are included in their averages.

The New York Stock Exchange is open from 10 AM to 3 PM Eastern time each weekday during which more than 2,000 stocks, with volumes up to 50 million shares, change hands. This tremendous marketplace provides the stock market investor with instant liquidity which few other investment vehicles can match.

Mutual Funds

A mutual fund is a way for many small investors to pool their money. The pool is invested on their behalf and, in effect, they own proportionate shares in the total. The pool is managed by full-time professionals who typically have resources of skill, time and research support beyond the reach of the average investor. The size of the pool enables them to reduce risks by diversifying. A single mutual fund might invest in the stocks of 50 or more companies. Mutual funds enable investors to do collectively what they could not do individually.

In the past, mutual funds invested heavily in common stock, primarily for capital appreciation. Within the stock market there is plenty of variety. At one end the aggressive growth stocks stress rapid appreciation with above average risks. This stock is mostly from small companies with above average potential. Another fund looking for less appreciation but also with minimal risk exposure might include mostly blue chip and middle size corporation stock. Yet another fund might concentrate on stocks which provide a mixture of dividends and capital growth. In the past few years, the average shareholder in a mutual fund has done fairly well. The funds typically exceed the rate of inflation and stock market rates as a whole.

Not only can the personal objectives of an investor be met through a specific mutual fund, but the ability to shift a shareholder's interest from a common stock fund to possibly a money market or a corporate bond fund offers flexibility few other investments possess.

Money Markets In periods of high interest rates, the well-to-do were always able to benefit from buying treasury bills, certificates of deposit of large banks and commercial paper of blue chip companies. These were really the IOUs of the government, the banking system and industry. They are all safe, high quality, short-term investments. The disadvantage has always been that the packages are so large that they have been out of reach of all but the wealthiest of investors.

With the advent of pooled funds (money markets) in 1974 these advantages became generally available for the first time. Suddenly it was possible to "get aboard" with only $1000 or $2500. These money market mutual funds have made a tremendous impact on the financial market.

Commodities

The main purpose of trading "futures" is to provide a system of forward contracting which gives commercial businesses an opportunity to minimize risks associated with volatile commodity prices. These businesses, known as hedgers, seek advance assurance of the buying and selling prices of their particular commodities. They are willing to forgo any possibility of savings to receive this assurance of a fixed price. The natural fluctuation of futures prices gives the prudent investor an opportunity to select the timing of risks in the speculation of higher prices of a certain commodity. These futures include cattle, cocoa, coffee, corn, cotton, gold, orange juice, pork bellies, silver, soybeans, sugar and many other commodities.

Increased price volatility over the past few years is one reason behind the high level of activity of commodity futures trading by hedgers and investors. For hedgers, volatile prices mean a greater need for protection, while at the same time, price changes give speculative investors increased opportunity.

There is no question, even among commodity brokers, that futures trading is a highly speculative investment. Most brokers suggest the commodities market only after an investor has satisfied himself that his "foundation" and "growth" investments are well in place. This form of speculating is not advised for those who cannot afford to lose the dollars they are investing. Most commodity investors/speculators would agree with the following list of advantages and disadvantages of the commodities market.

Advantages

Leverage Margin requirements for trading contracts are generally 5 to 20 percent of the market value of the contract. A market value contract of say $20,000 might require a margin of just $1400. An increase of 7 percent in the market value would yield $1400 to the investor, resulting in a 100 percent return on the initial $1400 deposit. Few speculative investments offer this type of leverage. Bear in mind, however, that a decrease of just 7 percent in market value also results in a 100 percent loss.

Liquidity In most cases an investor who wishes to buy or sell a futures contract can do so within minutes by calling a commodities broker.

Choice of risks The knowledgeable commodity speculator is able to choose from many possibilities entailing differing degrees of risk. The timing of this risk via the entry to and exit from the marketplace is one feature most other investments lack.

Transaction costs Commissions on commodity futures are considerably lower, in relation to value, than for almost any type of investment. Brokers refer to "round turn" fees which means the commission covers both the purchase and the eventual sale. The commission does not increase even though the value of the asset may have increased.

Continuous price information Futures are bought and sold continually in open competition on regulated markets, with the prices reported on a worldwide electronic communications network moments after the transaction. In addition, the *Wall Street Journal* publishes commodity prices daily.

Public information Many speculative investments depend on "inside" information. The facts and figures concerning supply and demand are published in government reports, and information concerning price-affecting developments is available but often difficult to interpret.

Disadvantages Because of its fast and furious pace, commodity speculation is not for everyone. It is not for the timid, nervous or slow decision-maker. Substantial price changes can occur rapidly. High leverage can create substantial rewards, but it can also produce fast and sizable losses. Investors unable to admit to their mistakes in market judgment can lose substantial sums while arguing in favor of their initial decisions.

More so than with any other investment, the commodity speculator must pay close attention to his investments and to the factors which influence them. The matter of timing is of utmost importance. A passive investment it is not! It has been said that one can always pick out the commodities speculator in a crowd—he is the individual with a phone growing from his ear. Another point to remember is that contracts have limited lives. Unlike other investments in which time may heal a bad buy, the commodity speculator's waiting period is limited.

Commodity Exchanges The principal commodity exchanges on which future contracts are bought and sold are located in Chicago, New York, Minneapolis, Kansas City, London and Winnepeg. All U.S. markets are designated contract markets and are regulated by the Commodity Futures Trading Commission.

These exchanges do not actually buy or sell the commodities, but instead provide the facilities and ground rules for activity. Prices are determined by competitive bids and offers from buyers and sellers or their representatives in an auction environment. By law all offers must be made by public outcry.

The apparent pandemonium of a commodities exchange actually comprises an orderly system of marketing. In the absence of some method of "forward pricing," the marketing of food and other commodities from producer to ultimate consumer *would* be absolute pandemonium. The futures market is one of the few remaining places where an arena of free and open competition exists.

How "Hedging" Works As mentioned previously, "hedgers" are primarily business firms of different kinds which buy and sell contracts for one basic reason—insurance against the price fluctuation of a particular commodity. Hedging is really nothing more than price protection.

Example A farmer is afraid the price of grain may decline before he is able to harvest and sell his crop. As price protection, he sells futures contracts calling for delivery about the time his crop will be harvested.

Example A national supermarket chain plans to feature an advertised sale on bacon over a period of several weeks. To protect itself against price increases, it buys futures contracts of pork bellies at a fixed price per pound.

Example An international export firm contracts to deliver soybeans at an agreed-upon price for the next 11 months. Because the export firm does not currently own enough soybeans to cover its commitments and is concerned that the cost might rise over its contracted selling price, it uses the futures market to establish a protected cost for any additional soybeans needed.

In all the above examples, the hedgers sacrificed the opportunity for greater speculative profit in order to offset risk. Hedgers are unwilling to assume risks produced by uncertain prices.

The hedgers' activity is what creates the opportunity for the speculator. The speculator takes the risks which the hedger avoids and hopes that by correctly sensing the direction and timing of the prices, he can realize a profit. In this respect a commodities speculator is no different than any other investor in the marketplace, regardless of the investment, who buys low and hopes to sell high.

Example Review the following scenario: For a period of several weeks during late winter, corn future prices have been moving slowly upward. There have been a few brief setbacks, but generally the trend has been steady. A speculative investor studies supply and demand reports and concludes that the price is likely to continue to rise.

He decides to purchase two July corn futures contracts, each contract being for the standard amount of 5000 bushels. To cover his margin requirement, $2000 is needed. This "good faith" money will be returned, plus or minus any profit or loss, when the contracts are sold. By early spring corn prices have indeed advanced, in the amount of 19 cents per bushel. The investor now decides to sell. His profit on 10,000 bushels of wheat is $1900 minus brokerage commissions.

At the same time the investor has been watching pork bellies and believes higher price levels are on the way over the next couple of months. He buys a futures contract for 38,000 pounds, putting up $2500. Each penny change per pound will represent $380 profit or loss. Two days after the purchase, a one cent per pound decrease is experienced, followed by a half-cent increase and then three half-cent decreases in a row.

The net decrease of two cents per pound in less than five days represents a loss of $760 to the investor. He decides to sell his position and pay his $760 loss plus brokerage commission out of his initial deposit of $2000. It is obvious that successful commodity speculating demands a strong stomach for risk and a sound strategy for speculation—if such a combination exists.

Precious Metals

Although there are many different types of metals available through the commodities market, many investors choose to invest in gold or silver as a potential hedge against inflation.

Silver For many years silver has been regarded as a symbol of wealth because of its lustrous appearance, durability and malleability. In addition, its unique chemical properties have made silver an essential industrial commodity. Most people are familiar with silver in its more common applications. Silver flatware is a traditional gift. Fine jewelry uses the metal and most countries use some silver in their coins.

More importantly to the investor, silver has many commercial uses, and industrial demand for silver is indeed the major factor in determining its market price. The photographic industry, for example, accounts for well over one-third of the country's silver consumption. Silver is used in electric and electronic equipment, for bio-medical purposes and as a catalyst in the chemical industry. New applications for silver are continually being discovered. This demand has brought about increasing silver prices which consequently attracts investors.

Investors are concerned exclusively with the price of silver, not the aesthetics of craftsmanship or age as are those who buy silver as art objects. Silver is preferred to be in bullion form since its value depends solely on its price, not on what it may be made into. Many silver investors prefer bullion to commodity futures since there is generally less risk involved. Remember, commodity market investors and hedgers are more concerned with speculative profit than with ownership.

Investors who buy silver classify the metal as a "hard asset." These are tangible goods which increase in value, thus preserving the buying power of money. Silver investors feel that hard assets will increase in value along with or ahead of the inflation rate because of the inherent value people around the world place on such metals. Silver can be a potential hedge against inflation, but the only profit to be made from silver comes in the form of increased value at the time of sale. There are no financial operational benefits to be realized. Silver is known for its swift price changes which can come about simply because of speculative rumors. Because of this lack of stability, even brokerage houses which offer group purchase programs suggest that individuals keep no more than 10 percent of their invested funds in silver.

Gold Probably no precious metal gets as much attention as gold. Gold, like silver, is used in jewelry and art, but it continues to be accepted as the ultimate storehouse of value.

As with most precious metals, large minimum purchase quantities plus shipping, insurance, storage and fabrication make investing in gold a cumbersome task. Many brokerage houses have a group purchasing plan which enables the investor to buy small quantities without the worry of storage, insurance or handling. If gold is in fact the ultimate storehouse of value, the price should theoretically increase during inflationary periods as the purchasing power of the dollar diminishes. In 1979, gold skyrocketed from $400 to $850 in six weeks; in January, 1980, it then fell back down to $500 in a matter of days. These price movements are caused not only by inflation but also by other variables such as interest rates, mining costs, political events and speculative rumors. Clearly, gold prices are not easy to predict.

Capital preservation and speculative profit are the only two reasons to invest in precious metals. They typically do not offer tax benefits or operational cash flow.

Strategic Metals There has been a recent upsurge of interest in strategic metals which are metals classified by Congress as essential for defense purposes. National directives have been issued to stockpile such items as chromium, manganese, cobalt and platinum.

A government directive of this type creates value since these stockpile purchases are over and above normal industrial demand. Again, the only profit to be realized is speculative.

Art and Gems

Although many investors purchase art or gems as potential assets which will increase in value, most people have the aesthetics and beauty of the item in mind long before the pure investment decision is made. Very seldom will an investor consider art or stones only as an economic investment.

There are of course many instances where value has steadily appreciated. In 1959, *The Storm* (a large painting of two young girls in a downpour) by Bourgereau sold at Sotheby Parke Bernet in New York for $1500. In 1979 this painting sold for $57,500. By 1981, its price was estimated to be over $100,000.

Whether an investor goes to a dealer or an auction house for art or gems, the new collector should bear one thing in mind. Viewing these items as investments should not obscure one of the most important truisms of collecting: "Art and gems should be enjoyed." Be wary of buying a painting or a stone simply because it may increase in value. Buying these items is a more personal form of investing than buying stocks or gold bullion. It is an investment which should enhance the quality of one's life.

Tax-favored Investments

Although real estate is certainly an investment vehicle which receives favored treatment from the IRS, there are a few others with which the real estate practitioner needs to be somewhat familiar. This list is certainly not complete, but it does include those vehicles most often compared to real estate in the investment decision-making process. Most of these items are partnership entities which purport to offer the investor an opportunity to invest a minimum of cash which he will get back immediately in tax refunds and which will earn additional tax refunds on the same investment in later years.

The IRS in recent years has documented more than 25,000 "abusive" tax shelters which have resulted in 200,000 audits and has collected over $5 billion in tax shelter revenue. In addition, the IRS is beefing up its manpower to conduct audits on at least 25 percent of all tax claims associated with what it deems to be "abusive tax-favored" partnerships.

Although an audit in itself is not an automatic disallowance of deductions taken, it is somewhat disturbing to know one's entire return is going to be scrutinized because of a particular tax-favored program.

Here are a few of the investments often sold as "tax shelters."

Real Estate Obviously, we will be investigating real estate in depth throughout this book, and we will analyze it as a particular kind of investment in the next chapter.

Oil and Gas There are three categories of investment in oil and gas:

1 *exploration* (wildcat) which involves as-yet unexplored areas and offers a high risk and a high reward *if* oil or gas is found;

2 *development* programs which involve exploring near fields known to yield gas or oil and which offer a lower risk and lower reward than wildcat exploration;

3 *production* programs in which existing wells are bought for cash flow and which involve the least risk.

The government, in its quest for energy independence, has subsidized oil exploration with what is known as Intangible Drilling Costs (IDC). The premise for IDC is that while one searches for oil, the costs should be deductible even if oil or gas is not found. All intangibles such as permits, transportation, personnel, maps, reports and travel become fully deductible items.

An exploration and drilling company usually acts as manager of the venture and raises money from the investors who then become partners of the management. Of perhaps a $10,000 investment as much as $7500 may be spent in the first year for drilling and/or exploration purposes. If a well turns dry, investors will have to be content to live with the deduction. If the company strikes oil or gas, they still get the deduction, plus the find's profit. Of the three categories of oil and gas investment, production programs generally will not offer IDC deductions, while the other two will.

Coal This fuel is similar to oil and gas, except that coal is fairly easy to find and mine. Less risky than oil or gas, coal is also less rewarding from a tax standpoint, but still appropriate for many people wary of wildcatting in the oilfields.

Cattle Feeding and Breeding Cattle investments fall into two distinct categories—cattle feeding and cattle breeding. Both are highly leveraged investments, but feeding is usually taxed as ordinary profit and breeding offers the possibility of capital gains. A cattle feeding investment is slightly more liquid than a breeding project, which is not very liquid and which generally entails a very high risk. However, with a feeding project, if there is a market downturn and a good sale cannot be made, the cattle still have to be fed and cared for until they are sold.

Building a herd of cattle for eventual sale is another game. Since such a venture has a longer maturation period, the write-offs and profits are spread over a longer period of time. Capital gains treatment is available but the element of time should be analyzed in the initial decision.

Equipment Leasing Investors are buying everything from computers to airplanes to railroad cars as tax-favored programs. For example, an investor puts a down payment on an airplane and finances the balance with a loan, using the plane as collateral.

In turn, the investor leases the plane to a commuter airline or user that would rather lease than own its own fleet. The investor takes advantage of the interest, cost recovery and maintenance deductions which affect his taxable income from other sources. Tax savings are the eventual goal through deductions and an investment tax credit. (This credit is a direct credit to any tax liability.) Meanwhile, the lease revenues are paying off the airplane which the investors or partnership will sell at the end of the program. The question, of course, becomes what will the airplane be worth at the end of the lease. The rapid growth of office computers and word processing equipment has opened up yet another avenue for investors wishing to get into an equipment leasing program as an investment alternative.

Summary

The overpowering comment heard from most authorities in the tax-favored investment field is, "Before entering a program of tax-favored investments, examine the pure economics in addition to the tax benefits which might accrue." This statement may be one to bear in mind as we discuss real estate as an alternative to any of the investment vehicles mentioned or to any others that may be available.

There are those investments which bring personal pleasure along with monetary gain. Art and gems are examples, but there is also the investor who pleads with his spouse that his vintage Mercedes is only an investment and the hours spent tinkering and polishing is his way of maintaining the value of the "investment."

There are investments which are heavily security-oriented. The savings account, certificate of deposit or money market fund are accessible sources of available cash when the need or emergency arises. These types of funds should not be totally construed as investment funds, but they do serve as an excellent measurement guide (since the returns are usually fixed and expressed as a percentage) for alternate investments.

The changes in the Economic Recovery Tax Act of 1981 bring the Individual Retirement Account (IRA) into the forefront for those hoping to provide for retirement. The current law permits up to $2000 per individual per year to be put aside into an account; the tax on the $2000 each year is deferred until after retirement when the liability will undoubtedly be less.

There are many available options for the IRA funds: banks, savings and loans, credit unions, mutual funds, stock brokerage houses, insurance companies or even the governments' Individual Retirement Bonds, but the underlying benefit is that the dollars are not taxed until they are withdrawn after retirement. A penalty is assessed if the funds are withdrawn early. Although an IRA program could be part of many investors' portfolios, the IRA itself is not really in direct competition for the real estate investor's dollars because of the minimal investment amount involved in the IRA.

Figure 1–3

LAST YEAR, A CAR OUT-PERFORMED 318 STOCKS ON THE NEW YORK STOCK EXCHANGE.
If you'd bought a new BMW 320i in the beginning of 1980, and sold it at the end, your investment would have retained 92.9% of its original value.
If you'd done the same with any of 318 NYSE stocks, you'd have done less well.
And you'd have forfeited an important daily dividend:
The unfluctuating joy of driving one of the world's great performance sedans.
BMW
THE ULTIMATE DRIVING MACHINE.

A knowledge of competitive investments is a necessity in real estate. The stock market is often used as a comparison tool for real estate investments and for many other kinds of purchases—even automobiles. (Advertisements printed in The *Wall Street Journal*, courtesy of BMW of North America, Inc.)

With so many investment alternatives available in the marketplace it is easy to understand why a thorough knowledge of both real estate and competitive investments is needed in order to succeed in the sales world.

2
REAL ESTATE AS AN INVESTMENT

Even with so many competitive investment alternatives available, it should be relatively easy to present real estate to a client and have him realize its benefits over other investments. However, sometimes it is difficult to remember that people are products of their environment and their life experiences. The term "real estate" has many different connotations to many people; we must be sensitive to the fact that to some people real estate as an investment may paint a mental image completely opposite from our own point of reference.

Our own personal perceptions play an important role in how we translate the term real estate. Real estate could mean home, vacant land, church, mobile home, farm, recreational project, shopping center, apartment, condominium, beach house, office building, industrial building, ranch or cemetery plot. These differences in perceptions become even more important as clients consider real estate as an investment.

If we accept the word investment to mean "a capital outlay of money with the view and expectation of obtaining cash flows in the future," the broker's role in investment sales becomes one of viewing real estate investments as future cash flows. But the astute practitioner realizes that buyers of real estate are people and people are emotional creatures with egos and pride.

Contrary to the opinions of some in the profession, investment real estate does not need any clever advertising, complicated referral services or 47-page computer analyses to sell. Since 1890 approximately 50 percent of all Americans have owned real estate. Many, of course, never considered their real estate an investment. Most simply called it home. In 1978, the Census Bureau reported that two-thirds of American residential units were owner occupied.

Nevertheless, the public awareness of investment real estate is keen and growing keener. One of the best selling books of 1980 was Albert J. Lowery's *How To Become Financially Independent by Investing in Real Estate*. Rest assured that the half-million copies sold were not purchased by real estate practitioners.

The public is ready to buy investment real estate. And, as the public's representatives in the real estate industry, we owe it to ourselves to dig, probe and study our product. It is our professional obligation. Real estate investors talk a strange language and it can all be very confusing when one thinks about a "net balloon wrapping around a constant cap allocated to the cost recovered preference on the basis of a recaptured 1031 IRR." We must learn to "translate" that language into the vernacular of the average investor.

Elements of Real Estate Investment

Participation in real estate investment offers financial and psychological benefits, emotional involvement and intellectual stimulation.

Real property environments serve many functions—home living space, medical services, education, food production, working environment, administration of activities, government, transportation, retirement and, inevitably, a final resting space. While some real estate consumers seek merely space, others aspire to highly personalized environments. Certain investors take real pride in owning property; others view real estate only in the strictest of financial terms. It is this combination of demand and the satisfaction thereof that makes real estate investing unique.

There are as many types, styles and degrees of real property as there are investors who want to purchase them. One consumer may not be served or satisfied by the same product which fulfilled the needs of another consumer. The matching of the investor's needs with a property that appeals to the investor's perception is sometimes a difficult task. Investment decisions are not always made strictly on a financial basis. Pride and emotions can play a large role.

In spite of the personal considerations often involved, real estate is fully susceptible to rational comparative analysis and management. Techniques that are useful elsewhere are also effective in real estate. At the same time, however, understanding some important and unique considerations can enable real estate investment participants to be more effective in their selection processes. Among these considerations are timing, planning, vision and creativity, product image and promotion. Disciplined management and careful analysis are fundamental requirements as they are in any enterprise where capital is at risk.

Overall, the real estate investment business is highly complex and the range of relevant disciplines is at times beyond the grasp of many. Specialized knowledge of the benefits of ownership is necessary as is knowledge of national economic trends. At the same time, an insight into the local economics and politics of the marketplace is mandatory. An investor or broker should be knowledgeable in advertising and promotion as well as marketing, planning and selling. The real estate investment business is so closely tied to the legal and tax counseling professions that no investor should venture forward without qualified representatives in these fields. It is a good idea to be personally involved in business and government relations if new projects are to be created.

Effective real estate investing is often the stage for interpersonal behavior; many times the insights of a psychologist would be most helpful. Since the real estate investment business is also highly cyclical and certain fads tend to be repeated, it also helps if an investor is something of an historian. These tremendous demands made on a real estate investor are part of the reason some individuals stray away from real estate as a primary form of investment. It is the practitioner's job to serve and coordinate activities with the investor to help him create a portfolio of real estate investments which help meet the investor's overall objectives.

Think of the need for coordination and interaction between financing arrangements and marketing and one realizes how important integration skills are for the broker active in investment sales.

Advantages of Real Estate

A wide overview of the elements which make real estate advantageous might include inflexibility of supply, growth of population, changing habits of buyers and federal legislation affecting the real estate market. Our discussion will center more on the specific advantages of real estate as an investment entity than on these general considerations. In few investment endeavors can one match the very specific and practical advantages of leverage, tax benefits, Cash Flow Before Taxes, appreciation, higher returns, equity build-up, personal control and inflation protection which real estate is often able to provide.

Leverage

Leverage, in perhaps oversimplified terms, is that characteristic in a buy-and-sell transaction which enables the buyer to realize a gain far out of proportion to the dollar investment he incurred in entering the transaction. For example, you are firmly convinced that the market in rare gems over the next few years will show a dramatic appreciation in price. You feel so strongly about it that you select and buy a brilliant, flawless unmounted diamond for $20,000. You pay cash for it and immediately put the stone in your safety deposit box to await the anticipated upswing in value. It turns out that you are correct in your premise and the stone doubles in price over the next five years. You then remove it from the safety deposit box and sell it for $40,000, a clear $20,000, 100 percent profit (unadjusted for time).

On the other hand, let's say you are convinced that a particular $50,000 piece of raw land is certain to appreciate in value. You arrange for the purchase, but instead of putting up the entire $50,000, you are required to put up only $10,000. Again you are correct in your original premise and the value of the land doubles in price because it sits in the path of progress of the city. You sell it for $100,000, or twice the price you paid. One-hundred percent profit? No. Your investment capital is only $10,-000 so your investment has actually increased in value not twice but five times. This is an example of leverage in its simplest form, and it is an element present in real estate transactions far more than any other type of speculation or investment.

Tax Benefits

Most important to the potential real estate investor are the tax benefits of real estate. While land itself does not depreciate in the government's eyes (hard to argue this since land is made of pretty sturdy stuff), buildings do depreciate in value and Uncle Sam is realistic enough to concede this to the point of permitting an allowance to be deducted annually to cover the ultimate cost of replacing it.

This amount is called the cost recovery allowance (it was called depreciation before the 1981 tax law). With a little thought, cost recovery can mean that a considerable portion of the risk of a real estate investment will be underwritten, for all intents and purposes, by the government. We will study cost recovery more thoroughly as we investigate individual investment projects in later chapters. To summarize, however, tax laws passed currently permit real estate to be depreciated over an 18-year period, which makes it entirely possible, in certain circumstances, not only to defer income tax payment on the real estate but also to spill that benefit over into personal income production. These tax savings from the ownership of real estate plus the favorable long-term capital gains treatment on property held for investment over one year offer the real estate investor considerable tax savings not available with other investments.

Without these incentives, risk capital might dry up and leave us in a sterile economy in which people sit quietly on their money in the safest form of investment possible, refusing to take a chance and refusing to contribute anything toward the perpetuation of the dynamic financial growth that has always set this country apart from others.

Cash Flow Before Taxes (CFBT)

Unlike many investments, real estate's cash flow really stems from two areas. One area of cash flow was mentioned briefly above, tax savings. That tax "world", however, is completely separate from the cash a property generates from operations (see Chapter 3 for a full explanation).

Insofar as a property is able to generate recurring income through rents, it generates dollars which, properly structured, can be untaxed. Cash Flow Before Taxes (CFBT) occurs when the gross rents exceed the expenses of the property and any debt service needed to service the mortgage. A commercial property with a long-term lease with a responsible tenant who maintains the building and pays all expenses of operation probably has a more secure CFBT than an apartment house with many tenants and expenses which are not easily predicted or controlled. With many properties such as this CFBT is nonexistent because of vacancies (reducing gross rents), expenses which run out of control or the amount of debt service needed for the mortgage payment.

CFBT will be figuring into every cash flow projection when we eventually get to the point of analyzing future cash flows from a real estate investment. It is a good idea to think of CFBT as a "checkbook" into which all rents are deposited, expenses paid and mortgage payments deducted. Hopefully, at the end of the year some money will be left over and can be put in the investor's pocket. When Uncle Sam determines tax liability on the real estate over in the "tax world," whatever is left over (if any) is the investor's and Uncle Sam doesn't really care. More on the "checkbook" and "tax world" in Chapter 3 of Section I.

Appreciation

In general, the tendency for well-located property is to appreciate in value. There are, of course, many exceptions but usually they are due to poor location or mismanagement. A growth in area income or production alone is enough to create sufficient demand to keep most income-producing properties substantially and profitably rented.

Multiplying the effect of increased demand is the incontrovertible fact of limited supply. Well located land tends to increase in value naturally as there is less and less available. Artificial limitations on the supply of real property also add to the increasing value of real estate. Concerns with pollution have led to environmental controls which limit new construction. Prevailing political attitudes in favor of controlled growth have also inhibited construction in many areas of the country. Natural gas and water shortages, sewer inadequacies, central city decline and resultant suburban expansion all help to increase the value of existing properties.

One further stimulus to appreciation is inflation. Historically, money tends to deflate in value over the years; therefore, more dollars are needed to purchase hard tangibles, such as real estate. Property commands a higher and higher price as inflation continues. With income-producing properties, as opposed to vacant ground, the benefits of appreciation come from increased rentals. Available financing also plays a role, but basically an increase in the net income of a property increases the value. These increased rentals, in turn, can only be obtained if the property is well located, well maintained and well managed.

Higher Returns

In general, carefully selected, well managed income-producing properties will show a higher cash return on the invested dollar than will most other types of investments. Disregarding any savings on income taxes which real estate offers, Cash Flow Before Taxes many times will equal what could be earned in a regular passbook savings account. Interest on deposits or bonds, dividends from stocks and other forms of investments rarely produce an equivalent return when one considers both CFBT and the tax benefits from real estate ownership. Add a possible increase in value and mortgage reduction and real estate usually outperforms other investment forms. (In Chapter 5 techniques which measure one investment against another are reviewed.)

Overall, the attraction of a higher return in real estate as opposed to other investment opportunities is a prime factor in creating a ready market when one seeks a disposition of the property.

Equity Buildup

Most income-producing property will utilize borrowed funds since leverage is an integral part of real estate investment strategy. With rare exception, all mortgages today call for monthly or quarterly payments which include both interest and a partial repayment of the principal. To the extent that the mortgage is reduced with each payment, the equity is correspondingly increased. If appreciation is also taking place, this combination can increase equity in a very short period of time.

The amortization or repayment of mortgage debt takes place continuously, but quietly, almost unnoticed month after month after month. When the debt is sufficiently reduced, some investors refinance the property with a larger mortgage and use the proceeds to pay off the reduced mortgage, thus making the difference available for some other investment.

Personal Control

Real estate investments provide the opportunity for a high degree of personal control. Purchase terms can be designed to reflect specific financial circumstances. Rents can be arranged to anticipate changes in future cycles. Various bookkeeping techniques can be adapted to reflect individual needs. For example, an owner can elect accelerated cost recovery over straight line cost recovery when such election works to an advantage in the overall tax structuring. In addition, property can be refinanced periodically to capitalize on the equity accumulated. The investor ultimately retains the power to decide when, how and to whom the property will be sold and under the terms most suitable to satisfy personal economic requirements.

Inflation Protection

Real estate has always been regarded as a prime hedge against inflation. Metals, diamonds and works of art have also been traditional inflation hedges, but real estate is the only such investment that produces income during its period of ownership. The combination of Cash Flow Before Taxes, tax benefits, potential appreciation and equity buildup is what makes real estate unique in the investment community as an investment entity.

Disadvantages of Real Estate

Because real estate is such a complex field and requires more than the normal amount of study before investing, as an investment it is a long way from being perfect. There are disadvantages to real estate and one would be foolishly shutting his eyes to the facts if the disadvantages were not strongly emphasized. They can be summed up as:

- Lack of liquidity
- Possible government intervention
- Management and administrative problems
- Lack of information on which to base investment decisions

Lack of Liquidity

The one most frequently cited objection to the ownership of real estate is the matter of liquidity, simply boiled down to the question of: "How fast can I get my money out of it if I need cash." Obviously, once the down payment is made on a piece of real estate, the problem of liquidity sits very securely in the lap of a potential sale or refinance. Even under the best of circumstances, selling a piece of real estate can be a time consuming matter. When one needs cash immediately a fast closing procedure of one to two months may not be fast enough. It is frequently difficult to sell quickly and there is little certainty about the final sales price. Unlike the stock and bond markets, where there are almost always buyers to be found if the price is low enough, sometimes real estate cannot be readily turned to cash.

Contributing to this low liquidity of income-producing property are the relatively large sums of money needed for property maintenance and reserve capital. Despite high leverage opportunities existing in the field, a sound investment must be backed by adequate capital to protect it in the event of unforeseen major crises. An unexpected reversal in the economic cycle of a community could result in a high number of vacancies and, at the same time, eliminate any possible market for disposing of a suddenly declining investment property.

Refinancing is always an alternative for limited liquidity, but often increased equity does not offer enough available cash to warrant the additional cost of refinancing. Refinancing should be an investment strategy decision and not a forced alternative because of cash needs.

Ironically, there are those who feel that the very fact that real estate has poor liquidity becomes an advantage rather than a disadvantage. The sluggish liquidity of real estate is fair insurance that the holder will not be tempted to jump too quickly in and out of one position in favor of another before the full market potential of the original choice has been realized. We have all met stock market speculators who spend most of the day complaining that they sold too early, taking a small profit on a block of stock when by holding it a year or two longer they may have realized ten times the profit that they did. Thus, the argument is frequently made that the temptation to take a small profit on a property (instead of holding on to it for greater profits two or three years hence) is materially lessened by the fact that it is difficult to execute a fast sale. A disillusioned real estate investor—thoroughly convinced that his investment program is failing and that he should sell while he can—will become discouraged or prohibited by the simple complexity of finding a buyer and going through the time consuming selling process. By the time he takes action, so goes this philosophy, he may well be out of the woods and no longer anxious to get rid of the property.

Government Intervention

There are numerous examples of government intervention which over the years have given many developers and property owners ulcers and cause for migraine headaches.

Example A local county assessor places an arbitrary assessed value on a piece of property because it has not changed hands for quite some time. The owner screams loud and clear that the assessed value is unreasonable but he still must go through an appeals process which might take years. Meanwhile, the tax bill must be paid on the "new" assessed value. A rebate will be paid if and when the appeals process determines a different value.

Example The planning commission on an island off the coast of Florida makes the decision that the growth of the island has been sporadic. A commercial building moratorium is enacted to give the island community time to "study" the growth situation. Length of time for the study—one year. No real estate developers are permitted on the planning commission since that would represent "conflict of interest." Current zoning and city requirements will permit only approximately 12,000 square feet of retail space to be built on a parcel more than three acres in size. Only 9 percent of the land area can be covered by a building on a parcel of over 131,000 square feet.

Management Problems

The problem of property management very likely deters more investors from real estate than any other reason. It is one thing to secure a good buy in the market. It is quite another to take on the role of absentee landlord for a piece of property inhabited by living and breathing people who are, at best, demanding and, at worse, freeloaders.

A real estate investment requires more active participation on the part of the individual investor than do most other investment opportunities. One can drive a hard bargain, project cash flows and draw sales agreements, but what happens the first holiday weekend when a tenant calls complaining that the sump pump has quit and water is two feet high in the basement? The tenant threatens a law suit because his washer and dryer are being ruined. Forget about the furnace! Or what about the commercial retail tenant who subtly shifts his operation into a semi-manufacturing endeavor in defiance of the lease and city zoning laws?

Example One broker was thrilled with the economics of his latest investment purchase. His college housing units were projected to yield more cash flow than he had ever imagined, considering the price and terms he had paid. Six months into the investment he complained that between the engineering students upstairs tearing the place apart and the law students downstairs keeping him tied up in court he had not had one good night's sleep since his "fantasy investment" was purchased.

This is not to say that investors should avoid real estate rental properties altogether if this kind of detail work is not attractive. It simply means that one should consider the cost of professional management in any property projection regardless of the size of the property. These services are not cheap, but they are mandatory for an investor who does not have the time or patience to handle the management and administrative nightmares of real estate proprietorship.

Lack of Information

A casual inquiry to a stockbroker about investing $50,000 in an obscure company will bring forth every bit of information you ever wanted to know about ABC, Incorporated, showering upon your shoulders. The

Figure 2–1
Advantages and Disadvantages of Real Estate

flood of material will contain gross revenues for the past 20 years, the property's operating profit margin and percentages, its net income, its working capital at any given time, its outstanding shares, its earnings per share, its dividends per share, its price range in the market, its price earnings ratio and its average yield for as far back as you care to investigate. You will have at your fingertips brochures outlining what the company has done in the past, what it is currently doing and what the experts believe it will be doing in the next five, ten or 20 years. By the time you are finished you might even know if the president likes gin or vodka martinis.

But what kind of information is available on a local piece of investment property? As brokers we try to back up our representations with facts about the area, vacancy rates and population trends. In general, the Department of Commerce and local planning boards do a fairly good job of providing us with information about populations, income, trends and consumer spending, but the interpretation of these facts as they pertain to one particular piece of rental property is difficult, to say the least.

Just because there is a shortage of office condos nationally does not mean that your new project will be instantly absorbed into the local marketplace. Real estate is local in nature and a 20 percent vacancy factor in Detroit does not translate to an overabundance of multifamily dwellings in Denver.

The identification of opportunities in the marketplace is a talent that only comes through investigation and research into an area and the variables at work within the community. Once identified, these opportunities can be pursued with vigor usually to the financial benefit of the real estate investor.

Market Characteristics of Real Estate

In addition to the advantages and disadvantages just discussed, there are a few characteristics of the real estate market that are unique because of the physical and legal attributes of real property.

Decentralized and Unorganized

Because of the immobile or fixed character of real property, its value will change with shifts in local supply and demand conditions and with alterations in the local environment. Notwithstanding the increasing participation of national corporations and financial institutions in the real estate market, the market still tends to be local and decentralized compared with the national markets for bonds and the securities markets which are controlled by and through the Securities and Exchange Commission.

Private Transactions

Many real estate transactions are conducted in private. In most communities no public record is made of the dollar amounts involved in a real estate transaction, and while some fee may be placed on transfer documents indicating transaction value, this is not always a reliable guide. The result is that there is relatively little available market data for investors, again compared with the securities and commodities markets.

Limited Supply

As previouly mentioned the supply of real estate is fixed, but this does not mean that increased demand for land around Washington, D.C. can be translated into higher prices for land in South Dakota. The limited land concept is most relevant when applied to land in *specific areas of growing demand*.

High Transaction Costs

The physical and legal complexities and lengthy negotiations which attend many real estate transactions often result in substantial professional fees for the investor. Real estate transaction costs may run substantially higher than those associated with stock and bond transactions.

3

THE FINANCIAL PICTURE OF REAL ESTATE

Assuming the reader is willing to accept the concept that investment real estate can be translated into a series of cash flows for the future, the task of the REALTOR® and the investor becomes one of gathering current information and projecting future data as it pertains to the property. Cash flow is generated by real estate from the following sources:

- Cash Flow Before Taxes
- Tax savings from ownership
- Appreciation
- Mortgage reduction

Not all investment real estate has all four cash flow areas working for it at any one time but generally any benefits from real estate ownership will accrue in at least one of these areas. One might suppose that a property which yields cash flow from all four sources would be superior to a property which only benefits the investor in, say, appreciation. The answer, of course, is "it depends." Each parcel must be analyzed on its own merit and then compared not only to other pieces of real estate but also to other investment alternatives. This is the reason an analysis of *all* cash flow benefits from an investment becomes so important.

Another reason real estate must be understood in depth if one is going to compare it to other forms of investment is that the government taxes real estate income somewhat differently than it does other investments. The basic premise is that all investment entities should be analyzed on an after-tax basis; otherwise, only part of the benefit or liability will be measured. Probably the best example of not looking at an investment on an after-tax basis would be a certificate of deposit. Assuming a 12 percent yield is used as a comparison with other investments, the decision process becomes somewhat distorted. If the investor pays 30 percent of his income to the government in taxes, the investor's yield is not really 12 percent, but only 8.4 percent since the tax is 30 percent times the 12 percent yield, or 3.6 percent. This distortion is the reason we need to

Figure 3–1
Cash Benefits of Real Estate

fully understand the four benefits of real estate and how to compare them after tax to other investment forms—in other words, apples to apples.

Cash Flow Before Taxes and the "Checkbook"

Like other investment forms, real estate is analyzed and measured on an annual basis. One of the most important variables of income-producing property is the amount of income the property will generate. Usually in the form of rents, the income pays all expenses and any mortgage payments needed to service the debt. Any cash remaining is referred to as Cash Flow Before Taxes. In some forms of investment (raw land, for example) there are no rents although expenses and debt service must still be paid. In this case, the Cash Flow Before Taxes is negative.

Below are some standardized terms which help brokers and investors communicate when they talk about Cash Flow Before Taxes:

Cash Flow Before Taxes (CFBT)

	Scheduled Rental Income
Less:	Vacancy and Credit Losses
Equals:	Effective Rental Income
Plus:	Other Income
Equals:	Gross Operating Income
Less:	Expenses
Equals:	Net Operating Income
Less:	Annual Debt Service
Equals:	Cash Flow Before Taxes

One helpful method used to explain the above process is the "checkbook" method. The thought process behind it is that all rents collected go into the "checkbook," expenses are paid, debt service is paid and the remaining dollars are Cash Flow Before Taxes (maybe positive, maybe negative).

For example, a property is purchased with a specific schedule of rents. Vacancies occur and the effective rents collected are deposited into the checkbook "account." Expenses are paid as they come due. A net amount of operating income is left in the checkbook as the amount of cash the property produces. This production of income is very important as we will soon find out. If there is a mortgage on the property, the debt must be serviced out of the net amount of operating income. Hopefully, after the debt payments are made there will be some money left in the checkbook. This amount, whether it be positive, negative (out of pocket) or $0 (break even) is the Cash Flow Before Taxes of the investment property.

This is but one of the benefits of real estate. Let's take a closer look at each of the components of this first benefit.

Scheduled Rental Income

This income is the annual gross amount scheduled to be produced by the investment property. If the property is an apartment building of 12 units, all scheduled to rent for $300 per month, the scheduled rental income would be

$$\$300 \times 12 \text{ units} \times 12 \text{ months}$$

or a total of $43,200 annually. This is the very beginning of a long road of analyses of cash flows for a particular piece of property. If this scheduled rental income is "pie in the sky" or way above what the market will accept, the entire analysis becomes fallacious and simply hypothetical. It is imperative that the broker investigate the market to make a projection of what an *accurate* scheduled rental income will be in the upcoming year. (If you look through a Multiple Listing Service book and pick out all the rental properties listed for sale, you will notice that practically every rental property listing carries the same four words, "rents should be raised.")

Information needed to determine the scheduled rental income of a shopping center or an office building is a little more difficult to obtain than that of an apartment building. Different lease termination dates and varied rental rates require close analysis to make an accurate projected scheduled income. If long-term leases are written on the property, determining this scheduled income may be a simple task. Probably the easiest type of property on which to calculate the scheduled income is a piece of land since generally raw land does not yield any income whatsoever.

Vacancy and Credit Losses

Vacancies and credit losses are a fact of life in real estate investments. Even if an accurate projection is done on the scheduled rental income, there will be losses from credit given to tenants as rent inducement or because of vacant apartments, unfilled offices or empty retail space. Even if an apartment project has a history of waiting lists and strong demand, some rents will be lost to vacancy even if it is only for a period of three days while the unit is being painted and prepared for the next tenant. Retail space generally takes much longer to rent than do apartments; consequently more rent is lost to vacancies. One long-term leasee may insure against vacancy if the tenant occupies the entire building and appears fairly stable. On the other side of that coin is the fact that when this lone tenant leaves, the *entire* building is vacant. That is called a 100 percent vacancy factor.

Vacancy factors are always fascinating. The whole world has a 5 percent vacancy factor! Don't believe it? Look at an apartment projection, look at an appraisal, look at packages from other brokers. Five percent is a nice round number and probably for some projects is right on target, but for everything across the board? Certainly not.

Example A local apartment project has a mixture of one, two and three-bedroom units. These are attractive units and there is a swimming pool, kiddie playland, tennis court—all the amenities. One day the owner became upset with the children's activities around the pool and moved all children and pets out of the units. Guess what happened to the vacancy factor, especially in the three-bedroom units? You got it; the threes are downright impossible to rent to families without children. Vacancy factor in the project? The stated 5 percent? Of course not! In reality it's much higher than a rule-of-thumb 5 percent.

Example A shopping center with half the space filled by a major grocery store is not going to have a vacancy factor in that half of the center. But there certainly may be a factor of vacancy in the local tenant space. Similarly, office buildings are difficult to figure for vacancy, but there are numerous publications available which give typical vacancy factors for many types of real estate investment properties. (See the section on office buildings in Chapter 4.)

Effective Rental Income

Many brokers and investors refer to the effective rental income as that income which is actually *collected* from tenants for the rental of property.

Other Income

Because many properties carry charges to the tenants other than rent, it is important to provide treatment of that income without it being reflected in a possible vacancy factor. Vending machine income, parking fees, laundromat income and tenant maintenance contributions are examples of other income a property generates which might not necessarily be included in rental income.

Gross Operating Income (GOI)

The GOI is generally considered to be the amount of all collected rents *plus* any extra income. Essentially, GOI is the amount of money in the "checkbook" before any expenses are paid or debt service is deducted.

Operating Expenses

Operating expenses should include any items which are directly or indirectly related to the operation of the property. These are such items as ad valorem taxes, insurance, utilities and legal, accounting and management fees. The estimation of operating expenses in itself is a science which can be enhanced by experience, research and sensitivity to items which are variable in nature.

The natural tendency for all of us is to project our real estate investments with somewhat unlikely expense figures. A sale of a parcel of real estate usually triggers a change in the assessment value, thus changing the ad valorem taxes. Insurance coverage is also often a variable item.

The REALTORS NATIONAL MARKETING INSTITUTE® has developed a checklist which is extremely useful in the determination of operating expenses. The Annual Property Operating Data (APOD) form can be used like a pilot's checklist before takeoff. (See Figure 3–2 for an example of this form.) Each item is listed as an expense; of course, the difficult part is determining the correct amount to list. A word of caution: the current owner's expenses always seem to be less than what one might experience

Figure 3–2

Annual Property Operating Data

Date ______
Price $ ______
Loans $ ______
Equity $ ______

Purpose ______
Name ______
Location ______
Type of Property ______
Assessed/Appraised Values

	$	%
Land	$	%
Improvement	$	%
Personal Property	$	%
Total	$	100 %

Adjusted Basis as of ______ $ ______

FINANCING

Existing	Balance	Payment	# Pymt/Yr.	Interest	Term
1st	$			%	
2nd	$			%	
3rd	$			%	
Potential					
1st				%	
2nd	$			%	

		%	2	3	Comments
1	SCHEDULED RENTAL INCOME				
2	Less: Vacancy and Credit Losses				
3	EFFECTIVE RENTAL INCOME				
4	Plus: Other Income				
5	GROSS OPERATING INCOME				
6	Less: Operating Expenses				
7	Accounting and Legal				
8	Advertising, Licenses and Permits				
9	Property Insurance				
10	Property Management				
11	Payroll-Resident Management				
12	Other				
13	Taxes-Worker's Compensation				
14	Personal Property Taxes				
15	Real Estate Taxes				
16	Repairs and Maintenance				
17	Services-Elevator				
18	Janitorial				
19	Lawn				
20	Pool				
21	Rubbish				
22	Other				
23	Supplies				
24	Utilities-Electricity				
25	Gas and Oil				
26	Sewer and Water				
27	Telephone				
28	Other				
29	Miscellaneous				
30					
31	TOTAL OPERATING EXPENSES				
32	NET OPERATING INCOME				
33	Less: Annual Debt Service				
34	CASH FLOW BEFORE TAXES				

The statements and figures presented herein, while not guaranteed, are secured from sources we believe authoritative.

Prepared by ______

after a purchase. It isn't that owners do not tell the truth about their property; it is often easy to forget an item or two when asked for a list of expenses. In a way, it is like the gas mileage of your car. Did you ever notice that your mileage per gallon when checked at the pump is *never* what you told people it was all week? Check the mileage per gallon in your car against the manufacturer's estimated MPG sometime. You get the picture.

The APOD form is really a checklist which is a useful tool to have when collecting income and expense data. It can also be used as a worksheet for any type of property. It can be used to list either the owner's income and expense information or the projected income and expenses for the next year assuming there will be a new owner. In the right hand corner of the APOD, information about financing is detailed.

Net Operating Income (NOI)

Of all the numbers we have reviewed so far in the determination of the Cash Flow Before Taxes the Net Operating Income (NOI) is probably the most important. (Not that the others weren't, since we used them to get here.) The NOI is the amount of money in the "checkbook" *after* all the rents are collected and operating expenses are paid. As with some other investments, this is the amount of money the investment produces on an annual basis. Later on we will measure how the value of a piece of real estate is tied to the NOI. All of the income tax calculations (savings we hope) will be made from the NOI number, so it is imperative that the NOI be as accurate as possible. Any financing which might be included on the investment is *not* reflected in this number, however.

Debt Service (DS)

If we have a mortgage and must service debt on that mortgage, we would pay it out of the NOI. The debt is not a direct expense of the property since it is the decision of the investor to place a burden on the NOI by servicing debt from the cash produced by the property. Practically speaking, most real estate investments carry some debt in order to take advantage of leverage and interest deductions.

Cash Flow Before Taxes (CFBT)

The bottom line to real estate investments on a before-tax basis is the Cash Flow Before Taxes which is basically:

$$\text{Income} - \text{Expenses} = \text{NOI}$$
$$\text{NOI} - \text{Debt Service} = \text{CFBT}$$

Here are a couple of examples for comparison purposes:

Raw Land

Scheduled Rental Income	-0-
—Vacancy	-0-
Gross Operating Income	-0-
Expenses:	
—Taxes	$2,400
—Maintenance	500
NOI	(2,900)
—Debt Service	12,000
Cash Flow Before Taxes	(14,900)

12-Unit Apartment House

		Broker's Comments
Scheduled Rental Income	$43,200	$300 per month x 12 units x 12 months
—Vacancy (5%)	2,160	
Effective Rental Income	41,040	
+Other Income	600	Laundry income
Gross Operating Income	41,640	
—Expenses (35%)	14,574	Did a lot of research on these expenses and I feel pretty good about this projection. The management company I'm using said it's probably a little high but that's OK.
NOI	$27,066	
—DS	26,400	$2200 payment per month
CFBT	666	Whew, that's not much but it beats the raw land's and its negative CFBT (at least at this level).

Tax Savings

Tax savings can emanate from the acquisition, operation and disposition stages of real estate ownership. However, it is necessary to understand the basic premise of how real estate is taxed in the operation stage before we venture into the more complicated areas of the tax law.

Taxable income from real estate is a benchmark by which one can assess the tax benefits of ownership. A negative taxable income can produce positive after-tax cash flows. Since tax rates change every year and all investors are not taxed at equal rates, the impact of taxes on real estate will vary from year to year and from investor to investor.

For our discussion, we will consider taxes as referring only to the federal income tax liability. It is of course necessary to take into consideration state and local taxes when analyzing investments, but here, for simplicity's sake, we will focus only on the federal income tax.

The basic tax advantages available to the real estate investor involve taking tax deductions today in exchange for tax obligations at a later date and shifting the subsequent obligation to a lower tax bracket than that applied to the initial deduction. The deduction taken against ordinary income may subsequently be taxed at capital gains rates. The value of these benefits can be enhanced by the use of borrowed money. In certain circumstances the investor is able to receive cumulative tax deductions equal to several times his initial equity investment. Thus, the investor does not avoid income taxes by investing in real estate; rather, he *defers* the tax obligation to a later date and possibly shifts it to a lower tax bracket. This is what many investors term the "tax shelter" aspect of real estate.

As noted earlier, income tax is levied against a taxpayer's *net* income rather than his gross income. In addition to wages and salaries, other income earned is also subject to taxation. Included in this other income category is the taxable income from the operation of real estate. When there is a positive taxable income, it is added to the taxpayer's other taxable income, and taxed accordingly. When there is a negative taxable income, this "loss" is deducted from the other taxable income, thus reducing the overall tax liability.

Recall that the Internal Revenue Service (IRS) permits us to deduct any costs involved in the annual operation of a property. After all expenses are recorded we end up with a Net Operating Income. This NOI is the foundation for the determination of tax liability, or savings, from real estate ownership. There are two items which are deducted from NOI to get to a taxable income for annual tax reporting:

NOI
– Interest
– Cost Recovery

Taxable Income

Interest

The interest expense is the amount paid in the form of annual debt service which is paid out of the NOI. The debt service is usually made up of both interest and principal, but it is necessary to separate the two because the principal is not deducted and, in essence, is taxed during the year of operations. (It may be possible through negative taxable income to shelter the principal and defer taxes to a later date.)

Study the following amortization schedule and notice what is happening as the payments are made. (The word amortize actually comes from a Latin derivative and in essence means "to gradually kill off.")

$50,000 mortgage

13% interest

Amortized over 25 years with monthly payments

5-year payoff (due date)

Payment: $563.92 monthly

$6767.01 annual debt service

EOY (End of year)	**Yrs Remaining**	**Interest**	**Principal**	**Remaining Balance**
1	24	$ 6483.52	$ 283.52	$49,716.48
2	23	6444.36	322.68	49,393.80
3	22	6399.80	367.24	49,026.56
4	21	6349.14	417.90	48,608.66
5	20	6291.45	475.59	48,133.07
↓	↓	↓	↓	↓
23	2	1891.61	4875.43	11,857.82
24	1	1218.64	5548.40	6,309.42
25	0	452.79	6314.25	-0-

Notice that in each year the annual debt service (ADS) is paid, the interest amount reduces and the principal amount increases. This is one of the variables which will be at work within the tax calculations when a projection is made for an anticipated holding period.

Although our purpose was to separate the interest from the ADS, it is also enlightening to note the gradual reduction of the balance as the loan is paid. This loan balance will become important later on when we discuss mortgage reduction, balloon payments and disposition.

Once the interest amount has been determined for the annual period being analyzed, our tax calculation for operations begins to take form. Let's work with the following $75,000 income-producing property (an apartment building) to see how the benefits of real estate come about. We will use the $50,000 mortgage shown above.

Assume we have kept close tabs on the apartments, and at the end of the first year of operation our "checkbook" looks like this:

Checkbook

Gross Operating Income	$10,000
—Expenses	3000
Net Operating Income (NOI)	$ 7000
—Annual Debt Service (ADS)	6767
Cash Flow Before Tax (CFBT)	$ 233

The tax calculation looks like this:

Tax World

Net Operating Income (NOI)	$ 7000
—Interest	6483
—Cost Recovery	______
Taxable income	

To complete our calculation of the first year's tax implications we need to understand the theory of cost recovery or, as many of us still think of it, depreciation.

Cost Recovery System

One of the most important attributes of real estate investment is the opportunity extended under the present laws to shelter a part or all of an investment's current earnings with an appropriate cost recovery deduction. In addition, and depending on the amount of the cost recovery deducted, "paper" losses may be generated from a particular investment; such losses may be utilized to shelter income from other sources. In fact, this tax sheltering aspect often becomes an investor's primary motivation for entering into a real estate transaction and therefore merits close examination. As mentioned, tax shelter is the reduction, postponement or elimination of tax.

Before the 1981 Economic Recovery Tax Act (ERTA) the cost recovery system was called depreciation. This term was at times confusing since real estate as an asset could have physical, functional or economic depreciation. The name change to cost recovery, although conceptually the same as depreciation, more accurately describes the asset allocation to be recovered year after year as a "paper" expense. In theory, cost recovery is the return of investment in business and income-producing property, prorated throughout its economic useful life.

Real estate investors think in terms of market value when buying, selling or financing real property. When buying, the purchase price is utilized to establish the "basis," or beginning book value of the investment on which cost recovery will be applied. When selling, the sales price will determine the amount of profit or gain secured as a result of the difference between the sales price and the adjusted basis (book balance) at the time of sale. Any cost recovery taken annually must be deducted from the basis of the property for calculation of gain at the time of sale (we will get to that concept shortly).

Cost recovery is determined after examining three factors: value of the land, value of the improvements and an estimate of the economic life of the improvement. The value of the land is included in the total market value; however, for cost recovery purposes, the value of the land is set apart from the improvements since land does not wear out and cannot legally be depreciated. Only the improvements made to and on the land are eligible for the deductions which cost recovery provides. Such improvements might consist of streets, sewers, buildings, pavement, fences, swimming pools and similar facilities.

Useful life determination used to give the investor a high degree of discretionary control in the ax structuring of an investment. Accordingly, the IRS would occasionally challenge, via an audit, an investor's discretionary choice of useful life. The whole area of useful life determination has been eliminated with the 1981 ERTA. The tax law now requires all real property to be depreciated over a 18-year period. It also allows a longer period of 35 or 45 years to be selected for certain types of property, but these longer periods of cost recovery will apply to very few investors in the day to day real estate business.

Depreciation methods The methods available have been simplified in the tax law. No longer does an investor have the option of choosing a type of accelerated depreciation or of breaking the property into many components, each with a different depreciation schedule.[1]

Two cost recovery methods are available. The straight line method recovers the same amount per year over the 18-year recovery period. This works out to be approximately:

$$\frac{100\%}{18 \text{ years}} = 5.555\% \text{ per year}$$

The other method available is the accelerated cost recovery system which is approximately 175 percent of the straight line amount per year except on a declining table. This method permits taxpayers to take larger cost recovery amounts in the early years of the ownership period.

1. See Stephen D. Messner, Irving Schreiber, Victor L. Lyon and Robert L. Ward. *Marketing Investment Real Estate*, 3rd ed. (Chicago: REALTORS NATIONAL MARKETING INSTITUTE®, 1985), Chapter 9, for a complete discussion of cost recovery.

The following tables outline the amount of cost recovery available for real property (except low-income housing) placed in service the first month of the tax year. According to tables published by the IRS.

Year	ACRS Available Cost Recovery	Straight Line
1	9%	5
2	9	6
3	8	6
4	7	6
5	7	6
6	6	6
7	5	6
8	5	6
9	5	6
10	5	6
11	5	5
12	5	5
13	4	5
14	4	5
15	4	5
16	4	5
17	4	5
18	4	1

Note from the table that the accelerated amount is less and less each year and eventually goes below the amount available under the straight line method (5 percent). This changing variable is another reason for projecting ownership into the future and subsequently monitoring the performance of an investment on an after-tax analysis.

Example 1 Here is an example of straight line cost recovery determination (properties placed in service first month of tax year):

Total Sale Price	$150,000
Land Value (per appraisal)	30,000
Improvement Value	$120,000

or

$120,000 × 5% = $6000

If it were determined that it would be to the investor's advantage to take the accelerated method of cost recovery, our example would change:

$120,000 of Improvement Value
× 9% (year 1 percentage from table above)
$ 10,800

Note how the accelerated method yields $10,800 of cost recovery instead of only $6000 obtained with the straight line method. Although the accelerated method looks superior from the above figures, it must be scrutinized. Later in this chapter we will look at the type of property, the investor's tax postion and the anticipated disposition of the property in relation to the method of cost recovery.

Example 2 For many years the IRS has agreed that the assessed tax valuation of a piece of property has some validity in the allocation of land/improvement value. For example:

Assessed Value		Market Value	
Total	$100,000	Total	$285,000
Land	$ 23,000 (23%)	Land	65,550 (23% of 285,000)
Improvements	$ 77,000 (77%)	Improvements	219,450 (77% of 285,000)

$219,450 × 5% = $10,972 Cost Recovery per Year

With $219,450 of improvement value, the first and second year's accelerated cost recovery amount would be:

$219,450 × 9% = $19,750

Notice that the third year's cost recovery amount would be:

$219,450 × 8% = $17,556

Since many properties do not get placed into service in the first month of the year, the IRS has published the cost recovery table shown as Figure 3-3 to determine the amount of cost recovery available in any one tax year, depending on when the property is placed into service.

"Tax World"

Now that we understand cost recovery, let's get back to the effect it has on our "tax world" calculation of taxable income from real estate (see page 47). Recall our example of the $75,000 property.

Figure 3-3a Straight-Line Depreciation Tables

18-Year Straight Line Using Mid-Month Convention
(For property placed in service after June 22, 1984)

If the Recovery Year is:	And the Month in the First Recovery Year the Property is Placed in Service is:					
	1–2	3–4	5–7	8–9	10–11	12
	The applicable percentage is:					
1	5	4	3	2	1	0.2
2	6	6	6	6	6	6.0
3	6	6	6	6	6	6.0
4	6	6	6	6	6	6.0
5	6	6	6	6	6	6.0
6	6	6	6	6	6	6.0
7	6	6	6	6	6	6.0
8	6	6	6	6	6	6.0
9	6	6	6	6	6	6.0
10	6	6	6	6	6	6.0
11	5	5	5	5	5	5.8
12	5	5	5	5	5	5.0
13	5	5	5	5	5	5.0
14	5	5	5	5	5	5.0
15	5	5	5	5	5	5.0
16	5	5	5	5	5	5.0
17	5	5	5	5	5	5.0
18	5	5	5	5	5	5.0
19	1	2	3	4	5	5.0

Figure 3-3b

18-Year Real Estate Other Than Low-Income Housing
(Put into service after June 22, 1984)

If the Recovery Year is:	And the Month in the First Recovery Year the Property is Placed in Service is:											
	1	2	3	4	5	6	7	8	9	10	11	12
	The applicable percentage is:											
1	9	9	8	7	6	5	4	4	3	2	1	0.4
2	9	9	9	9	9	9	9	9	9	10	10	10.0
3	8	8	8	8	8	8	8	8	9	9	9	9.0
4	7	7	7	7	7	8	8	8	8	8	8	8.0
5	7	7	7	7	7	7	7	7	7	7	7	7.0
6	6	6	6	6	6	6	6	6	6	6	6	6.0
7	5	5	5	5	6	6	6	6	6	6	6	6.0
8	5	5	5	5	5	5	5	5	5	5	5	5.0
9	5	5	5	5	5	5	5	5	5	5	5	5.0
10	5	5	5	5	5	5	5	5	5	5	5	5.0
11	5	5	5	5	5	5	5	5	5	5	5	5.0
12	5	5	5	5	5	5	5	5	5	5	5	5.0
13	4	4	4	5	4	4	4	4	4	4	4	5.0
14	4	4	4	4	4	4	4	4	4	4	4	4.0
15	4	4	4	4	4	4	4	4	4	4	4	4.0
16	4	4	4	4	4	4	4	4	4	4	4	4.0
17	4	4	4	4	4	4	4	4	4	4	4	4.0
18	4	3	4	4	4	4	4	4	4	4	4	4.0
19		1	1	1	2	2	2	3	3	3	3	3.6

To determine cost recovery we must first "allocate" land and building. A quick check at the county tax office shows that our building is being taxed on an 80 percent/20 percent allocation—80 percent improvement value/ 20 percent land. If we multiply the $75,000 purchase price times 80 percent we find that a justifiable allocation for our building is $60,000. If we use the available 18-year life for straight line cost recovery we can take $3000 per year:

$$\$60{,}000 \times 5\% = \$3000$$

in the "paper" recovery of the asset.

Another alternative would be to use accelerated cost recovery, using the same $60,000 allocation and the same 18-year recovery period but to utilize the accelerated cost recovery table to determine the amount of cost recovery available. The first year amount available is 9 percent of the allocated basis or $60,000 times 9 percent, which equals $5400. One can readily see how the accelerated method provides more cost recovery in the early years of an investment. We will see later, however, how the tax posture of the individual investor determines which cost recovery table to use.

For our example, let's assume we choose straight line cost recovery. The taxable income determination now looks like this:

Tax World

NOI	$7000	
— Interest	6483	
— Cost Recovery	$3000	(SL $60,000 improvement value)
Taxable Income	(2483)	

Establishing Tax Liability

It is at this point that the active broker selling investment properties must understand the concept used by the IRS to establish tax liability for individuals. Although real estate can be owned by other entities such as corporations, trusts and estates, we will concentrate on the benefits of real estate as they accrue to an individual. The taxable income from real estate is added to the individual's other taxable income.

The simplistic approach to understanding an individual's tax liability (although the IRS tax code is anything but simple) is to:

- Anticipate or estimate the gross amount of dollars earned
- Subtract any exemptions and deductions
- Apply taxable income to the appropriate tax rate schedule

Since tax rate schedules are designed in a progressive manner, one can view them as a set of stairsteps that increases the amount the government will "take according to how much we make." The 1981 ERTA reduction in taxes implemented the tax rate schedules shown in Figure 3–5. Notice that the top rate an individual can pay in tax is 50 percent. This is a reduction from the 70 percent "marginal bracket" in force before 1982. The "marginal bracket" is the level of tax levied on the last dollar of taxable income. For example, in 1982 if an individual reported $29,900 of taxable income, the next dollar earned would be taxed at 33 percent. This percentage is what a person refers to when he says, "I'm in a 30 percent tax bracket."

The marginal bracket and progressive tax schedule are what give rise to tax savings in real estate. Refer again to the $29,900 taxable income level on the "married, filing jointly" schedule for 1982.

The tax liability is

$29,900 taxable income = $5574 tax

If, say, $1000 taxable income is added to the $29,900, the tax liability now becomes

$30,900 = $5574 tax + 33% of $1000

or

$5574 + $330 = $5904

Figure 3–4

The more you make, the more *he* takes.

Figure 3-5 Tax Schedules

1985 TAX RATE SCHEDULES

SINGLE TAXPAYERS

If taxable income is: Over—	but not over—	The tax is:	of the amount over—
$ 0	$ 2,390	-0-	
2,390	3,540	11%	$ 2,390
3,540	4,580	$ 126.50 + 12%	3,540
4,580	6,760	251.30 + 14%	4,580
6,760	8,850	556.50 + 15%	6,760
8,850	11,240	870.00 + 16%	8,850
11,240	13,430	1,252.40 + 18%	11,240
13,430	15,610	1,646.60 + 20%	13,430
15,610	18,940	2,082.60 + 23%	15,610
18,940	24,460	2,848.50 + 26%	18,940
24,460	29,970	4,283.70 + 30%	24,460
29,970	35,490	5,936.70 + 34%	29,970
35,490	43,190	7,813.50 + 38%	35,490
43,190	57,550	10,739.50 + 42%	43,190
57,550	85,130	16,770.70 + 48%	57,550
85,130	. . .	30,009.10 + 50%	85,130

HEADS OF HOUSEHOLD

If taxable income is: Over—	but not over—	The tax is:	of the amount over—
$ 0	$ 2,390	-0-	
2,390	4,580	... 11%	$ 2,390
4,580	6,760	$ 240.90 + 12%	4,580
6,760	9,050	502.50 + 14%	6,760
9,050	12,280	823.10 + 17%	9,050
12,280	15,610	1,372.20 + 18%	12,280
15,610	18,940	1,971.60 + 20%	15,610
18,940	24,460	2,637.60 + 24%	18,940
24,460	29,970	3.962.40 + 28%	24,460
29,970	35,490	5,505.20 + 32%	29,970
35,490	46,520	7,271.60 + 35%	35,490
46,520	63,070	11,132.10 + 42%	46,520
63,070	85,130	18,083.10 + 45%	63,070
85,130	112,720	28,010.10 + 48%	85,130
112,720	. . .	41,253.30 + 50%	112,720

Figure 3-5 Tax Schedules (Continued)

1985 TAX RATE SCHEDULES

MARRIED FILING JOINT RETURNS AND QUALIFYING WIDOWS AND WIDOWERS

If taxable income is: Over—	but not over—	The tax is:	of the amount over—
$ 0	$ 3,540	-0-	
3,540	5,720	11%	$ 3,540
5,720	7,910	$ 239.80 + 12%	5,720
7,910	12,390	502.60 + 14%	7,910
12,390	16,650	1,129.80 + 16%	12,390
16,650	21,020	1,811.40 + 18%	16,650
21,020	25,600	2,598.00 + 22%	21,020
25,600	31,120	3,605.60 + 25%	25,600
31,120	36,630	4,985.60 + 28%	31,120
36,630	47,670	6,528.40 + 33%	36,630
47,670	62,450	10,171.60 + 38%	47,670
62,450	89,090	15,788.00 + 42%	62,450
89,090	113,860	26,976.80 + 45%	89,090
113,860	169,020	38,123.30 + 49%	113,860
169,020	. . .	65,151.70 + 50%	169,020

MARRIED FILING SEPARATE RETURNS

If taxable income is: Over—	but not over—	The tax is:	of the amount over—
$ 0	$ 1,770	-0-	
1,770	2,860	11%	$ 1,770
2,860	3,955	$ 119.90 + 12%	2,860
3,955	6,195	251.30 + 14%	3,955
6,195	8,325	564.90 + 16%	6,195
8,325	10,510	905.70 + 18%	8,325
10,510	12,800	1,299.00 + 22%	10,510
12,800	15,560	1,802.80 + 25%	12,800
15,560	18,315	2,492.80 + 28%	15,560
18,315	23,835	3,264.20 + 33%	18,315
23,835	31,225	5,085.80 + 38%	23,835
31,225	44,545	7,894.00 + 42%	31,225
44,545	56,930	13,488.40 + 45%	44,545
56,930	84,510	19,061.65 + 49%	56,930
84,510	. . .	32,575.85 + 50%	84,510

The $1000 income caused an additional $330 tax liability for the individual. If the $1000 taxable income were negative, or a $1000 loss (such as the case with most real estate investments), the $29,900 taxable income now becomes $28,900. The tax on $28,900 is:

$28,900 taxable income = $5284 tax

compared to

$29,900 taxable income = $5574 tax

Notice that the ($1000) created a tax liability $290 *less* than the liability on the $29,900. This tax savings is a direct result of the negative taxable income from real estate. Generally, it can be said that a negative taxable income from real estate will create tax savings which should then be attributed to the real estate.

Notice in the example that the $290 savings is 29 percent of the ($1000) taxable savings. This is why investors use a marginal bracket as an estimate for tax liability or savings. However, the danger in estimating a bracket can be seen in the tax rate schedules (see Figure 3–5). Not only do the schedules change from year to year, but an investor's taxable income would have to be the same amount year after year for an accurate projection. This is, of course, not always realistic but it is the most commonly used way of determining tax savings. Another note of caution: The marginal bracket determination of tax savings can be misleading if the taxable income increases enough to jump more than one bracket.

Let's go back to our $75,000 property example (page 46) and determine the actual tax savings and a marginal bracket estimation of savings for the first year.

Our $75,000 apartment project had the following taxable income, as determined by our interest calculation and cost recovery selection:

NOI	$7000
— Interest	6483
— Cost Recovery	3000
Taxable Income	(2483)

The negative taxable income in this example will translate to tax savings but the *amount* of tax savings depends on the individual investor. The level of taxation, or the marginal bracket of the investor, becomes important at this point. For our example, let's make the assumption that the investor considering the investment property is married, filing jointly for 1984, and has a taxable income of $29,500. According to the 1984 tax rate schedule, this investor is in the "25 percent bracket" which many people immediately multiply by the taxable income to get the actual tax savings.

The more precise way to view this concept is that the negative taxable income from the real estate reduces the overall tax liability, thus creating tax savings. Generally speaking, we might calculate this way:

NOI	$7000	
— Interest	6483	
— Cost Recovery	3000	
Taxable Income	(2483)	
	× 25%	tax bracket
	$620.75	tax savings

Actually, here is what is happening: Without the real estate our investor would have paid more income tax on $29,500. Using the 1984 schedule:

	Taxable Income
$24,600 – 29,900	$3465 + 25% on excess over $24,600
or	
$29,500	$3465 + 25% of $4900
	for a total tax of $4690.

With the real estate, the total tax liability is not figured on $29,500 but rather $29,500 plus the real estate taxable income of ($2483) or $27,017. The tax on $27,017 is $3465 plus 25 percent of $2417, or $4069. We can now make a direct comparison.

Tax Without Real Estate	Tax With Real Estate
$4690	$4069

The $621 difference which the investor did not have to pay in tax (tax savings) was a direct result of the real estate ownership. Also, the amount of tax savings after all the calculations is exactly the same as we determined by multiplying the taxable income from real estate ($2483) times 25 percent. The reason is that the amounts of taxable income were all within the line of $24,600–29,900 on the schedule.

The tax schedules being the "stairsteps" that they are create interesting results when large amounts of taxable income are added. The marginal bracket method becomes somewhat misleading under the following circumstances, for example. Let's use the same investor ($29,500 taxable income for 1984), but assume for a moment the taxable income from the real estate is ($21,900). The question now becomes what bracket to use since adding ($21,900) to our investor's $29,500 taxable income will result in only a $7600 taxable income. Notice how he dropped all the way down to the 14 percent bracket from the 25 percent bracket. Obviously, it would be difficult to determine a tax savings from these circumstances without actually calculating the tax. One's first inclination might be to apply the 25 percent bracket to the ($21,900) and calculate $6351 in tax savings. Let's take a closer look:

Tax Without Real Estate		**Tax With Real Estate**	
Total Taxable Income	$29,500	Total Taxable Income	$7600
Tax	$ 4690	Tax	$ 483

Taking the ($21,900) times 25 percent creates $5470 tax savings which would not be possible since the total tax on $29,500 is only $4690. The actual tax savings because of the real estate is $4207 ($4690 less $483).

This concept of graduated tax rate schedules and the tax savings from real estate is very important in the sales field since tax benefits are a strong "suit" of real estate investments. Many times a broker will not have specific tax information for an investor and thus will use an example tax bracket rather than disregard the tax benefits altogether. (We will see some of this in Chapter 7, "Presenting the Package.")

We have described the tax savings from our $75,000 property, but did you notice that our property has really had two cash flow benefits so far? A summary of the first year's cash flows for our investor might look like this:

Checkbook		**Tax World**	
Net Operating Income (NOI)	$7000	Net Operating Income (NOI)	$7000
— Annual Debt Service (ADS)	6767	— Interest	6483
Cash Flow Before Tax (CFBT)	233	— Cast Recovery	4000
		Taxable Income	(2483)
		Investor's Marginal Bracket	× 25%
		Tax Savings	$ 621

The cash flow of the $233 in the checkbook and the $621 saved in taxes gives our investor a total Cash Flow After Tax (CFAT) of $854 for the first year. These two benefits come from the operations portion of the real estate and continue year after year into the ownership period. Each year's cash flow will undoubtedly be different than that of the year before because of the variables involved. The next year's gross operating rents might be different due to increases or vacancies, and expenses will change, affecting the NOI and the before-tax cash flow. In the "tax world," the interest deduction will be less and less as the principal payment increases each year. If we had used the Accelerated Cost Recovery System (ACRS) instead of straight line, the cost recovery amount would change each year. Finally, our investor's overall taxable income might change, thus changing his tax liability from year to year. All these variables, constantly changing, make real estate one of the most interesting and challenging investment vehicles to project over a period of time. Projections are needed, however, to closely analyze real estate's potential benefits.

It was mentioned earlier that real estate-generated benefits come from four areas: Cash Flow Before Taxes, tax savings, appreciation and mortgage reduction. We have discussed the first two as they accrue in the operation of real estate ownership. Appreciation and mortgage reduction are also at work, but cash rewards from these will not be realized until the property is sold (or possibly refinanced). Since these benefits will not be collected until time of sale it only makes sense to look at these benefits on an after-tax basis. As a matter of fact, all investments should be analyzed on an after-tax basis so they can be accurately compared.

Appreciation and Mortgage Reduction

Real estate has a tendency to increase in value. This increase or appreciation in value may be due to desirability, improvement, inflation, market conditions or increased rental income. With income-producing property this rental income (Net Operating Income) could be increased by higher rental rates, lower expenses or more effective management. Regardless of the way the value of the property increases, appreciation has historically been one of the main reasons investors buy real estate.

Combined with the leverage position under which most real estate investments are purchased, appreciation helps the astute investor increase the amount of equity (value minus mortgage amount) in the investment. This increase of equity is not realized or taxed until some later date when a disposition occurs.

The reduction of mortgage is another benefit which many people overlook in the cash flow analysis of real estate investments. Recall from the $75,000 apartment example that a $50,000 mortgage at 13 percent interest amortized over 25 years had $284 of principal paid in the first year.

The principal amount in Year Two was $323 and by the end of Year Five the balance on the original $50,000 mortgage was $48,133. The $1867 mortgage reduction is actually paid by the property; it is sheltered from tax by cost recovery and will eventually end up in the investor's pocket after favorable tax treatment. This increase of equity through appreciation and mortgage reduction is illustrated in Figure 3–6.

Figure 3–6
Equity Build-up

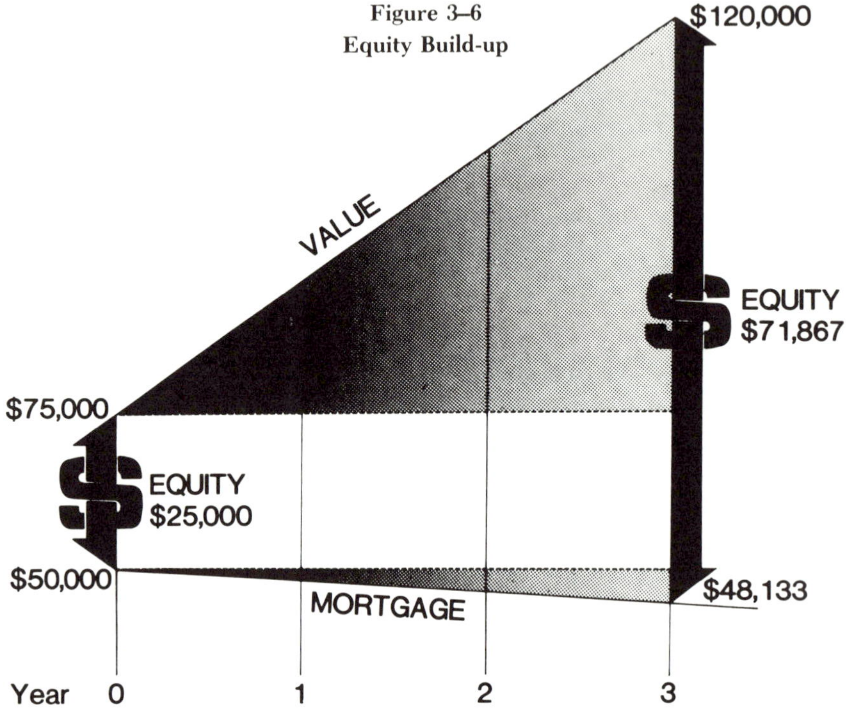

In the example shown in Figure 3–6 the original property value of $75,-000 grew to $120,000 in five years because of inflation. All the while the mortgage was methodically being reduced to a balance of $48,133. This new equity value minus the mortgage position of $71,867 ($120,000 less $48,133) was created in spite of the investor's activities. It might have been possible that effective management policies dictated the increase in value, but many an investor has been spared financial ruin by this very concept. Remember, the growth of $25,000 equity to $71,867 equity does not represent the whole picture since all investments must be viewed after tax. The reduction of these cash flows to an after-tax basis will give us an opportunity to view not only the cash flows from operations after tax but also disposition proceeds.

Taxation of Sale Proceeds

There are, of course, alternatives to an outright sale of property with its tax implications, but for the following explanation we will approach taxation of sale proceeds in a straightforward, simplistic manner. Just as it does in the "tax world" of operations, the IRS has its own language in the area of taxation on the disposition of investment real estate. There are a number of items and terms to keep in mind.

The IRS will tax the transaction on the difference between the sale price and the original purchase price after certain adjustments have been made to both. The original purchase price (original basis) is the starting point for this calculation.

Adjustments required to be made to the original basis are:

- plus any capital improvements, i.e., new roof, garages or driveways
- minus all cost recovery taken during ownership
- minus any partial sales, i.e., extra land
- equals adjusted basis

The adjusted basis is the amount to be subtracted from the sale price to determine the gain on the sale for tax purposes.

Example

$100,000 Apartment

$100,000	Original Basis	(original purchase price)
20,000 +	Capital Improvements	(say a garage and driveway)
16,000 –	Cost Recovery	(total cost recovery taken over holding period)
10,000 –	Partial Sale	(sold a small lot which was 10% of original purchase)
$ 94,000	Adjusted Basis	(at time of sale)

Assume a sale price of $160,000 which is reduced by the amount of sales costs paid to sell the property. Let's assume sales costs are $11,500 and there has been a three-year holding period. Our determination of gain for the IRS would then look like this:

Sales Price	$160,000
–Sales Costs	11,500
–Adjusted Basis	94,000
Gain	$ 54,500

This is the way gain on sale is determined:

- As a capital asset, real estate is eligible for long-term capital gain tax treatment if the asset has been held for more than six months.
- Tax is paid on 100 percent of ordinary income, but only on 40 percent of long-term capital gain.
- Financing has no effect whatsoever on gains.
- The gain must be reduced by any cost recovery taken over and above the straight line amount (called excess cost recovery).
- The excess cost recovery will be "recaptured" and taxed at ordinary income rates at the time of sale.
- This *recapture* of excess cost recovery takes place any time the accelerated cost recovery system (ACRS) is used.
- Straight line cost recovery is not recaptured.

Cost Recovery and Recapture

The 1981 Economic Recovery Tax Act lists the following rules for recapture of cost recovery:

Property	Rule
All real estate using straight line method	No recapture
Residential properties using accelerated method	Excess of accelerated over straight line
Commercial and industrial properties using accelerated method	Full recapture

In the example above the gain of $54,500 would receive different treatment depending on the type of property and the type of cost recovery taken. If straight line cost recovery were used, no recapture rules apply, so $54,500 becomes a capital gain; the taxable amount the IRS will recognize becomes $54,500 times 40 percent, or $21,800.

If the property in the example were a commercial property and accelerated cost recovery were taken, all cost recovery taken would be recaptured. The balance of gain would receive capital gains treatment:

$54,500	Total Gain
–16,000	Cost Recovery Taken
$38,500	Capital Gain

The $16,000 would be taxed at ordinary income rates while the capital gain of $38,500 times 40 percent, or $15,400, would be recognized by the IRS as taxable.

However, since our example is a residential property (an apartment building), only the excess amount of cost recovery over the straight line amount would be recaptured. The balance of the gain would receive capital gain treatment:

Excess Determination

	Total Cost Recovery Taken	$16,000	
Less:	Straight Line Cost Recovery	10,000	
	Excess Cost Recovery	$ 6,000	
	Total Gain	$54,500	
Less:	Excess Cost Recovery	6,000	(taxed at ordinary rate)
	Long-Term Capital Gain	$48,500	(receives capital gain treatment)

The $6,000 would be taxed at ordinary income rates, while the capital gain of $48,500 times 40 percent, or $19,400, would be recognized by the IRS as taxable.

Although these taxable amounts vary with each specific property, the real test of investment strategy comes at the beginning of the holding period since that is the time a decision whether to use straight line or accelerated cost recovery must be made. An investor not only needs to project the future of the property and its sales price; he also must consider his personal tax posture since the amounts of taxable income from the sale will be piled on top of personal taxable income.

Capital Gains Rates

The hoopla that you probably heard about the 1981 tax bill was that capital gains tax rates were lowered to 20 percent. That is not strictly the case. We saw above that only 40 percent of the capital gains is recognized. The tax rate schedules in 1982 were reduced so that the highest bracket is 50 percent. What is really meant by a 20 percent capital gains tax is that the maximum tax on capital gains is 40 percent times the 50 percent bracket, or 20 percent.

Many times an investor will determine the maximum tax on capital gains simply by multiplying the capital gains amount by 20 percent (50 percent of 40 percent), thus calculating the tax liability. Actually, an accurate analysis is somewhat more complicated if one is interested in the exact amount of tax which a sale triggers. This analysis becomes even more important if projections or "what if's" are being calculated to help make a decision about the method of cost recovery to be used.

Determining Tax Liability on Sale

The process for determining tax liability from a sale is exactly the same as determining tax liability during a year of operation except that the amounts of taxable income are usually larger. Let's take a look at an example of the after-tax proceeds calculations necessary to determine the amount of cash coming from the sale of a piece of real estate. Review the following as a road map before we apply it to the numbers:

1.		Sale Price
	Minus	Sales Costs
	Minus	Adjusted Basis
	Equals	Total Gain
	Minus	Accumulated Excess Cost Recovery
	Equals	Long-Term Capital Gain

2.		Long-Term Capital Gain
	Times	40%
	Equals	Taxable Portion of Long-Term Capital Gain
	Plus	Excess Cost Recovery
	Equals	Taxable Income From Sale

The actual tax liability *on* the sale of real estate is then determined by first looking at the particular investor's taxable income in the year of sale, but without the sale. A comparison of this tax liability can then be made to the total tax liability encountered after the taxable income from excess cost recovery and capital gains is piled on top of the ordinary income. A sale causes some additional tax to be paid. The additional tax above what would have been paid without the sale is directly attributable to the sale.

Example Assume Mr. and Mrs. Brown have a taxable income of $35,-200 in a particular year without selling the real estate they own. They look at a tax schedule and determine their total tax liability that year will be $7323. They entertain an offer on the real estate and find that because of taxable capital gains and some excess cost recovery, an additional $10,-600 of taxable income will be piled on the $35,200 taxable amount. They then compare the tax on $45,800 to the $7323 tax on $35,200. If they sell the property, the total tax for the year will be $11,457 (see Figure 3–7).

The outright sale of the real estate would trigger a taxable event of an additional $4134. This tax is directly attributable to the real estate and thus should be paid out of any sale proceeds before Mr. Brown tells his poker buddies about the tremendous profit made on the sale.

Figure 3–7
Mr. and Mrs. Brown's Tax Liability

The scenario is something like this: Having made the decision to sell at a lower-than-expected price, Mr. and Mrs. Brown anxiously await the day of closing. Since they owe only $55,000 on the mortgage note, a sale price of $110,000 looks pretty attractive. Once at the bank, however, the closing statement starts to nibble away at the $110,000 "profit." First there are the costs of sale, which include the broker, the attorney and the appraisal fees; these amount to $8700. Then the bank takes the amount needed to pay off the old mortgage of $55,300. Having paid these two items, the Browns leave the bank with a check in the amount of $46,000 and a smile on their faces.

No sooner do they pop out of the revolving doors of the bank when a skinny old man with a white beard, white and red striped pants, a blue shirt with white stars and a tall top hat taps them on the shoulder and says, "Don't forget your Uncle Sam!" A quick look at the tax table, a few calculations, and the Browns discover the sale has cost them an additional $4134 in tax. The Browns quickly plunk down $4134 to Uncle Sam and go on their way with a total of $41,866 after tax from the sale. A far cry from the amount Mr. Brown led his poker buddies to believe.

The only way to view and understand real estate investment is to thoroughly comprehend the basic tax concepts presented in this chapter. A conceptual understanding of real estate investment on an after-tax basis is an absolute necessity for the broker active in investment sales.[2]

It is not the purpose of this text to concentrate on methods of taxation, but rather to give an explanation of the benefits as they accrue to a real estate owner.

The simplistic approach presented here is by no means complete. Traps lie around every turn. Minimum tax, tax preference items, dealer status, mortgage over basis, imputed interest, basis of gift or inheritance are all areas that can lead the real estate practitioner down the path of misrepresentation through ignorance. Although we are constantly dealing with real estate on an after-tax basis, we are not accountants. Some real estate brokers have more interest than others in certain areas or certain tax laws, but it is important not to try to know "everything about every-

---

2. Numerous tools and methods are available to the practitioner to help him serve his clientele. Two of the most widely used vehicles of sale are the installment sale and tax deferred exchange. Both methods either spread out or defer taxable income from the sale to a later date when the tax implications may be less severe. It is difficult to understand how anyone active in investment sales can function without the knowledge of these sale tools. Both the exchange and installment sales process are treated in isolated splendor in *Real Estate Exchanges* by Mark Lee Levine and in *Marketing Investment Real Estate* by Stephen Messner, Irving Schreiber, Victor Lyon and Robert L. Ward. Both are published by the REALTORS NATIONAL MARKETING INSTITUTE®.

thing." This author believes that the most important item for the active broker to know about the tax code is his accountant's phone number! For a real estate practitioner, knowing when to ask the question is more important than knowing exactly what section of the code refers to which items.

Case Study

The following piece of property is anticipated to be held for two years. A Cash Flow Analysis form on this investment is shown as Figure 3–8.

The facts:

Property 2000 square-foot office building, five years old. Smith Insurance Agency is tenant and has two years left on lease, with option to renew.

Income Net lease, $1250 per month; tenant pays all expenses. Rent will increase to $1800 per month at the end of two years.

Purchase Price and Terms $125,000. Owner has agreed to carry $100,000 at 12 percent interest for only five years; new buyer has the right to assign contract anytime after first year.

Anticipated Sale Two-year holding period; sale price of $175,000 (rental increase will cause increase in value). Project outright sale since it will have the best tax impact.

Investor Last year the married investor had taxable income of $35,000. Even though he anticipates an increase in income, he figures his deductions will also increase. All calculations will therefore assume a taxable income of $35,000.

Note that on the tax schedule $35,000 falls on the marginal line of 30 percent for 1983 and 28 percent for 1984. It is safe to say that any taxable loss will save approximately 30 percent in tax liability in 1983 and 28 percent in 1984. The taxable income from the sale at the end of Year Two will have to be figured instead of using a bracket amount.

Projected Purchase Date: January 1, 1983

Projected Sale Date: December 31, 1984

Since this is a commercial property, straight line cost recovery will be used instead of the Accelerated Cost Recovery System (ACRS). If accelerated were used, *all* cost recovery would be recaptured and taxed at ordinary rates at the time of sale.

The Scratch Paper Method

The Financial Picture

	Year 1	Year 2
Gross Operating Income	15,000	15,000
— Expenses	-0-	-0-
Net Operating Income	15,000	15,000
— Debt Service	12,000	12,000
Cash Flow Before Taxes	3,000	3,000
Net Operating Income	15,000	15,000
— Interest	12,000	12,000
— Cost Recovery*	5,208	5,208
Taxable Income	(2,208)	(2,208)
Marginal Bracket	30%	28%
Tax Savings	662	618
Tax Savings	662	618
Cash Flow Before Taxes	3,000	3,000
Total After-Tax Cash Flow	$3,662	$3,618

After-Tax Cash Flow from the Operations: Year 1 3,662
Year 2 3,618

*$93,750 improvement value, 18-year straight line

Tax Implications of a Sale

Step 1:	Basis in Property		
	Original Basis	$125,000	
	— Cost Recovery	10,416	
	Adjusted Basis	$114,584	
Step 2:	Gain		
	Sale price	$175,000	
	— Cost of Sale	13,250	
	— Adjusted Basis	114,584	
	Gain	47,166	
	— Excess Cost Recovery	-0-	(straight line)
	Capital Gains	47,166	
		40%	
	Taxable Portion of Capital Gains	$ 18,866	

Step 3:	Taxable Income			
	Other Taxable Income	$ 35,000	Tax without Sale:	$ 6,218
	+Capital Gains	18,866		
	Taxable Income	$ 53,866	Tax with Sale:	$12,837

Step 4:	Tax with Sale	$ 12,837
	— Tax without Sale	6,218
	Tax Because of Sale	$ 6,619

Sale Price	$175,000
— Cost of Sale	13,250
— Mortgage	100,000
— Tax Liability	6,619
Proceeds After Tax	$ 55,131

Note the four areas of cash flow benefits from this property:

Cash Flow Before Taxes	$ 3,000 per year
Tax Benefits	$ 662, Year 1 and $618, Year 2
Appreciation	$55,131 after tax
Mortgage Reduction	-0-

These after-tax cash flows can be more accurately viewed:

Year	$
0	(25,000) (down payment)
1	3,662
2	3,618 + 55,131 (from the sale)

The Cash Flow Analysis form shown as Figure 3–8 guides one through the steps of calculating Cash Flows After Tax. Take a minute to compare this form to the "scratch paper" method above. Both accomplish the same goal—reducing the real estate investment to cash flows on an after-tax basis.

Figure 3–8

Cash Flow Analysis

For Mr. Investor

Purpose Smith Insurance Building Projection

Date

Purchase Price $125,000

Encumbrances 100,000

Investment 25,000

Mortgage Data

	Encumbrances	Beginning Balance	Remaining Term	Number of Payments Per Year	Interest Rate	Payment	Annual Debt Service	Remarks
1	1st Mortgage	100,000	Interest only	12	12	1000	12000	Due in 5 years
2	2nd Mortgage							
3	3rd Mortgage							

Taxable Income

	Ownership Analysis of Property Income:	Year: 1983	Year: 1984	Year:	Year:	Year:
4	Gross Scheduled Income	15 000	15 000			
5	Less: Vcy. & Credit Losses	0	0			
6	Gross Operating Income	15 000	15 000			
7	– Operating Expenses	0	0			
8	Net Operating Income	15 000	15 000			
9	– Non-Operating Expense	0	0			
10	– Interest – 1st Mortgage	12 000	12 000			
11	– Interest – 2nd Mortgage					
12	– Interest – 3rd Mortgage					
13	– Cost Recovery	5 208	5 208			
14	Real Est. Taxable Income	2 208	2 208			

Cash Flows

		Year: 1983	Year: 1984	Year:	Year:	Year:
15	Net Operating Income	15 000	15 000			
16	– Annual Debt Service	12 000	12 000			
17	– Funded Reserves	0	0			
18	– Capital Additions	0	0			
19	Cash Flow before Taxes	3 000	3 000			
20	– Minimum Tax	0	0			
21	– Tax Liability on Real Est.	(662)	(618)			
22	Cash Flow after Taxes	3 662	3 618			

EOY	Mortgage Balance
	1st Mortgage
	2nd Mortgage
	3rd Mortgage

Analysis of Sale Proceeds

Year:

	Adjusted Basis		Excess Cost Recovery (CR)		Tax Liability on Sale	
23	Original Basis	125 000	Total CR	10 416	Excess Recapture Tax	
24	+ Capital Improvements	0	S/L CR	10 416	Capital Gain Tax	
25	– Cost Recovery	10 416	Excess CR*	0	Tax Liability on Sale	6 619
26	– Partial Sales	0	Exc. CR Carryover			
27	AB	114 584	**Gain**		**Sale Proceeds**	
28			Sale Price	175 000	Sale Price	175 000
			– Cost of Sale	13 250	– Costs of Sale	13 250
			– AB	114 584	– Mortgage	100 000
			Gain	49 250	Proceeds before Taxes	61 750
			– Excess CR	0	– Tax Liability on Sale	6 619
			Capital Gain	47 166	Proceeds after Taxes	55 131

*NOTE: On non-residential property, if accelerated CR system is elected, all CR claimed is recaptured as ordinary income in the year of sale.

The statements and figures presented herein, while not guaranteed, are secured from sources we believe authoritative.

Prepared by Realtor John

$47,166 x 40% = $18,866 Taxable

Conclusion

With total understanding of the real estate financial language one can communicate with investors regardless of their colloquialisms.[3] In a way it's like having the English language at your command. The language of the deep south, New Jersey and California certainly have their idiosyncrasies, but with a basic understanding of English, communication takes place effectively.

Random thoughts concerning the "financial picture of real estate":

- Some clients might be interested to know that in Canada the tax laws prohibit real estate taxable income from ever going below $0. The net result is that Cash Flow Before Tax and principal reduction is not taxed at that time, but real estate cannot "shelter" other income from tax liability (there is one type of property that is an exception to this rule). ("We are indeed fortunate in the U.S., Mr. Client, to be able to use real estate as a way of reducing our personal tax liability.")
- Refinance proceeds are not taxed until a sale occurs. Mortgage amount has no bearing on the determination of gain from which taxable income is determined.
- With so many variables at work, plus the investor's tax posture playing a major role in the determination of cash flows from real estate, "what is good for the goose is *not* always good for the gander."
- Syndicators will look for "soft costs" they can include in the first year of operation expenses. Although the seller may think of these items as down payment monies, tax structuring becomes a game in which the purchaser "writes off" as much of the cash down payment as possible in the early years. Why? Simple: Early tax benefits for the syndicators' partners. Be careful with the seller's tax position. What's your CPA's phone number?
- The term "split fund" usually means to split the down payment over a couple of tax years. Advantageous? It depends for whom, when and how. Pick up the phone and call your client's accountant.

---

3. The REALTORS NATIONAL MARKETING INSTITUTE® offers intensive courses on commercial-investment real estate. In addition, RNMI has developed the Cash Flow Analysis Form (shown as Figure 3–8 of this chapter) which will help the practitioner in everyday calculations and work with clients. Information about these courses and other educational tools can be obtained from REALTORS NATIONAL MARKETING INSTITUTE®, 430 N. Michigan, Chicago, IL 60611.

- Some investors familiar with other "tax shelter" programs will talk in terms of "1- to 1 write-off." Make sure you understand their terminology. Most of the time this refers to the taxable income amount, i.e., $100,000 down payment requires ($100,000) taxable income (loss) the first year.

Figure 3–9
After-Tax Proceeds Scenario

4

TYPES OF PROPERTIES

Before selecting a specific real estate property to analyze for possible acquisition, an investor should determine the general category of property best suited to his investment goals, experience and resources. This approach is somewhat analogous to that of a stock market investor who selects the security most appropriate to his investment objectives (common or preferred stocks or bonds) and then proceeds with an analysis of individual securities within the chosen category.

Investment real estate opportunities are so vast that it is probably impractical for a broker in the investment field to be an expert on all real estate investment alternatives. However, since each property offers unique opportunities for investors, it is important that the broker at least have a general knowledge of each type, its attributes and the risk factors involved in each. The purpose of this chapter is to present a brief overview of properties and the variables that make each unique. An abbreviated form of financial analysis will be presented on each type of property to give the reader at least one example of the financial benefits of ownership. Obviously, the examples are not cast in stone since income and expense variables change from region to region and from property to property.

Investing in Land

Land purchased for resale will be discussed here as opposed to land for development since development usually includes entrepreneurial profits instead of strictly investment benefits.

General Characteristics

In economics land is defined as one of the three factors of production. It is the natural factor; the other two factors are labor and capital. We are concerned here with surface land even though mineral or air space rights which generally accompany land title are severable and many times valuable.

The present and future use for a particular piece of land will depend in

Figure 4–1

It is impractical for a broker to be an expert in all types of real estate investments.

part on the location and the physical attributes of the land. The supply of land is limited, it does not decrease in value with age, it does not become obsolete and it does not require maintenance. Land can, of course, suffer from location obsolescence if its location becomes less desirable for certain uses, if traffic routes change or if adverse environmental conditions exist.

Land located near populous areas has tended to increase in value over the years because of a growing demand working against a limited quantity. In many areas, this land value has increased as fast as the rate of inflation or in some cases even faster. This growing value comes from a general increase in population and a rising per capita demand for land.

Because any profit from undeveloped land will probably be in the form of price appreciation, appropriate judgments on the expected value of a particular piece of land become extremely important. Probably the most important variable in land evaluation is its location. The land itself is fixed or immobile, so future changes in the surrounding environment will bring changes in the value of the land. Most pieces of land have a highest and best use depending on location, zoning, physical characteristics and market needs. This use will have a direct impact on the value of the land as it relates to the value a user would be willing to pay for it.

Land is usually purchased by an investor or a developer. The developer usually will determine a value he can pay for the land based upon expected future cash flows from a proposed income-producing project. The investor purchases land in hopes of selling it at a later date for a price higher than the original purchase price.

Investment Characteristics

While some land might require some degree of attention and maintenance responsibilities (such as leased farm land), most land investments can be considered to be relatively passive. It can also be said that of all real estate investment alternatives land is the least liquid form of investment. The market is restricted to the developer or the land investor and it can take months or even years for land to convert to cash through a sale. There are, of course, exceptions in the case of highly sought-after pieces of land.

The primary investment goal for a purchaser of undeveloped land which is to be resold in its existing state is price appreciation. Many land investments offer opportunities for extremely high returns, sometimes even the highest returns of the various alternatives of real estate investment. The risks associated with these returns are also some of the highest.

Risks generally fall into two categories: (1) the inability of the investor to meet the cash flow requirements of carrying the property and (2) the failure of the property to rise in value enough to offset the carrying and subsequent transaction costs.

When considering land as an investment vehicle, keep the following in mind:

1 Like common stocks, land depends on appreciation rather than periodic cash flows and tax benefits for its economic return. Land is not the most appropriate vehicle for those seeking periodic income, cash flows or tax benefits. There is no cost recovery available for land—consequently tax losses are "hard," or out-of-pocket, dollar losses.

2 Sharp increases in land value are usually tied to a new use for the land. Land used strictly for farming will be valued for less than the same farm land ready to be utilized for residential lots or commercial use.

3 Generally, land represents a relatively small portion of the cost of a total real estate investment project. If a large hotel developer has found land that meets the criteria for a project, the difference of a couple of thousand dollars per acre will not noticeably affect the overall economics of the project. In recent years the percentage of land costs for residential projects has risen sharply and has spawned numerous high density residential developments.

4 Liquidity is a major problem with land. Investment planning is difficult since land cannot always be sold when cash needs are projected.

5 As an investment land could be purchased on the assumption of holding it indefinitely. This, hopefully, will not be the case, but this attitude helps when negotiating terms of purchase.

6 Substantial appreciation must take place to overcome carrying and disposition costs. Although an increase of 20 percent might sound attractive, carrying costs of 8 percent and selling costs of 7 percent plus any tax liability eat up profits in short order.

7 Only well located properties are wise buys since there literally may not be any purchasers at any price for poorly located land.

8 Purchase and sales decisions should not be based totally on asking and selling prices of similar properties, but rather on eventual use value. It is important to project the future use of the property, when that use will take place and how much the land will be worth at that time. This

procedure should help provide a discounted present value of the property to compare to actual prices prevailing in the area.

9 In the case of raw, undeveloped land it may be desirable or even necessary to sell off part of the acreage at a profit and retain the balance. The tendency is to sell off the best part of the acreage first, usually because of unsolicited offers and increased marketability. Invariably, this is unsound strategy as the poorer parcels end up being the last to be sold. In general it is advisable, if possible, to sell the poorer sections first and wait for development of these portions to further appreciate the value of the better parcels that have been retained. This creation of value will always be more advantageous for the better parcels than for the poorer ones.

10 Raw land ownership is strictly an unprofitable situation until the time of sale. Remember that if a developer buys the property, he is generally concerned with frontage on highways or access roads, so it is important to control as much frontage as possible in a speculative buy.

11 There are primarily three risks in the speculation of raw land: (1) the cost of carrying the purchase may prove burdensome or even impossible; (2) the land may already be overpriced as one speculator passes it on to another, with each succeeding price reflecting optimism which may or may not be justified; (3) the land may have physical or legal defects which might be impossible to resolve, such as lack of sewer or utilities, drainage problems, soil stability problems or public easements.

Land Investment Profile

Since many times it is possible to use leverage in the purchase of raw land, the profile shown in Figure 4-2 includes a debt-free analysis compared to a 70 percent leverage purchase.

Using a discounted cash flow analysis percentage (IRR) which is similar to a rate of return as quoted on savings accounts (see Chapter 5), we can compare the two alternatives shown in Figure 4-2. Of the two alternatives presented, the leveraged position yields 34.6 percent as opposed to 16.5 percent for the debt-free purchase. Note that both situations involve negative cash flows until the time of sale. Even though the calculation of the yields is somewhat distorted by these negative cash flows, one can readily see the advantage of leveraged property in this situation. This profile is a prime example of an investment which has benefits in the area of appreciation only; its disadvantages are negative Cash Flow Before Taxes, minimal tax savings and no mortgage reduction (in the case of the free and clear purchase).

Figure 4-2
Land Investment

	Free and Clear Purchase	70% Leverage Purchase
Price	$150,000	$150,000
Loan	-0-	105,000 (10%, interest-only)
Down Payment	150,000	45,000
Holding Period	3 yrs.	3 yrs.
Estimated Selling Price	293,000	293,000 (25% increase per year)
Estimated Selling Expenses	29,300	29,300
Gross Income	-0-	-0-
Expenses	2100	2100
Cost Recovery Value	-0-	-0-
Income Tax Rate	50%	50%
Capital Gains Tax Rate	20%	20% (maximum)

Annual Cash Flows

	Free and Clear Purchase	70% Leverage Purchase
Gross Operating Income	$ -0-	$ -0-
–Expenses	2,100	2,100
Net Operating Income	(2,100)	(2,100)
–Debt Service	-0-	10,500
Cash Flow Before Taxes	(2,100)	(12,600)
Net Operating Income	(2,100)	(2,100)
–Interest	-0-	(10,500)
–Cost Recovery	-0-	-0-
Taxable Income	(2,100)	(12,600)
x 50% bracket		
Tax Loss (Savings)	(1,050)	(6,300)
Cash Flow After Taxes	(1,050)	(6,300)

(continued on page 79)

Figure 4–2 (continued)

Sale Proceeds

	Free and Clear Purchase	70% Leverage Purchase
Sale Price	$293,000	$293,000
–Sale Costs	29,300	29,300
–Adjusted Basis	150,000	150,000
Gain	$113,700	113,700
	x 20%	x 20%
Maximum Tax on Capital Gain	$ 22,740	22,740
Sale Price	293,000	293,000
–Cost of Sale	29,300	29,300
–Mortgage	-0-	105,000
–Tax on Sale	22,740	22,740
Proceeds After Tax	$240,960	$135,960

Summary of Cash Flows

Free and Clear Purchase vs. **70% Leverage Purchase**

Time	$	Time	$
0	(150,000)	0	(45,000)
1	(1,050)	1	(6,300)
2	(1,050)	2	(6,300)
3	(1,050) + $240,960	3	(6,300) + $135,960
Internal Rate of Return (IRR)	16.5%		34.6%

Land Investment Profile

Broker A purchased 22 acres of commercially zoned land adjacent to a local shopping center. Armed with demographic information and data on growth patterns, he invited two local businessmen to join him in the partnership. "Of the 22 acres, only 12 have frontage but we could put in a road or two and expand our frontage," Broker A explained. "I have arranged 36 months of interest only financing and certainly by that time we can roll the land over."

The average selling price of surrounding land at the time of purchase was approximately $100,000 per acre, but Broker A paid an average of only $65,000 per acre for the 22-acre package. The total purchase price of $1,430,000 was structured with a $130,000 down payment; the seller financed at 10 percent interest on the balance of $1,300,000, to be paid on a quarterly basis, with the entire balance due 36 months from the time of purchase. Although carrying costs amounted to $163,100 per year, the first interest payment of $32,500 was not due for 90 days after closing.

Two developers expressed interest in at least four acres even before the original purchase. The proceeds from these acres were thought to be sufficient to pay interest on the balance of the note. Figure 4-3 is the financial projection for the three-year period.

From a $50,000 original investment, $147,300 is returned—almost a 200 percent return! Broker A exclaimed. As you might imagine, however, the transaction did not exactly work out as projected even though Broker A was conservative in his projections. He had, after all:

- Projected sales at $100,000 per acre for each year even though land was *currently* selling for $100,000 per acre
- Put extra cash on principal to reduce carrying costs
- Accounted for extra road work and contingencies

Here is what actually happened:

- Four prime acres sold immediately for $95,000 per acre.
- First year carrying costs were paid out of proceeds of the four-acre sale.
- One more acre sold in the first year; this reduced the note $50,000 and paid each partner his first year cash flow.
- Balance going into second year was $1,050,000 with first quarter interest payment of $26,250 due. Price reduced on another acre to $85,000 for a quick sale.
- Six acres now sold; interest payments up to date going into second quarter of second year.
- At this point, land sales slowed down (the best acres were gone) and the partnership needed cash to meet interest payments.
- Road work was needed to create more frontage but without a sale no cash was available. Partners had to use personal borrowing power to borrow cash to pay quarterly interest on main note.
- Partners were now faced with a $1,000,000 note, slow sales and paying interest on borrowed money. The interest on the borrowed money for the main note was over 20 percent.

Figure 4-3
Financial Projection on Land Investment

Year 1		
Sell 7 Acres at $100,000	$700,000	
–Release Fee	350,000	
–Broker's Fee (direct sale)	-0-	(helps partnership get rolling)
Net Before Taxes	$350,000	
First Year's Carrying Costs	163,100	
Net Cash Flow	186,900	
–Principal Payment	150,000	
Distribute to 3 Partners	$ 36,900	
Year 2 (15 acres left)		
Note Balance	$800,000	
Sell 8 Acres at $100,000	$800,000	
–Release Fee	400,000	
–Broker's Fee	60,000	
–Road Work	40,000	
Net Before Taxes	300,000	
–Second Year's Carrying Costs	95,000	
Net Cash Flow	$205,000	
–Principal Payment	100,000	
Distribute to 3 Partners	$105,000	
Year 3 (7 acres left)		
Sell 7 Acres at $100,000	$700,000	
–Balance on Note	300,000	
–Broker's Fee	50,000	
–Road Work	50,000	
Net Before Taxes (To be distributed to 3 partners)	$300,000	

Each partner puts in $50,000 at the time of purchase (organizing partner's original down payment was $30,000) and receives:

1st year	$ 12,300
2nd year	35,000
3rd year	100,000

- With only three months left until the entire balance was due, the partners were looking for a way out without suffering any more personal financial loss.

- The way out was a developer who bought the remaining 16 acres for the $1,000,000 ($62,500 per acre) owed on the note (extending the due date). The developer spent $100,000 on road improvements and created frontage, value and demand for the remaining acres.

What started the demise of Broker A's project was his partnership distribution in the first year. When the three partners had to use personal borrowing reserves (at 20 percent interest) to pay interest on the main note, it became evident that the carrying charges of the property were much too heavy for the individuals involved. It is a shame that the partnership did not have the "staying power" since their projection prices were actually below what was happening in the marketplace.

It has now been five years since Broker A's original purchase and the developer who purchased the property has very little land left. His latest sale was reported at $145,000 for just under an acre of land.

Summary

Land is a specialized investment entity which takes time, staying power and patience. An investment strategy should take into account the absorption time of land into the marketplace. Although there are times when land can yield cash flows, as in a ground lease or farm rental, for the most part raw land is a cash drain on the investor. Anticipation of the negative cash flows should convince the investor to carefully project and structure land investment strategy. The lack of tax savings through cost recovery and the lack of cash flows in land require that appreciation carry the land through the investment program for the investor. In short, there are tremendous benefits to be had in the speculation of raw land, but it is probably not the place for the investor new to real estate.

Investing in Single Family Homes

Of all real estate investments, the most basic is the single family home. Residential properties offer a fundamental need to all of us—shelter. Compared to other real estate investments, single family homes are relatively easy to buy, sell and manage. They can also be one of the least profitable. As with all types of investments, single family homes offer some risk and opportunity. Historically they have been a starting place for many investors since the capital needed to purchase one house is minimal compared with what is needed for other investments.

General Characteristics

Many investors who buy single family homes for rental are successful because they adhere to a simple philosophy. They look for properties in favorable locations. Schools, shopping, churches, public utilities, recreation facilities, libraries, fire protection and quiet streets are all factors to be considered when purchasing a home for rental and eventual resale.

Many of the financial "gurus" who write books on real estate have been preaching that all an investor has to do is purchase a house, make some cosmetic adjustments and sell it for twice the original purchase price. While this strategy is certainly not fool-proof, it is, of course, true that one can increase the marketability of the property by making certain interior and exterior changes.

With this in mind, an investor should systematically view the house as an ultimate resident/buyer might, even though initially the property is purchased to rent. The value may be created solely by inflation or possibly through a cosmetic remodeling job.

An investor should bear in mind that upgrading a single family house many times becomes a remodeling project. Although value can be created instantly through work and aesthetic improvement, many investors simply do not have the time, energy or patience for such activities. In this discussion, single family home investing will be viewed as capturing potential appreciation with minimal improvements to the property.

The two most important variables to consider when buying single family homes for resale are location and timing. Investors should buy in the very early stages of a boom in housing demand or inflation. A weakening market might indicate an investor should wait until a later date for the single family home purchase. It would be much more advantageous to buy at the end of a stagnant period than to buy at the end of a boom. If one buys at the "low" end, time probably will work positively. Conversely, if a purchase is made at the "high" end, the timing might not be so favorable in the realization of price potential. Timing should place an investor in a position where the property can reach its maximum potential.

Most investors tend to stay in their immediate locale, but it might be wise to check out the local employment and income rates. Are incomes on the increase? Will there be demand for housing when a new company opens a plant? What will happen to housing if the employment centers of the area are closing their doors? Cities do not grow evenly. What area is growing? Are there areas which will open up as streets are expanded? What area is popular for young families who *need* housing?

Once the location is determined, stay with homes which have wide market appeal—those popular floor plans, popular styles and features buyers tend to notice. Forget the unusual, one-of-a-kind property unless the risk seems to be minimal and you have a gambling nature. Many investors go overboard and buy a "dog" because they were told, "After all, you are not going to live there." Investing in single family homes should be a conservative business.

Investment Characteristics

Single family homes are purchased most often for the appreciation benefits. The Cash Flow Before Taxes will probably be negative since the current rental is usually not nearly enough to carry the expenses and the debt service. There are other benefits, however. Tax benefits are available to the investor since the improvement value can be "recovered" using cost recovery. The amount of leverage available in single family homes is usually higher than in other types of investments since lenders are accustomed to lending policies based on the borrower's income instead of the property's ability to pay. Owner financing is frequently available at lower rates than typical conventional financing. These financing variables need to be considered when analyzing a single family home as a potential investment. One reason many investors are satisfied with so little cash flow is that they have put up very little cash to buy the property in the first place.

There are a number of problems with single family homes as investments. The major hurdle for many investors is in the area of management. Usually, houses are the first real estate venture for investors, who enter the arena unprepared to make decisions about operating the property. Property showings, collection of rents, ordering of repairs and accounting procedures put the investor in property management in a big way for little profit. Maintenance and repairs can be expensive if a skilled workman is called for every job. Suddenly an investor finds himself a do-it-yourselfer for his tenants' living quarters. When the investor tires of this, he usually approaches a management firm, only to find his property is "too small" for the management company to handle.

Although many tax benefits are available relative to the amount of money invested, most investors find that the tax benefits and potential appreciation of owning one house do not warrant the management headaches. Some investors in this case offer leases in which the tenant is responsible for all repairs other than major items. Although this is reflected in the gross rental charge, it does free the investor of some management responsibility. Other investors have decided that single family homes are attractive investments and set up a portfolio of many homes which can support their own management and maintenance employee.

Summary

Single family homes can be an attractive investment, especially to investors new to real estate. However, problems of management, maintenance and negative cash flows must be overcome. The purchase of numerous homes may be needed to spread the risk and to make a portfolio workable for an investor. The strategy suitable to most investors is one based on the projected increase in the price of the house. Most prices change because of inflation, but by timing the purchase at the end of an economic dip, one can take advantage of increased demand plus any appreciation that might transpire. Of prime importance are the physical characteristics and location of the house since they ultimately affect its marketability.

If the intent is to invest as a hedge against inflation without regard for cash flow, the single family home, properly structured into an investment portfolio, can be a suitable vehicle.

The visual presentation shown as Figure 4-4 was developed by a sales associate to explain the benefits and disadvantages of investing in single family homes. Notice his technique for handling the problem of negative cash flows created by the rental properties.

Many brokers specialize in such programs and are paid a fee to purchase, manage and eventually sell homes for investors.

Figure 4–4

XYZ Realtors® is accepting client applications from investors interested in acquiring single family residential units.

Figure 4–4 (continued)

An Investment Opportunity in Residential Real Estate

Investment Rationale

- Historically, when money has become expensive, the economy tends to slow, and housing sales drop. These past few months have seen a dramatic drop in demand for single-family housing. As a result, prices have stabilized and owner financing plans have become available. In many cases, stress situations have forced owners to sell homes for far less than market value and with soft financing terms.
- If an individual could economically afford to take advantage of this slow down and purchase homes at a reduced price with favorable financing, he would be in an extremely favorable position when the housing market opens up.
- The Mortgage and Real Estate Executives Report of October 15, 1978, sited a continuing strong demand for single-family homes which is being reinforced by two demographic changes in the market:

    1. The median age of first-time homeowners has fallen from 38 in 1968 to 34 in 1977. During this same period, the younger age group became a significantly larger portion of the total population.
    2. A significant number of single persons are opting for home ownership rather than renting.

- Houses can be readily financed. Institutional lenders will often loan up to 95 percent of the purchase price. There are numerous governmental programs such as FHA, VA and FHA 235 Loan Insurance Programs available to assist in financing. Moreover, home sellers seem to be more willing to accept purchase money financing than are sellers of other types of property.
- Houses are one of the most liquid types of real estate. A house priced at a fair market value can usually be sold in a relatively short time in a normal market.
- Renters tend to pay a higher rent for a single-family house than for an apartment with the same amount of space.

Investment Obstacles and Risks

- There is absolutely no guarantee that the property value will increase during the projected holding period. Unknown and unpredictable circumstances can cause property values to stabilize or decrease for extended periods of time.
- In the event of a vacancy, the property is 100 percent vacant. Even though there is no income, the mortgage payments and expenses continue and must be met from other cash resources. In some cases, vacancies can continue for extended periods of time.
- It is not possible to guarantee at what price and how long it might take to sell a specific property.

Figure 4–4 (continued)

- There is the possibility of financial loss from tenant damage to the property and from nonpayment of rent requiring legal eviction of a tenant.
- It is difficult for one investor to purchase and support a program of residential investment.
- It is also difficult for one investor to purchase enough properties to minimize his risk and avoid putting all investment "eggs" in one basket.
- Real estate investment requires a constant monitoring of the market on a daily basis.
- Management of a real estate portfolio with regard to collection of rents, payment of bills, complaint calls, etc. requires a full-time management group, which increases cash operating expenses.

Investment Solutions

- Pool individual investment capital to form a group for the purpose of purchasing single-family investments.
- The group investment philosophy is to buy in a depressed market (individual or general) or to buy a depressed property, rent the property until it has been held long enough for measurable appreciation and then sell when conditions warrant, normally 12 to 24 months.
- Utilize the professional management and marketing divisions of the *XYZ* Company to ensure the efficient day to day handling of the properties while they are being rented and to ensure wide marketing exposure of these properties at the time of sale.

Investment Benefits

- Tax Advantages: Rental homes allow for interest and cost recovery deductions, resulting in tax savings from ownership.
- Appreciation: Investors benefit from increase in value at time of sale.
- Risk: Capital is insulated by multiple purchases so as to minimize risk.
- Management: All management functions will be handled by the *XYZ* Company, thereby relieving investors from any day to day responsibilities.
- Market Knowledge: Timing and selection of purchases would be done by professionals with thorough knowledge of the local market.
- Mortgage Reduction: Investors would benefit from reduction of mortgages paid by tenants.

Figure 4–4 (continued)

Sample Purchase Portfolio

$ 100,000	Cash Invested
- 10,000	Broker's Fee
- 20,000	Reserves (to subsidize rents and make repairs during holding period)
$ 70,000	Available as down payment

Purchase range: $35,000 to $70,000 homes ("Mid Market" range of homes)

Nine homes are purchased:

Value

2 at	$35,000	
2 at	40,000	
3 at	45,000	
1 at	55,000	
1 at	60,000	
	$400,000	Total Sales Price
	70,000	Down Payment
	$330,000	Financed at aggregate of 11 percent, 25 yrs.

Cash flow for the nine homes for one year looks like this:

Scheduled Income	$46,200
-Vacancy (10%)	$4,620
Gross Operating Income	$41,580
-Expenses (39%)	
Taxes	$4,410
Insurance	2,600
Management	2,000
Repairs	3,000
Services	1,296
Sewer	1,944
Miscellaneous	900
Total	$16,150

(2 Homes at $350 per month, 2 Homes at $400 per month, 3 Homes at $450 per month, 2 Homes at $500 per month)

Net Operating Income	$25,430
-Annual Debt Service	38,812
$330,000 at 11%, 25 yrs.	
Cash Flow Before Tax	($13,382)

To subsidize negative cash flow, $20,000 reserves would be needed. Assume the balance of reserves will be spent on capital improvements.

Figure 4–4 (continued)

First Year After Tax Position

30 percent Tax Bracket Investors

Net Operating Income	$25,430	
— Interest	36,169	
— Cost Recovery	17,777	18 year S/L, on $320,000 improvements
Taxable Income	($28,516)	
	× 30%	Bracket
Tax Savings	$ 8,554	(to be dispersed)

In addition to the $8,554 of tax benefits, appreciation must be considered. If the original purchase of $400,000 worth of property increases in value 25 percent over a one-year period, the partnership could consider selling the homes. If 25 percent seems high, consider: (1) properties will be purchased in a somewhat stagnant market and (2) a $35,000 home needs to sell for only $43,750, a $50,000 home needs to sell for $62,500. Location of the homes and timing of purchase is extremely important in this project.

Assume the $400,000 investment has grown to $500,000 in value:

$ 500,000	Total Sales Price
- 38,400	Total Selling Expenses at 7.7%
- 327,357	Mortgage Balance
$ 134,243	Proceeds to be Dispersed

Partnership Benefits to be Dispersed

Tax Savings (1st year)	$ 8,554
Cash from Sale	134,243
Total Benefit	142,797
Maximum Tax on Sale (Capital Gains Treatment)	−15,875
Total Cash After Tax	$126,922

If an investor were to invest $10,000 for one year under the above projected program he would receive $12,692 in return ($10,000 investment plus $2692 for the 10 percent ownership position).

This $\frac{\$2692}{\$10,000}$ is equal to a 26.92 percent return on an after-tax basis!

The key to this program is to buy properties which appeal to a wide market, to rent properties during the holding period, to sell for increased value (because of timing and selected purchasing) and finally, to effectively manage and market the properties.

Investing in Apartments

Rental apartments are a popular form of living unit in the United States. Ranging in size from two-units and three-units to four-flats to "garden" style units and including giant high rise complexes, rental units vary widely in price, style, design, amenities and profitability. Apartments have been very popular as living quarters for singles, couples and young families getting a start in the housing market. An apartment is typically a couple's first homestead, and many times an apartment turns out to be their home again after the family is raised and on their own.

One of the primary concerns of an owner (lessor) is the stability and harmony of the landlord-tenant relationship. The owner wants the apartments to be occupied by contented, responsible tenants who pay the rent on time. He chooses tenants carefully and checks into credit ratings to see if they can afford to pay the monthly rent. Tenants (lessees), on the other hand, want peaceful occupancy of well-maintained living quarters at reasonable market rates. They want as many amenities and conveniences as their monthly rent checks can purchase.

The tremendous increase in the adult population in the 1970s brought about a strong market for apartment rentals. As people in the age groups of 30 and below flooded the housing market looking for living quarters, developers built and built apartment units. By the mid-1970s many cities saw overall vacancy factors hovering around 20 percent. As these vacant units were absorbed into the marketplace, many apartment owners continued to raise rental rates. The sudden overabundance of apartments halted new project construction in the late 1970s, and those owners who had suffered through a few years of vacancy problems suddenly found themselves with apartments filled with tenants paying much higher rents than ever expected. Many owners sold their apartment projects for substantial gains.

New buyers bought on the premise that rents could always be raised to cover whatever negative cash flow existed. After all, rents had steadily increased all through the 1970s. There was no reason to believe that rent schedules could not continually be raised. "Why, we might even raise the rents as soon as we buy the property." This was the prevailing attitude among buyers since the brokerage community promised them that the rents on their purchases could always be raised.

As late as 1975 brokers suggested that an investor pay no more than, for example, $19,500 for an apartment unit which rents for $300 per month. Such rules of thumb eliminated many buyers from the market and convinced many others that with increased prices rents certainly would have to be raised substantially.

Nevertheless, during the 1970s, the "darling" investment was indeed the apartment project. Most projects had enough income to support expenses, pay debt service and yield Cash Flow Before Taxes to the investors. Long-term fixed financing at 9 percent or lower was not uncommon. An increase in rental income automatically raised the market price of the units, and many sellers took advantage of this rapid "appreciation." Short holding periods were common as investors sought out quality projects.

The beginning of 1980 saw a different scenario for the apartment investor. Cash Flows Before Taxes were no longer available. All rental income was utilized to pay increased expenses and higher-priced debt service. Suddenly the projects no longer "penciled" out as they had in the past. Apartments continued to be sold only as investors grew to accept negative cash flows and concentrated on tax benefits and future appreciation. "Demand will certainly create increased prices since the cost of construction and increased (if not impossible) financing costs seem to be here to stay," one investor was quoted as saying.

Many investors are still conditioned to believe that their apartment units will increase in value due to inflation almost overnight. Many have learned this may not be the case.

A mix of interesting variables is currently at work in the apartment market:

- Vacancy rates are at an all time low. In San Francisco the vacancy factor is less than 1 percent in rental apartments. The law of supply and demand would dictate that since apartments are scarce their prices would rise and there would be a mad scramble to produce more apartment units. This has not happened.
- Rents generally are on the rise, in some areas of the country as much as 12 to 15 percent increase per year. However, even this increase of rental income has not spurred new construction.
- Condominium conversions of quality apartment units, although slowed by financing woes, continue at a steady pace. There has been some opposition from community groups who feel that taking rental units off the market displaces the poor and elderly.
- Some markets which experienced an increase of sale prices of multifamily units of more than 17 percent per year are suddenly experiencing a slow-down to less than a normal pace. Some speculate that

investors sense the end of the greater fool theory—pay any price regardless of economics as long as there is a greater fool behind you—the last one in line loses.

- The high cost of financing has forced prices *down* as investors watch cash flow go to the lender. Owner financing is being provided but only as a temporary "fix" since balloon due dates tend to roll around faster than one can imagine. (It has been said that if you want to see time fly, structure a short balloon due date into your next purchase.)
- Construction of new units is practically at a standstill because of higher material costs, higher labor costs and stringent code requirements. The availability and cost of capital has kept many builders sitting on their hands during a period which, theoretically, should be a time to satisfy a demand for new units.
- Even though a change in tax laws has increased the tax benefits available, investors are now becoming very conscious of the *present* economic benefits as well as the benefits of appreciation. They are no longer willing to accept the large negative cash flows, hoping that inflation and/or condominium conversion will bail them out. The reduction in the top marginal federal tax brackets has even reduced available tax savings.

These variables create a climate of reluctance to "buy the future." It is almost as if the pendulum is starting to swing away from purchases of reckless abandon and negative cash flows. Future sales activity will certainly depend on the ability of financial institutions to provide capital and the investors' attitudes toward an inflationary market.

General Characteristics

Although apartments come in all shapes, sizes and styles, there are basically two classifications which investors discuss: garden style and high-rise apartments.

Families need a place to live and many times spend a large part of their income for housing and related amenities. Housing is expensive because land and construction costs are high. The easiest way to reduce costs per housing unit is to put more units on a parcel of land. As far as construction costs are concerned, the most economical way to build is to stack units higher. If the stacking exceeds a few stories then the type of construction must change and the cost increases sharply. Another easy way to reduce costs per unit is to put a few units together using common walls. Thus townhouses, the modern version of the old rowhouses, reduce per-unit land costs and some construction costs by using common walls. A garden apartment style of construction is an even better way of keeping housing costs low. Multi-level flats offer the advantage of using cost-saving construction techniques.

The fact that garden apartments can provide more housing per dollar than other types of rental housing is important to the investor. This so-called bread and butter investment will always rent because of the heavy demand for housing at a modest cost. The broader the market, the safer the market.

Such a low risk investment also tends to be pushed up in value as investors bid the price to the point where the benefits are less than in many other real estate investments. The benefits of garden style apartments are comparable to other types of property but the risk factor tends to be lower than with other investment properties.

High-rise apartments tend to appeal to a different market than do garden apartments. The magnificent view, occasionally above the clouds, the gentle sway of the building on a windy day, high speed elevators, prestige and countless amenities are all part of high-rise living. These factors attract higher income level tenants and consequently make high-rise apartments more expensive to build and operate.

The major risk in high-rise apartments is attracting tenants in a soft market. Unlike garden style units where a reduction of $25 per month might attract a host of new tenants, the high-rise tenant will not be attracted by a reduction in the rent structure. High-rise tenants largely search for amenities and status. Features such as modern elevators and inside parking play an important role in keeping buildings filled.

Investment Characteristics

Compared with other real estate investments, the apartment investment requires the greatest management participation in terms of physical maintenance and keeping tenant goodwill. As the number of apartments increases, the responsibilities of management increase accordingly. This active form of investment requires substantial time and attention by the investor.

It is always interesting that when a client seeks a real estate investment he usually begins with a small apartment complex. The capital requirements are many times less than with other investments and the tax benefits are available, but apartments are management-intensive. An investor untrained in apartment management soon wonders how or why he ever got into the real estate arena in the first place. Somehow the benefits do not seem worth the management effort.

Professional management most often is the solution to the problem of owner-tenant relationships. Regardless of the apparent cash savings with the do-it-yourself approach, management should be included in the cost of operating an apartment project. Of course, one has to ascertain the management capabilities of the investor, but by and large professional management is a bargain at twice the price.

There are two reasons why apartment prices have been driven past the point of current economic value: (1) negative cash flows have been accepted because of the many tax benefits connected with apartments and (2) investors feel it is easy to raise the rents on multifamily projects.

Before 1981 many new apartments were sold because 200 percent declining balance depreciation could be taken. Investors talked of "heavy tax shelter" because of "double declining depreciation." This rapid acceleration method was not available on other types of property. The Deficit Reduction Act of 1984 changed the cost recovery method to a predetermined schedule over a 18-year life (see Chapter 3). This increases the amount of cost recovery available but it also opens other types of real estate investments to this accelerated schedule. Apartments generally carry a higher improvement value compared to land than other investments do, thus making more cost recovery available. A large taxable loss can still be generated by apartments, but many times the heavy negative cash flow erodes the tax savings to a minimal amount. The reduction in the marginal tax brackets in the new tax law also affects the amount of tax savings available.

Overall, apartments have always been known as the best "tax shelter" vehicle in real estate because of the large taxable losses. The tax savings generally are strong enough to offset negative cash flows while the rents are raised year after year. The high amount of leverage used in the purchase of apartments helps create a taxable loss but reduces the investor's Cash Flow Before Tax.

The only way to view the benefits of a project accurately is to analyze a particular property as it pertains to a specific investor. The before-tax benefits of a project are somewhat difficult to project unless one is currently familiar with the income and expense analysis of similar projects.[1]

1. The Institute of Real Estate Management (IREM) (430 N. Michigan, Chicago, IL 60611) produces an annual *Income/Expense Analysis*. This analysis is a statistical compilation of income and expenses from over 500,000 apartment units. Trends over the past year in gross income, individual operating expenses, net operating income, vacancies and turnover rates are charted. Units are broken down as to type of building, age of building, number of units in building and region of the country.

Property Profile

The income and expenses shown on the Annual Property Operating Data (APOD) form (Figure 4-5) are for a five-year-old, 48-unit garden apartment project in the Midwest. Notice that expense items are expressed as a percentage as well as a dollar amount. This percentage amount enables an investor to make a quick comparison against other properties.

With some investigation a broker can become familiar with the income and expense variables in his local area. This knowledge can help in the overall analysis and marketing of an apartment project.

Garden apartments typically incur expenses between 40 and 50 percent of the collected rents. The lowest (and therefore most favorable) operating ratios occur on the west coast with the highest ratios occuring in New England and the Northeastern part of the United States. Townhouse-style units usually have only 35 to 40 percent operating cost ratios because of the lack of common hallway utilities and interior maintenance costs. Elevator buildings consume a larger share of every dollar collected on operating expenses than any other type of building.

The major cost factor in any style of apartment project is the cost of utilities. Many apartments provide heat for tenants. Although reflected in the rental cost of the unit, gas and/or electric costs are important variables in the overall operation of an apartment project. With energy costs soaring out of control, many investors have opted for apartment projects which are individually metered for tenant utility costs. Naturally, when utilities are included, cold weather areas of the country have higher overall operating costs than those of the South or West.

To examine how these income and expense variables affect the ultimate cash flow from an apartment project, let's go back to the APOD for the 48-unit garden apartment (see Figure 4-5) and look into the cash flow and tax benefits. We will need some additional information to make a first year overview. Here are the facts:

- Property was purchased for $1,200,000 ($25,000 per unit): 82 percent improvement value, 18 percent land.
- There are three investors, all in the top marginal tax bracket (50 percent).
- Investors' accountant wants to use accelerated cost recovery system.
- Property is purchased in the first month of the year.

Figure 4–5

Annual Property Operating Data

Date ______
Price $ ______
Loans $ ______
Equity $ ______

Purpose Income/Expense Hypothetical
Name ______
Location ______
Type of Property 48-unit garden style gardens

Assessed/Appraised Values

Land	$	%
Improvement	$	%
Personal Property	$	%
Total	$	100 %

Adjusted Basis as of ______ $ ______

FINANCING

Existing	Balance	Payment	# Pymt/Yr.	Interest	Term
1st	$			%	
2nd	$			%	
3rd	$			%	
Potential					
1st				%	
2nd	$			%	

		%	2	3	Comments
1	SCHEDULED RENTAL INCOME			149 760	
2	Less: Vacancy and Credit Losses	5%		7 488	
3	EFFECTIVE RENTAL INCOME			142 272	
4	Plus: Other Income (laundry)			2 000	
5	GROSS OPERATING INCOME			144 272	
6	Less: Operating Expenses				
7	Accounting and Legal	.1%	200		
8	Advertising, Licenses and Permits	.4%	800		
9	Property Insurance	3.4%	4 900		
10	Property Management	5%	7 216		
11	Payroll-Resident Management				
12	Other				
13	Taxes-Worker's Compensation				
14	Personal Property Taxes				
15	Real Estate Taxes	7.3%	10 531		
16	Repairs and Maintenance	4.4%	6 347		
17	Services-Elevator				
18	Janitorial	2.5%	3 600		
19	Lawn	1.6%	2 300		
20	Pool				
21	Rubbish	2.6%	3 800		
22	Other (snow)	1%	1 250		
23	Supplies	1.1%	1 600		
24	Utilities-Electricity common area only	6%	8 600		
25	Gas and Oil (all elec. heat)				
26	Sewer and Water	3.3%	4 770		
27	Telephone				
28	Other				
29	Miscellaneous	2.1%	3 000		
30	Leasing fees	1.5%	2 200		
31	TOTAL OPERATING EXPENSES	42.4%		61 114	
32	NET OPERATING INCOME	57.6%		83 158	
33	Less: Annual Debt Service				
34	CASH FLOW BEFORE TAXES				

The statements and figures presented herein, while not guaranteed, are secured from sources we believe authoritative.

Prepared by ______

- Seller/developer agreed to carry financing at 11 percent interest only for five years with a 20 percent down payment.

The cash flow looks like this for the first year:

NOI	$ 83,158	
— Debt Service	105,600	$960,000 11% interest only
CFBT	($ 22,442)	Out of pocket! Ouch!

NOI	$ 83,158	
— Interest	105,600	
— Cost Recovery	88,560	$984,000 improvements × 9%
Taxable Income	($111,002)	
	50%	Tax bracket
	$ 55,501	Tax savings

CFBT	($ 22,442)
+ Tax Savings	55,501
CFAT	$ 33,059

The first year outlook for the property shows total after-tax cash flow of $33,059. Typical of an apartment complex is the large amount of tax savings generated to offset the negative cash flow. The Accelerated Cost Recovery System helped generate a $111,002 loss to be used against other income. A couple of questions present themselves at this time:

- Can the investors absorb negative cash flows?

Excess cost recovery is a tax preference item during the year it is taken and is subject to the alternative minimum tax calculation. This becomes extremely important now that economic lives are shortened to 18 years. Any time property has a large amount of excess cost recovery, double check to see if the excess is substantially more than straight line. Even with a $40,000 exclusion for married filing jointly taxpayers the alternative minimum tax may be more than the regular tax calculation. This extra tax should be considered. Call your accountant for an in depth discussion on the subject!

- Will the investors stay in top marginal tax brackets so as to maximize tax savings?
- Can rents be raised to offset negative cash flow as years go by?
- When investors need to dispose of property or refinance (to pay off the developer at end of Year 5), will the value be sufficient to pay balance due?
- Since rents may change and cost recovery available will *decrease* every year of the holding period, what will subsequent years of ownership look like on an after-tax basis?
- Are tax savings alone strong enough motivation for investors to buy property in the first place?
- What effect will available financing have on the value of the property five years into the future?

These questions and many others need to be answered before a purchase is made. But analysis begins when a potential purchaser looks at the income and expense statement for an apartment investment property.

Conclusion

For investment purposes, the two- or three-unit or larger multi-unit apartment projects provide investors with many tax sheltered, profit-making opportunities. Because it involves a large degree of personal commitment to management, multifamily rental apartment ownership requires more of an owner's time and effort than do most other forms of real estate investment. Depending on the size of the project, these responsibilities can be delegated to a professional management team.

In recent years, values of apartment projects have often been determined primarily on the basis of cost, since the value of the project from a cost approach has in many instances far surpassed the value of the project based on income alone. The market in many areas has not permitted rents to rise as rapidly as operating expenses and construction costs. These factors plus increased borrowing costs have left most apartment projects in a negative cash flow position; tax savings and appreciation are the only benefits investors have received. Some investors are starting to feel that appreciation may or may not be realized because of financing availability. Consequently, the current economic factors of an investment, rather than a market value in the future, are becoming more and more important.

Multifamily housing is treated favorably at the time of sale since only the excess cost recovery is taxed at ordinary rates. All other gain is given capital gain treatment, resulting in substantial tax savings to the investor. However, it is easy to become so enamored with a high leverage apartment purchase which produces a high tax loss that one disregards the cash needed to absorb the shock of a tough market.

Many investors are now turning to other avenues to help apartment projects "pencil out." Subsidy programs, solar energy units to help tenants save fuel costs, apartments mixed with commercial units, unique site characteristics and condominium conversions are just some of the ways investors are coping with the current apartment rental market.

Investing in Shopping Centers

The Urban Land Institute defines a shopping center as a group of commercial establishments—planned, developed, owned and managed as a unit, related in location, size and type of shops to the trade area the unit serves and providing on-site parking in definite relationship to the types and sizes of stores.[3]

The sharp rise in the use of automobiles for shopping since World War II and the accompanying population shift to the suburbs were important factors in the fast rising number of shopping centers. New centers tend to locate in suburban areas where the automobile is the mode of transportation, where substantial purchasing power is located and where land is usually less expensive than in the city—an important factor because of the need to provide large, free parking areas. *Shopping Center World's* Census of Shopping Centers showed 22,050 operating centers at the end of 1980 with approximately 632 new additions underway in 1981. In 1955, there were only 1000 shopping centers in the United States but by 1973 an estimated 14,000 centers were in operation. The rapid growth of these investment vehicles has proved to be very attractive for many investors even though the characteristics of a shopping center as an investment are somewhat unique.

General Characteristics

The Urban Land Institute, in its triennial publication *Dollars and Cents of Shopping Centers*, has categorized centers into four basic types. This standardization has helped define the type of center not by size but rather by major tenant or tenants.

A *neighborhood center* provides for the sale of convenience goods (foods,

---

3. *Dollars and Cents of Shopping Centers* (Washington: Urban Land Institute).

drugs and sundries) and personal services (dry cleaning, beauty shops, shoe repair) for day-to-day living needs for the immediate neighborhood. Typically, this type of center will not be larger than 50,000 square feet.

A *community center* offers convenience goods and personal services similar to a neighborhood center, plus a wider range of soft and hard goods (apparel for men, women, children and hardware and appliances). Such a center is built around a supermarket and a junior department store as its major tenants. It usually does not have a full line department store. These centers typically measure approximately 150,000 square feet of gross leasable area.

The *regional center* provides for general merchandise, apparel and furniture as well as a range of services and recreational facilities. It is usually built around one or two full line department stores of at least 100,000 square feet each. These centers generally are about 400,000 square feet total gross leasable area.

A *super regional center* is generally made up of at least three major department stores of 100,000 square feet each. It offers an extensive variety in general merchandise, apparel and home furnishings as well as a variety of services. In practice these widespread centers are approximately 1,000,000 square feet gross leasable area in size. Super regional centers are often enclosed malls, with the large anchor tenants spread out and the smaller tenants in between.

Although not classified by the Urban Land Institute, there are two other types of smaller centers that line the streets of most cities in America. The *strip center* may be a center of only 10,000 to 20,000 square feet but generally the stores provide convenience goods and services to a small local area. *Specialty centers* are also becoming quite popular. These centers offer small boutique-type operations. These specialty shops are always local in nature and often are side line operations for the owners.

A long-range goal of many real estate investors is to own at least one regional shopping center. The appeal of this form of realty is that it requires minimal personal involvement with management and offers relatively high, risk-free yields. With a Sears, Wards or Penneys anchoring a shopping mall, there is little chance for failure. There were those center owners who, of course, felt very secure with a long-term W. T Grant Company lease. After the W. T. Grant Company went bankrupt, many an owner found himself with a center half full of small tenants depending on the draw that the large department store was supposed to provide.

With shopping centers, like no other real estate form, success of the investment is tied very closely to the success of the tenants as entrepreneurs. If a tenant cannot show a profit in a particular location, no matter how low the rent is he will probably not be able to pay it. On the other hand, if a tenant has success as an entrepreneur, it leads directly to locational longevity—a landlord's dream!

Investment Characteristics

The overriding factor in any shopping center, large or small, is the ability of the tenants to sell merchandise. This factor alone will enable the investor to own a real estate investment which will see rents and real estate value increase over the holding period.

While everyone needs an apartment or house to live in, the comparative ease of renting or owning a piece of residential property in contrast to a shopping center is pretty decisively offset by the fact that the commercial tenant is a lot less likely to stop up the plumbing with empty beer cans, move out in the middle of the night or set fire to the draperies. The commercial tenant may indeed pay more attention to his place of business than his home. His place of business reflects his image to the community.

The need for tenants to do well in their respective businesses creates a new set of investment variables for the investor to consider. Whether a potential project is being studied or the purchase of an existing center is contemplated, several questions must be answered. Certainly not a complete checklist, the following factors are unique to a shopping center's success since they relate to variables that may determine the financial success of the tenants.

- What are the general economic conditions of the city or community?
- What are the employment trends?
- Where is the market area?
- Are there natural or man-made traffic patterns which serve as boundaries of the potential market or trade areas?
- How large is the trade area and how many families live in it?
- What are the population characteristics of the market area?
- What are the age groups, income levels, occupations and family make-up of the trade area?
- Where are the competitive facilities?
- Where are existing or proposed roadways in the site area?
- Does the site have adequate parking?

- Are entrances and exits convenient and free-flowing?
- Are tenant sales volumes on the increase?
- What is the proposed tenant mix and are the tenants compatible?

Definitions

The shopping center investment world has a language unique to itself, with several terms not used in other forms of real estate investment. The following is a partial list of some of these terms.

Gross Leasable Area (GLA) is the total floor area designed for tenant occupancy and is expressed in square feet. Income and expenses of shopping centers tend to be reported in terms of cost per square foot of the GLA.

Common Area is the total area within the shopping center not designed for rental to tenants but which is available for common use by all tenants and customers.

Base Rent is the amount of rent paid regardless of sales volume produced.

Overage Rent is the rent paid on any volume done over and above the base amount. Example: The tenant agrees to pay rent based on a 5 percent of volume vs. base rent. Base rent equals \$15,000 per year. The tenant would have to do over \$300,000 in sales before overage rent would "kick" in

$$\frac{\$300{,}000}{.05} = \$15{,}000$$

If tenant did \$400,000 of volume, the annual rent would be \$400,000 × 5 percent or \$20,000. The \$5,000 extra would be overage rent.

Percentage Lease Once in a while, an owner will sign a percentage lease (no minimum or base rent) with a tenant. This is determined by multiplying the sales volume times the agreed-upon percentage. The *Chain Store Guide*[4] publishes typical percentage amounts for many different tenant establishments.

Sales per Square Foot is the annual sales volume divided by square foot amount of the store. *Dollars and Cents of Shopping Centers*[5]

---

4. *Chain Store Guide*, (New York: Lebhar-Friedman, Inc.)
5. *Dollars and Cents of Shopping Centers*, (Washington: Urban Land Institute)

publishes tables of sales per square foot for various tenants as guidelines for shopping center investors and owners.

Common Area Maintenance (CAM) is an amount charged back to the tenant as the owner's expense in maintaining and operating the common areas. CAM is usually expressed in cents per square foot and is based on the percentage of space occupied by the tenant. Generally, the larger anchor tenants pay a minimum amount of CAM compared to local tenants.

Merchants Association is an association of the tenants which promotes the image of the center as a collective unit instead of each business acting separately. The association is helpful in formulating centerwide policies and enforcing regulations which affect all the tenants.

Major or Anchor Tenant is usually the largest tenant in the center. A supermarket or full line department store might act as an anchor tenant. This tenant provides the "draw" of shoppers so important to the smaller tenants. Typically, rental concessions are made to this tenant because of its importance to the overall success of the center.

There are many periodicals and books an investor or broker involved in shopping centers can purchase; the following are highly informative:

Chain Store Guide, Lebhar-Friedman, Inc. New York

Dollars and Cents of Shopping Centers, Urban Land Institute, Washington, D.C.

ICSC Newsletter, International Council of Shopping Centers, New York

National Mall Monitor, Cherry Hill, NJ

Shopping Center World, Communication Channels, Inc., Atlanta, GA.

Survey of Buying Power, of *Sales and Marketing Management Magazine*, New York

These periodicals provide up-to-date information on leasing trends, income amounts, expense guidelines and problems encountered in the shopping center investment arena.

Economic Factors

Regardless of the size of the shopping center, the key to success lies in the strength of the lease. The income to a shopping center owner is provided by a relatively small number of tenants compared to, for example, an equal investment in an apartment project. There may only be 10 to 15 tenants under lease terms which range from 5 to 25 years. The investor must pay close attention to these terms so that expenses such as increased ad valorum taxes, parking lot maintenance or insurance costs can be passed on to the tenant. Any rental increases will probably come about in the form of percentage rents. Percentage leases are the key to growth of rental income and value in shopping centers since minimum rents are usually level throughout the term of the lease. It is important to calculate accurate expenses and make sure that the minimum rents cover on-going expenses and debt service if an investor expects favorable cash flow.

Because of long-term leases, shopping centers tend not to have the dramatic appreciation that many other forms of investments have experienced. Since the value of the center is tied to income produced, many owners like to sign shorter leases with local tenants so rents can be escalated more often. Owners also like to get as much of their fixed costs (debt service and expenses) covered by the major tenants as possible.

The after-tax benefits of a shopping center, like other real estate investments, are largely a result of the cost recovery available. Although the accelerated cost recovery method is available, most investors use 18-year straight line cost recovery to avoid the recapture tax implications. Careful structuring is needed if the accelerated method is used since all cost recovery taken is treated as ordinary income at time of sale. The combination of straight line cost recovery and high land value compared to other investments makes shopping centers somewhat less of a tax-oriented transaction than apartments. Tax benefits being less than other investments, shopping center investors look closely at income and expenses to insure a positive before-tax cash flow.

The returns from shopping center investments are generally stable and predictable. While many centers can be purchased with relatively small amounts of cash in relation to the purchase price, most shopping center projects represent major undertakings. They are not really as suited to the new investor as small residential properties which can be invested in on a very small scale. However, for those in a position to undertake shopping center investments, there are some attractive risk return features.

The principal risk in center investments is vacancies; in a successful center an increased vacancy rate could be caused by a drop in the trading area buying power. This buying power loss could be created by lowered employment during a major plant layoff or by the closing of a large employment center. Because continued sales will depend on continued employment in the area, the risks are greatest for the shopping center located in an area dependent for its prosperity on a few major employers.

Another less severe risk would be a gradual drop off in sales, with the consequent reduction in overage rent. This could be caused by a shift in the buying habits of those in the trade area, which is usually a result of the development of another competitive center.

There are many relatively attractive risk protection features of shopping centers which include:

1 Some rental income in larger centers comes from AAA rated tenants with long-term leases. (AAA to most investors means a company with $1,000,000 net worth.)

2 Many times minimum rents will cover annual debt service requirements.

3 The low level of operating expenses reduces risk of negative cash flows due to vacancies.

4 Investors have inflation protection in two ways: (1) rental income increases as merchandise prices increase, because of overage rents or escalation clauses, and (2) the tenants are required to pay for increases in property taxes and insurance premiums.

5 Established centers offer capital protection since new competition will have to base rents on higher construction and debt service costs. Further protection against new development is provided if no other large tracts of land are available in the immediate trade area.

Investment Profile

Figure 4–6 is a profile of a new, 50,900 square-foot, neighborhood shopping center in the Southeast, with a supermarket and a drug store as major tenants. Note the breakdown of rent per square foot, CAM per square foot, base rent vs. percentage rent, lease terms and major tenant rent as a percentage of total income.

Rents on this property are tied to relatively long leases (three to five years). This does not give one the opportunity to raise rents on an annual basis. Also, straight line cost recovery offers less tax benefits than might be available from other types of investments. Accelerated cost recovery could be used, but the investor would have to face full recapture at the time of sale (see Chapter 3).

Figure 4-6
Neighborhood Shopping Center
50,900 Square Feet

Tenant	Square Footage	$ Per Sq. Foot	Minimum Annual Rent	% Rent	CAM Per Sq. ft.	Lease Term
Supermarket	20,000	$4.25	$85,000	2% vs. Base	.10	20 yrs.
Drug Store	5,000	5.75	28,750	4% vs. Base	.15	15 yrs.
Auto Supply	2,000	8.50	17,000	3% vs. Base	.25	5 yrs.
Paint Store	3,600	8.00	28,800	4% vs. Base	.25	5 yrs.
Real State Office	1,200	9.00	10,800	–	.25	3 yrs.
Plant Store	1,200	9.00	10,800	6% vs. Base	.25	3 yrs.
Beauty Salon	2,400	9.50	22,800	5% vs. Base	.25	5 yrs.
Ice Cream Parlor	1,200	9.00	10,800	8% vs. Base	.25	5 yrs.
Dance Studio	2,400	8.50	20,400	–	.25	3 yrs.
Radio & TV Service	1,400	9.00	12,600	–	.25	1 yr.
Insurance Office	1,200	9.25	11,100	–	.25	3 yrs.
Hardware Store	3,600	8.25	29,700	5% vs. Base	.25	5 yrs.
Animal Clinic	2,100	9.50	19,950	–	.25	5 yrs.
Gift Shop	1,200	9.00	10,800	6% vs. Base	.25	1 yr.
Sandwich Shop	2,400	8.50	20,400	5% vs. Base	.25	3 yrs.
TOTALS	50,900		$339,700			

Income and Expense Analysis

Tenant	Square Footage	Minimum Annual Rent	Annual CAM	Total	% of Total Rent
Supermarket	20,000	$ 85,000	$2,000	$ 87,000	25 %
Drug Store	5,000	28,750	750	$ 29,500	8.5%
Locals	25,900	$225,950	$6,474	$232,424	66.5%

Gross Income	$348,924	
–Vacancy (6% of Local Tenants)	$ 13,945	
Effective Rental Income (ERI)	$334,979	
Less Expenses:		
Ad Valorem Taxes	47¢/SF for 50,900 SF	$ 23,923
Insurance	11¢/SF for 50,900 SF	5,599
Management	5% of Effective Gross	16,748
Repairs	10¢/SF for 50,900	5,090
Maintenance	22¢/SF for 50,900	11,198

(continued on page 108)

Figure 4–6 (continued)

Utilities	8¢/SF for 50,900	4,072
Advertising	Contribution To Merchants Association	6,000

–Total Expenses (21.6% of ERI)	72,630
Net Operating Income (78.4% of ERI)	262,349
–Debt Service ($1,800,000 @ 13% for 25 yrs., 5 yr. Balloon)	243,612
Cash Flow Before Taxes	$18,737

After-Tax Overview (First Year)
(50% Tax Bracket)

Net Operating Income	$262,349
— Interest	233,406
— Capitalization of points*	9,000
— Cost Recovery**	88,888
Taxable Income	($ 68,945)
Tax Bracket	× 50%
Tax Savings	$ 34,472
+ Cash Flow Before Taxes	18,737
Cash Flow After Taxes	$ 53,209

*Capitalization of points:

5 Points ($90,000) were paid at time of origination of loan (10-year loan)

$90,000 ÷ 10 years = $9,000 per year

**18-year straight line on $1,600,000 improvements

Conclusion

The future periodic income and cash flow returns to the investor and the future value of a shopping center will depend on the buying power as well as the buying habits of the population served by the project. The risks of shopping center investing are tied to the same factors. A complete knowledge of the trade area, competitive centers and average disposable income is necessary before making a commitment to buy or develop a shopping center. Since future value of the center will be directly related to the rents generated, a strategic leasing plan must be developed to permit the investor to share in increased sales volume through percentage rents and common area charges.

Investing in Office Buildings

Our nation's current business activities are oriented to an office environment. Each profession, government agency, financial institution, corporation or business needs an office to house its service activities. The recent surge in computer utilization has created more demand for office space than ever before. Even industrial firms require a main office in which to centralize their management operations in addition to office space located within the manufacturing plant.

The demand for office space has steadily increased over the years as our economic base has progressed from agrarian to industrial to service-oriented employment centers. It is estimated that over 75 percent of the work force today is engaged in occupations which utilize office space.

Akron, Ohio is a prime example of a shifting work force. A city that once housed the world's largest tire manufacturers has gradually shifted from rubber manufacturing to service-oriented industry. Large tire plants sit empty while the demand grows for office space to house the continually growing white collar work force.

Although the skyscraper office building dominates the metropolitan skyline, it is not the only type of office space available in today's marketplace. Suburban office buildings house the growing number of office users who want to be located close to business streets, in office parks or adjacent to airports. The transportation and parking problems of a communities' downtown area have also provided impetus for growth of suburban offices.

General Characteristics

Whether the project is a towering high rise in Manhattan or a two-story building in Iowa, the characteristics of office space are essentially the same. Most tenants require quality space in a location that is easily reached by their particular clientele. Many companies, large and small, have a desire to own their own office space. This many times creates "monuments" to their success that can mislead even the most careful market analyst because the owner may not be paying market rent.

Types of Office Investments

Office building ownership can range from the owner occupied converted home to a multi-story high rise owned by a large corporate conglomorate or syndicate. Because of the heavy financial burden placed on an owner in early years of development, most central high rise buildings are owned by large institutional investors who are more able to withstand the limited cash flows. The smaller office building investors, unable to compete with the institutional giants, have largely turned to the suburban market for profitable office investments.

Low Rise Offices

These smaller office buildings have ownership structures similar to the small apartment project in terms of turnover, maintenance and management. Even though office tenants typically sign longer leases than apartment dwellers, long-term leases are still difficult to find for this type of office space.

Prime location is not the overriding factor with this type of space. Tenants who do not need high traffic exposure are attracted to these converted homes or one-floor offices tucked away on a secondary street. Appropriate access and off-street parking facilities usually must be provided to attract tenants, however.

Owners of older low rise office buildings generally pass on all interior maintenance responsibility to the tenants since the offices usually are not large. In a multi-office situation, the owners may provide cleaning service to help keep an overall quality appearance to the building. These properties are relatively easy to manage but may never appreciate as much as newer office buildings since the amount of rent collected is limited because of the lower rent appeal.

Suburban Offices

As suburbs grew, many businesses and professionals found themselves in downtown locations far from the homes of their customers. The suburban office concept has become very popular since about 1965. A concept that has worked very well for many "owner investors" has been to build approximately two to three times the amount of space needed for their operations and lease the balance to quality tenants. Many lawyers, accountants, real estate brokers, contractors, insurance agents and doctors have utilized this concept successfully in the past ten years.

These suburban offices range from 5,000 to 100,000 square feet and almost always are located in a quality growth area on the edge of the residential suburbs. A modern variant of this type of office space is the small mixed-use commercial center which is constructed around an inner courtyard with retail shops on the first floor and offices on the balcony level above with entrances facing the courtyard.

Another interesting phenomenon in this office market is the owner occupant who defies all market feasibility and builds a building to suit his own tastes, disregarding the rental market completely. A developer can easily be led away from the needs of the market and rents being generated by existing office space if he does not discount the owner occupants in the office marketplace.

The suburban office market has its own language and definitions which is helping to standardize the industry. The Institute of Real Estate Management (IREM) has adapted from the Building Owners and Managers Association the following terms.[6]

To qualify as a suburban office building (and to be included in the IREM analysis), the property must meet the following criteria:

1 Project is within a 30-mile radius of a "metropolitan location"—outside the central business district.

2 Minimum floor area is 5000 square feet.

3 80 percent or more of the rentable area is occupied by office space (the balance retail, parking, etc.).

Gross Area of Entire Building The gross area of the building is the sum of the areas at each floor level, including cellars, basements, mezzanines, penthouses, corridors, lobbies, stores and offices. It also pertains to garages in the building that are included within the principal outside faces of exterior walls, not including architectural setbacks or projections.

Gross Rentable Area Gross rentable area is computed by measuring the inside finish of permanent outer building walls or from the glass line where at least 50 percent of the outer building wall is glass. Gross rentable area includes all area within outside walls *less* stairs, elevator shafts, flues, pipe shafts, ducts and balconies.

Net Rentable Area Net rentable area is computed by measuring inside finish of permanent outer building walls or from the glass line where at least 50 percent of the outer building wall is glass. Net rentable area includes all area within outside walls *less* stairs, elevator shafts, flues, pipe shafts, vertical ducts, balconies, air conditioning rooms, janitor closets, washrooms, public corridors and other such rooms not actually available to the tenant.

Tenant Alteration Allowance This is the amount of money per square foot (based upon rentable area) which the building owner allows for tenant renovation. It usually varies depending on the length of the lease.

---

6. *The 1981 Income/Expense Analysis of Suburban Office Buildings* (Chicago: Institute of Real Estate Management, 1981).

Mechanical This term refers to machinery, heating, ventilation and air conditioning equipment, plumbing and electrical systems.

Medical Clinics

Another type of office space which has become increasingly popular is the medical clinic which allows doctors, dentists and other medical practitioners to offer services located in one central location. Under some circumstances the ideal location might be near a hospital. Some medical practitioners prefer to be in the suburbs closer to the homes of patients.

Although clinic designs vary, most include the doctors' offices as complete, self sufficient units. Other clinics have been designed around a central reception and waiting room. Here the doctors share the cost of a central filing system as well as a pool of nurses, receptionists and medical technicians.

The high cost of plumbing and electrical requirements of medical offices greatly exceeds comparable costs of other forms of office construction. Therefore, the rents are higher and leases longer than with standard office space. As a result of the high cost of rent, many medical groups have formed partnerships to develop clinics which they themselves own, often as condominium ventures.

One risk in this type of office building is that the number of practicing medical professionals in any one area is somewhat limited and does not dramatically change from year to year under normal conditions.

Office Suites

Recently, many office owners have offered a full service office suite to the tenant who does not need or cannot afford a full office space. The "suite" concept offers the smaller user a central answering service, a common conference room, secretarial service and all the amenities of a large office, but on a shared basis.

Somewhat more expensive to develop, this style of office space offers the owner an opportunity to collect substantially higher rents since the rent payment also includes services which the independent user could not afford on his own. A lawyer on the West Coast has gone so far as renting an entire floor of a downtown high rise and is subleasing to one or two associate firms. Amenities included are two luxury conference rooms, an extensive law library and sophisticated word processing capability. These specialty uses command much higher rent than any comparable space.

Office Parks

As office buildings made their way into the suburbs, office parks started to develop. In addition to accessibility from the residential areas, office parks are also able to offer other amenities to attract tenants. Security service plus recreation, cultural and dining facilities within the park create a preplanned, well maintained atmosphere for the tenants and their clients. The image projected by the office park is sometimes as important as the office space itself.

High Rise Office Buildings

In most metropolitan areas the largest amount of office space is contained within skyscraper office buildings. Built to house either the single institutional tenant or a group of tenants, the skyscraper can offer the major tenant the ability to expand its operations when needed.

Many corporations construct their own wholly occupied high rise towers in strategic midcity locations. Some companies, for publicity purposes, incorporate unique architectural designs or characteristics in their buildings. The Sears Tower in Chicago, acclaimed as the tallest building in the world, is an example.

Investment Characteristics

Investing in buildings which house offices is different from investing in residential buildings. The risks of not renting available space are greater with office buildings than with residential apartments, the services expected by tenants are generally more expensive and there is a higher risk of obsolescence. Choosing an attractive location and projecting what the market demand will be when the space is completed are all-important.

The overall demand for office space always fluctuates. While there may always be someone willing to move into housing units, users of office space are not sensitive to bargain prices unless they specifically need to move. When office users upgrade, it is usually the quality of the accommodation and the location which determine the move. Office rental is tied to the needs of the modern professional community. Status locations offering amenities will command higher rents.

In addition to reviewing income and expenses, there are a number of variables to consider when viewing a new or existing office building as an investment:

- Is the location positively a quality prestige area in town?
- Do the leases contain strength and length in case of the need to refinance?

- Is base rent sufficient to cover the high cost of operating a full service building?
- Do the leases offer rent escalations to cover variable expenses such as taxes, insurance, cleaning service and utilities?
- Is indoor parking available?
- Is food service available for personnel of tenants?
- Can an early leasing program be instituted for the new building?
- Interior alterations for tenants are expensive. Can cost be passed on to tenants? Is cash flow sufficient to make alterations in case of tenant turnover?
- Is cash flow sufficient to pay leasing fees in case of turnover?
- Is a dependable service available for cleaning?
- Are the elevators fast? Is cash flow sufficient to cover high cost of maintenance on elevators?
- Is the heating, ventilation and air conditioning adjustable on a room-by-room basis?
- Is the layout of the building efficient? (High percentage of net rentable space compared to gross area)
- A new building may be needed today, but can the space be absorbed into the market one year from now after the construction time lapse?
- Can tenant improvements be standard enough for cost projections and exclusive enough to attract financially acceptable tenants?

By no means a complete list, the above questions nevertheless will help the active investor consider some variables which may be unique to the office building investment.

In existing buildings the principal risk is the location. A quality location will attract other good office buildings. Good locations become better locations with the addition of newer and competitive office buildings in the same general area. It seems that office buildings are judged many times by the company they keep.

Office rents must be carefully monitored in order to keep up with the costs of operation. These costs must be kept down so the rent charged does not exceed that of competitive space. Buying out old leases to accommodate larger tenants who seek expansion can be expensive.

Cash flows, on the other hand, can be steady, with stable tenants in a quality location. The higher cost of land reduces the ratio of the improvement value for cost recovery but an office building still yields substantial tax savings if properly structured. One advantage of office buildings is that when an investor decides it is time to sell the property, the market will not only be other investors but also potential users.

Investment Profile

The following profile (Figure 4-7) is of a typical suburban office building in a small midwestern town which is owned by investors and leased to the investors' real estate brokerage operation. The total square footage of the office building is 16,750. Net rentable space is 15,000 square feet. There are two floors, a full atrium and an elevator. Note the high cost of operations since the building is a full service building. Note also how the rental charge is varied. The original improvements needed by the tenant helped determine the rental cost. (A survey of rents nationwide would find that rents in smaller Midwestern towns lag considerably behind many parts of the country.)

If the owner of the building were to charge the real estate firm market rent, the building would probably break even or show a positive cash flow. This is why many times it is difficult to determine market rent or the value of a building when an owner-occupant is involved.

Figure 4-7

Suburban Office Building
(15,000 Square Feet Net Rentable)

Tenant	Square Footage	$ per Sq. Ft.	Annual Rent	Lease Term
Real Estate Office*	7,500	8.50	$ 63,750	1 year
Insurance Agency	3,000	9.25	27,750	5 year
Travel Agency	1,000	9.50	9,500	2 year
Accountant	1,500	9.25	13,875	3 year
Investment Advisor	1,000	9.00	9,000	1 year
Developer	1,000	9.00	9,000	1 year
Total	15,000		$132,875	

*Owner's company

(continued on page 116)

Figure 4–7 (continued)
Income and Expense Analysis

	(% of ERI)	
Gross Income		$132,875
–Vacancy (2,000 sq. ft. for 3 months)		4,500
Effective Rental Income (ERI)		$128,375
–Less Expenses	(% of ERI)	
Advertising & Promotion	.5%	$ 642
Commission (lease or renewal)	1.8%	2,310
Elevator	.1%	128
Window Cleaning	.6%	770
Insurance	.2%	2,560
Janitor Services	.9%	11,553
Management	.5%	6,418
Outside Maintenance	1.1%	1,412
Painting & Decorating	.5%	641
General Repairs	3.8%	4,873
Rubbish	.5%	641
Taxes	6.4%	8,250
Utilities	15.8%	20,282
Total Expenses	47.1%	$60,480
Net Operating Income		$67,895
–Debt Service ($550,000 at 13%, 25 yrs.)		$74,437
Cash Flow Before Taxes		(6,542)

After-Tax Overview
First Year
(30% Tax Bracket)

Net Operating Income	$67,895
— Interest	71,318
— Cost Recovery*	33,333
Taxable Income	($36,756)
Tax Bracket	× 30%
Tax Savings	$11,026
Tax Savings	11,026
Cash Flow Before Taxes	(6,542)
Cash Flow After Taxes	$ 4,484

*18-year straight line on $600,000 improvements

Specialty Real Estate

In addition to the more traditional forms of real estate investment—land, apartments, houses, offices, shopping centers—there are numerous opportunities to participate in profitable ventures in specialized real estate. These specialty properties are usually classified as such because of their thin market in terms of available tenants who can utilize the facility.

These are opportunities which require special knowledge, marketing or management capabilities above and beyond the capabilities of the average real estate investor. Specialty properties may be so management-intensive that the investor is in essence operating a business instead of managing a real estate investment. In other cases the property may be so unique that there is a limited market for it.

Fast Food Restaurants

Throughout the United States investors have watched the fast food restaurant business experience rapid growth. The need by these operations for expansion capital gave investors a chance to provide real estate leased on a long-term basis to fast food companies. Based on the strength of the company, an investor usually signed a 25-year lease on a building built specifically for the tenant. Unique sizes, shapes and rooflines limited any secondary uses, but most investors were not worried since the lease was on a "net lease" basis (tenant pays *all* expenses of operation).

Truly an investor's dream? Even though many times fast food chains pay the investor a percentage of gross receipts over a stipulated amount, the investor has little chance to increase the cash flow as years go by. The limited increase in rents carries over to the valuation of the property at the end of the holding period. Thus, many investors found themselves with a single purpose building and a level income stream and were unable to sell the property for its original price. Usually the culprit is financing. As financing increases in cost, the value of real estate is affected. Without periodic income increase, the investment community offers lower prices to create desired yields on the equity invested.

Careful screening of an investor's objectives is needed if a level cash flow investment vehicle such as a fast food lease is being considered. The disappearance of long-term financing also puts the burden on the investor to structure a lease which meets the needs of the financing.

Industrial Buildings

The industrial building is typically used in the production, storage or distribution of tangible goods. Industrial property includes the many plants, lofts and warehouses located throughout the nation. The users of these buildings are a lot like the fast food industry in that their funds are best used in the business venture and not as equity in real estate.

The sale leaseback technique is frequently used with this form of investment. The owner-manufacturer sells the building to an investor and leases the facility back on a long-term basis.

The characteristics of industrial buildings differ somewhat from other real estate opportunities. Heavy electrical and gas usage may be needed, for example. In recent years the disposal of waste and water capacity have become major problems for industrial developers. Often, industrial parks need to build their own disposal plants, thus adding substantial costs to the land development process. Since the movement of goods and products is of great importance to the typical manufacturer, highway, railroad and airport capabilities are concerns unique to this type of investment.

Industrial real estate can be highly sensitive to shifts in the market or technology. It also has a great degree of sensitivity to local taxes; often a manufacturer will receive tax abatement in return for locating in a certain community.[7]

Self-Service Storage

The self-service storage or "miniwarehouse" concept began in the early 1960s. It was probably the brainchild of some businessman who knew that one-fourth of the population moves each year across the hall, across town or across the country.

Surveys of tenants of self-service storage units show that as many as 69 percent have lived in their current locations for less than three years and as many as 55 percent for less than one year. In addition, housing has changed. As the prices of single-family homes have escalated, more and more Americans have opted for multifamily units.

Opportunities in self-service storage exist but only for those who realize that although the units are structured like a typical real estate investment, they are more of a business venture than a pure real estate investment. The industry maintains that warehouses do not sell space but, instead, sell solutions to people's space storage problems. These solutions can range from small deposit drawers for valuables to oversize garage

---

7. *Industrial Real Estate*, 2nd ed., by William N. Kinnard, Stephen D. Messner and Byrl N. Boyce (Washington: Society of Industrial REALTORS®, 1979) is a comprehensive text on the subject.

size units or extra space for heavy warehousing of goods for a local manufacturer.

Rules of thumb for the industry are plentiful as to the number of units per population count, driving time and target markets. Two variables remain constant: (1) consumers will not drive long distances to get to the facility, thus location is important, and (2) accessibility must be easily available at all times of the day and from all directions.

The field is wide open to those entrepreneurs who combine real estate investment techniques with a facility of basic design requiring few frills and amenities. Construction and operating costs are low compared to most real estate investments.[8]

Racquetball Clubs

In the early 1970s the hottest investment idea to hit the real estate market was the commercial courtclub concept. Racquetball was discovered by both men and women as a fine form of physical exercise.

Investment brokers found themselves helping groups of investors find land for the "ideal" courtclub. As more and more clubs were built, however, the market made a shift and suddenly the facilities were no longer a "sweetheart deal." Like bowling alleys and tennis clubs before them, not all facilities would survive.

Racquetball clubs usually contain eight to 20 racquetball courts (20 by 40 feet and 20 feet high), locker rooms, running tracks and viewing areas. Their income is solely dependent on the ability of management to create programs to keep memberships active and people using the facility. Courtclubs require special construction including high ceilings, glass walls, jacuzzis and saunas. By most standards they are very expensive buildings to build, maintain and operate.

The first clubs were built in areas with heavy population in the 18-35-year age groups. Clubs typically could service 10,000 people per court and a driving radius of 10 to 15 minutes. Depending on the facility, income of $30,000 per court per year was not unusual. The author was personally involved in a few clubs which in their first year of operation in the mid-1970s showed Cash Flow Before Taxes of $100,000 each.

8. The Self-Service Storage Association (SSSA) began in Dayton, Ohio in 1975 as a trade association and has continued to grow to its current size of over 850 members representing over 3,000 storage facilities. The association offers professional advice on all aspects of locating, building and operating a storage facility. It is currently located in Eureka Springs, Arkansas.

The courtclub industry is beginning to deal with the problem of saturation. A club that started out servicing 15,000 people per court suddenly, because of competition, is servicing 4500 per court. The industry has watched club after club fail with no alternate use for a 25-foot high building with no windows but two shower and steam rooms.

The biggest problem for most clubs has been that they were built by racquetball players who thought it would be nice to own a courtclub. They have intensive management needs; full-time devotion is needed.

As an investor in the building only, one might consider the alternate use problem and require nonrecourse financing (if financing is available at all). The courtclub industry is not nearly as active as it was in the mid-1970s, but there are still parts of the country where a well placed, well managed facility can provide physical fitness services to a somewhat limited market. There is probably an opportunity for the broker or developer who can create an alternate use for the many clubs in the country that are operating at a loss year after year.

Condominium Conversion

The recent demand for housing at affordable levels has sparked many condominium conversion projects around the country. Given the right conditions, the purchase of an existing rental property with subsequent conversion and sale of units as condominiums can and has yielded substantial profits for many investors. It could prove to be a top real estate opportunity for owners of rental property.

A number of conditions need to be considered before a conversion is undertaken. There should be a large demand for homes and apartments in the area. Newer properties with similar amenities should be generating 25 percent more rent than the subject property. Single family homes should cost 25 to 30 percent more than the anticipated unit sales price. There should be a low turnover in the current list of tenants; ideally 30 to 35 percent of the present tenants will become the owners of their own units.

Apartments in a converted building should have the features and floor plan similar to those of a house. Condo buyers are looking for more than pure shelter from the elements; they want the features found in a single family home. Typically, apartment houses catering to singles have not done well in conversion. Kitchen and bathrooms tend to be an area of concern in the marketing process. Extra amenities such as pools, tennis courts and parking facilities also help sales.

The ideal situation for pre-sale is to poll the present tenants and find how many might buy their units. If 35 percent or so would buy, losses from vacancies could be cut substantially with a condo conversion. Tenants can be offered discounts and allowances which often help them make the decision to buy.

There are a number of questions that a broker or investor should consider before any conversion project, some of which include:

1 Will the property sell for more as condos than a discounted outright sale?

2 What are the costs of marketing, including advertising, promotion, rent loss and sales commissions?

3 Is there suitable financing available for the individual condo buyer?

4 Are existing leases a problem?

5 Is there competent, conversion-experienced legal assistance available?

6 Is there a competent marketing sales force available?

7 How much will the condos bring on the market and how long will it take for them to be absorbed into the market?

8 Is interim financing needed and what are the costs involved?

9 What are the after-tax costs to a perspective buyer? Are they realistic in the marketplace?[9]

Remember, a conversion will most likely be taxed as ordinary income. After conversion the price must be high enough to offset the loss of capital gains treatment on the sale proceeds. An astute investor would certainly figure a sale both as an apartment building and as a conversion to determine the after-tax economic feasibility of each.

---

9. *The Condominium Home, A Special Marketing Challenge* by Janet Scavo (Chicago: REALTORS NATIONAL MARKETING INSTITUTE®, 1981) outlines conversion and marketing techniques for the real estate broker.

Section II
CASH FLOW ANALYSIS AND MEASUREMENT TECHNIQUES

Chapter 5

The Analysis of Cash Flows

What exactly is GRM, cash on cash, IRR and FMRR? We still use cash on cash to sell property; is there a way to sell clients on the shortcomings without offending them? How do I explain IRR to a client? Is there a measurement that measures all the benefits of real estate?

Chapter 6

Measurement Techniques as Sales Tools

What techniques do investors really use? How can I get owners to list their property at realistic prices? What do I say to a client who wants too much money for his property? Is there a way to prepare a presentation to help the owner see the buyer's side of the transaction? How can I use IRR as a sales tool instead of an academic exercise? How do I explain cash flow analysis in a sales presentation?

5

THE ANALYSIS OF CASH FLOWS

An investment is made today so that cash flows can be received in the future. Therefore, the most important task a broker performs in analyzing cash flows with a client is the "crystal ball" forecast of what will happen to the property (especially the cash flows) tomorrow and beyond. After forecasting income and expenses, the second stage of the property presentation is the analysis of the cash flows. These cash flows are then reduced to a return percentage for comparison with other opportunities in the investment marketplace.

For years, investors have done well in real estate in spite of their analysis decisions. It has been said that there are no "bad" pieces of real estate, only parcels that were bought or sold at the wrong time. Since the Depression in the 1930s, most of us have been conditioned to believe that real estate always goes up in value. Inflation usually saw to that. Long-term fixed financing and increasing rents meant a favorable equity position at the time of sale regardless of the criteria utilized to analyze future benefits. That is not the case today.

Measurement Techniques

Market conditions necessitate a more in-depth view of financing and tax implications. As investors become more sensitive to sophisticated analysis techniques, we in the real estate industry need to understand and speak the language of the investment community. The following techniques are used in the investment community to analyze real estate investments. Used by themselves, most of them are fallacious at best. Regardless of their shortcomings, however, real estate practitioners must understand them and be able to relate to the investors who use them.

Generally, the higher the price of the investment, the more sophisticated the investors will be in making analysis comparisons; still, billions of dollars of real estate have been purchased utilizing very simple rules of thumb. A major problem arises as investors and brokers, all talking "rates of return," measure the benefits of a real estate investment at different levels. It is imperative that the broker know and understand

Figure 5–1

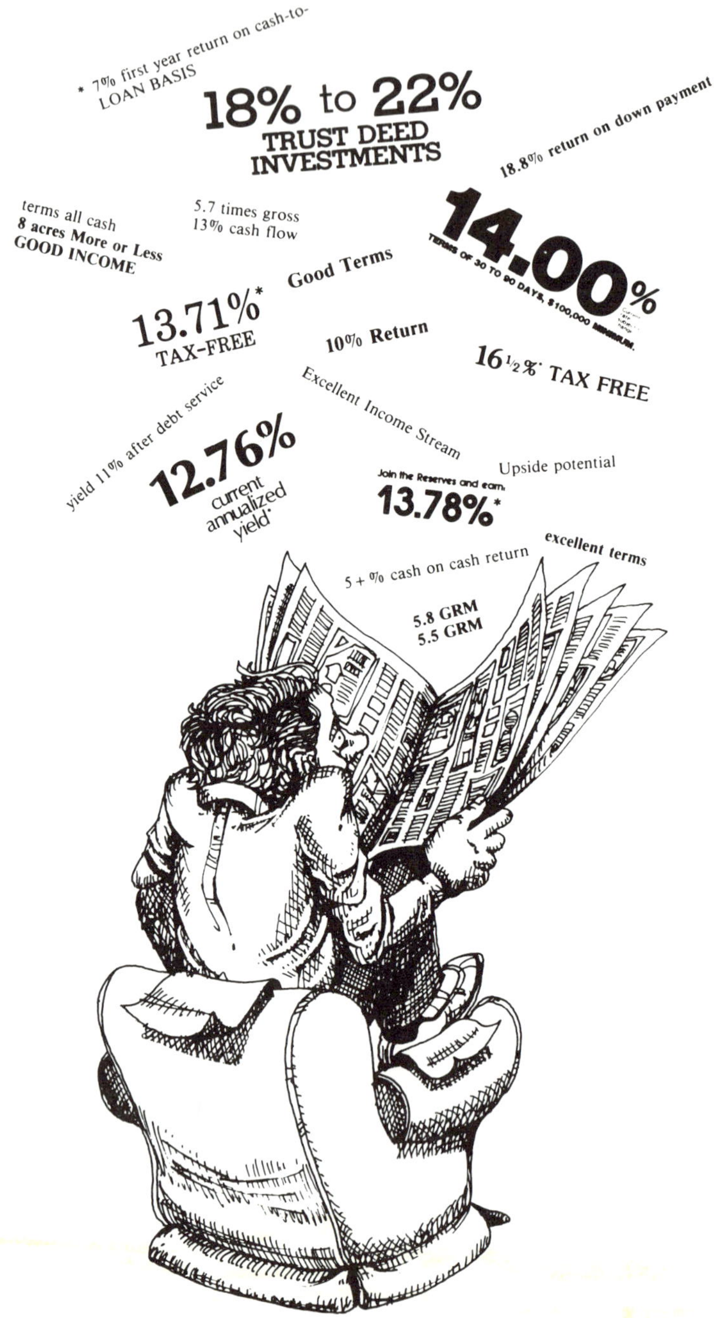

The marketplace is full of confusing percentage returns and measurements.

the measurement criteria the investor is using in his decision-making process.

Payback

The "payback" simply computes the time it takes an investment to pay back the original down payment to the investors. Certainly not a true measurement device, the payback simply converts Cash Flow Before Tax into a period of time as related to the original investment. No treatment of present value of cash is utilized, only the payback period. Even though this technique disregards the benefits of real estate in terms of taxes, appreciation and mortgage reduction, many investors view the payback period as a true measurement of risk.

Here is an example of how payback is figured:

Down Payment	$20,000
Annual Cash Flow Before Taxes	2,000

$$\frac{\$20{,}000}{2{,}000} = 10 \text{ Years Payback}$$

As we saw earlier, different types of real estate yield different tax benefits, thus destroying the credibility of any measurement that does not include an after-tax analysis of cash flows. Note on the primary evaluation technique index (Figure 5-2) that 17 percent of the respondents used the payback period as a *primary* evaluation technique in the decision-making process. (This chart and its history will be discussed further in Chapter 6.) One must also be aware of the fact that many times an investor will be using Cash Flows After Tax instead of before tax to determine the payback period of the investment.

Gross Rent Multiplier

Most often used by apartment investors, the gross rent multiplier (GRM) is a quick determination of value. It is nothing more than a relationship of gross rents and price; i.e., a price of $100,000 divided by gross rents of $10,000 equals a GRM of ten. The most that can be said for the technique is that the lower the multiplier the lower the value—fine for a purchaser, not so swell if you are the seller. As a comparative tool, the GRM cannot be measured against any other standard except another GRM. Comparing two GRMs could be accurate if both investment alternatives have the same expenses, same vacancies, same financing arrangement, same fee ownership, same after-tax benefits, and so on. As an investment measuring device, the GRM lacks credibility. This is not to say that investors avoid buying (especially apartments) based on gross rent multipliers or, even worse, on a per-unit cost basis.

Figure 5-2

Primary Evaluation Techniques

Technique	Payback	Internal Rate of Return	Present Value of Cash Flows (specific desired yield)	Financial Management Rate of Return	Gross Rent Multiplier	Net Income Multiplier (Cap Rate)	Before Tax Cash/Equity	After Tax Cash/Equity	After Tax Cash & Amortz./ Equity	After Tax Cash & Amortz. & Apprec./Equity
Average Project Size (in millions)										
Less than $2.5	16%	16%	22%	22%	7%	13%	35%	48%	23%	29%
$ 2.5 – $ 5.999	20%	62%	29%	9%	7%	20%	53%	47%	13%	22%
$ 6.0 – $ 9.999	14%	62%	24%	19%	14%	24%	81%	38%	24%	24%
$10.0 – $14.999	18%	71%	24%	18%	–	6%	77%	49%	24%	24%
$15.0 and above	18%	29%	35%	24%	–	18%	49%	35%	24%	6%
Type of Firm										
Life Insurance	15%	75%	24%	9%	6%	15%	73%	49%	21%	18%
REIT	15%	54%	8%	15%	8%	23%	77%	39%	8%	8%
Pension Fund Advisor	17%	83%	17%	33%	–	17%	83%	50%	33%	33%
Syndicator	19%	48%	28%	16%	5%	13%	36%	52%	20%	30%
Private Devel. Firm	20%	55%	29%	24%	9%	20%	47%	43%	20%	24%
Public Devel. Firm	–	80%	10%	30%	10%	10%	50%	30%	40%	20%
Overall	17%	62%	25%	18%	6%	16%	51%	46%	21%	24%
Fortune 1000	12%	49%	19%	N.A.	N.A.	N.A.	N.A.	N.A.	N.A.	N.A.

From a survey conducted by Dr. E.J. Farragher, Associate Professor of Finance, DePaul University, Chicago.

Many brokers "track" GRMs in their local markets to look for trends in price ranges. When a property is placed on the market, they immediately know if the gross rents and the price lie within customary guidelines. It can only be hoped that these brokers will look further than a first year relationship between gross rents and the "magic GRM" to determine a property value, but this is how they do it:

First Year Gross Annual Rents:	\$10,000 x 7 GRM =	\$ 70,000 value
	10,000 x 8 GRM =	80,000
	10,000 x 9 GRM =	90,000
	10,000 x 10 GRM =	100,000

Note in the survey shown in Figure 5-2 that relatively few buyers of real estate over a \$2.5 million value utilize the GRM. But be prepared for the first-time investor to be familiar with the GRM. He may have read about it in a book written by one of many self-proclaimed investment "gurus" who purport the wisdom of buying based on GRMs and per-unit cost.

Capitalization Rate

The capitalization rate, or overall rate (OAR), of a property has long been used to value investment real estate. Utilized by appraisers to place a value on real estate via an income approach, the "cap" rate is a most useful tool to the active broker and investor. As a relationship between Net Operating Income (NOI) and value, the cap rate is a quick way to look at the initial cash return of a real estate project if financing is not used.

The cap rate or OAR is only as pure as the numbers that make up the Net Operating Income, however. The *quality* of the Net Operating Income figure can be inconsistent depending upon who creates the income and expense statement. Assuming that a Net Operating Income is accurate, an investor can measure the amount of first year cash (before financing) against the value of the investment.

By definition, the capitalization rate is determined by dividing the NOI by the market value. The handy relationship:

$$\frac{\text{Net Operating Income}}{\text{Cap Rate x Market Value}}$$

will help the practitioner find the cap rate on any given property or find the value if the income and rate is known, always solving for the unknown variable.

However, the question of how a capitalization rate is determined without knowing both the NOI and the market value is always a mystery. Appraisers continually amaze investors and brokers with their ability to pull a capitalization rate from the marketplace and draw conclusions from it as to the value of a particular parcel of real estate.

Historically, the capitalization rate has been created by many methods. Two of the most common methods are the band of investment method and the market comparison approach.

Band of Investment Method Under this method, individual rates of return are given to individual interests in the property. Mortgages and equity investments are weighted to arrive at the capitalization rate of the market.

To illustrate, assume a 70 percent loan-to-value mortgage on a property at 13 percent interest with the equity investor requiring a 12 percent return on the 30 percent equity position. The capitalization rate would build as follows:

	Ownership %		Rate of Return		Weighted
Mortgage	70%	x	13%	=	9.1%
Equity	30%	x	12%	=	3.6%
Total	100%				12.7%

Capitalization Rate = 12.7%

Market Comparison Approach This is the more common method for the real estate practitioner. Data on recent transactions might appear as follows:

Comparable A

$$\frac{\text{NOI}}{\text{Sale Price}} = \frac{\$\ 12{,}000}{100{,}000} = 12\%$$

Comparable B

$$\frac{\text{NOI}}{\text{Sale Price}} = \frac{\$\ 15{,}000}{130{,}500} = 11.5\%$$

Comparable C

$$\frac{\text{NOI}}{\text{Sale Price}} = \frac{\$\ 17{,}500}{141{,}000} = 12.4\%$$

If all comparables were relatively the same as the subject property, one could surmise the market rate for capitalization of the first year's net income would be approximately 12 percent.

Many investors will refer to this evaluation as "12 times net" or

$$\frac{\text{Net}}{.12}$$

Although indicating what the market may currently be paying for property, this technique says absolutely nothing about financing, increases or decreases in value or tax benefits of the investment.

Capitalization Rate and Leverage The capitalization rate is utilized by many investors to analyze the leverage position of financing upon acquisition of a property. If the cap rate is higher than the mortgage constant, which is

$$\frac{\text{Annual Debt Service}}{\text{Loan Amount}}$$

positive leverage exists, thus making it possible to achieve higher Cash Flows Before Taxes when borrowing with high loan-to-value ratio. Positive leverage exists whenever the cap rate exceeds the mortgage constant.

Conversely, if the capitalization rate is lower than the mortgage constant, negative leverage exists and the investor might consider structuring a lower loan-to-value ratio to realize any Cash Flow Before Taxes.

10 Percent Cap Rate This author has always felt that the entire market uses a 10 percent cap rate to value property since it is easy to figure without a calculator. This is certainly not the case with all properties but it *is* interesting to note how many properties use a 10 percent cap rate for valuation, regardless of financing costs.

Cash on Cash

When an investor uses the term "cash on cash," reference is usually being made to the first year's Cash Flow Before Taxes divided by the initial investment (usually the down payment). Many investors think of this percentage as "the" return a property yields.

Because real estate yields benefits in four major areas, the cash on cash percentage should not be the sole criteria for decision making. We have seen that a real estate investment usually benefits the owner in the following areas: (1) Cash Flow Before Taxes, (2) tax benefits, (3) appreciation, and (4) mortgage reduction. We know that not all investments offer all four benefits, but by using a measurement device which only views the Cash Flow Before Taxes, an investor may be passing up an investment which has overshadowing benefits in other areas.

Here is an example of how cash on cash is determined:

Purchase Price	$1,800,000
Down Payment	360,000

Annual Net Operating Income	$ 200,000
Less: Annual Debt Service	175,000
Annual Cash Flow Before Tax	$ 25,000

Cash on Cash Percentage $\frac{\$\ 25{,}000}{\$\ 360{,}000}$ or 6.9%

Note on the primary evaluation techniques survey shown earlier (see Figure 5-2) the high percentage of investors who utilize the cash on cash method. Although the method gives an immediate percentage return of the first year's cash flow, it can hardly be compared to other methods which may or may not be returns expressed on an after-tax basis. For example, it is a simple process to compare the first year's Cash Flow Before Tax to a savings account percentage, but because of the tax ramifications of real estate, the results could be grossly misleading. One might think that a higher cash on cash return indicates a better investment when in fact other variables might influence the property's ability to produce financial benefits.

Like the gross rent multiplier, the payback, and the cap rate, the cash on cash return fails to measure any future benefits from the property in terms of operations, refinancing or eventual sale proceeds.

The problem the broker will face in the investment community is that cash on cash is widely used as a measurement tool. It is our job as active practitioners to understand how and when this return method can be justified in the decision-making process.

Cash on Cash After Tax One step better than the basic cash on cash before tax is a measurement of return which views the property on an after-tax basis of the first year's cash flow. This return can be compared to a savings account if the savings account is reduced to an after-tax return. Cash on cash after tax can be compared to, say, a tax-free bond, but it must be pointed out that growth of the investment is still not considered.

Although this type of analysis takes into account Cash Flow Before Taxes and the first year's tax benefits from real estate, it still fails to measure after-tax benefits of future years or any proceeds at the time of sale.

Cash on cash after tax is the first step the investor may take to the understanding that all investments must be viewed on an after-tax basis for each and every opportunity.

Here is an example of cash on cash after tax:

Purchase Price	$900,000	
Down Payment	250,000	
Mortgage	$650,000	13.5%, 25-year amortization

Checkbook		Tax World	
NOI	$100,000	NOI	$100,000
–Debt Service	90,920	–Interest	87,546
CFBT	$ 9,080	–Cost Recovery	45,000
		Taxable Income	($ 32,546)
		Tax Bracket	50%
		Tax Savings	$ 16,273

CFBT	$ 9,080
Tax Savings	16,273
CFAT	$ 25,353

$$\frac{\$\ 25{,}353}{\$250{,}000} = 10.1\% \text{ Cash on Cash After Tax}$$

After Tax Plus Amortization

As investors come to realize that equity build-up and appreciation are in fact a very real portion of the return from real estate, they struggle to account for the dollars returned by including them in their percentage calculations. Prevalent in today's marketplace are the following two procedures which, for what they do, are not all bad. However, as we will see, they are not comparative tools for *all* future benefits of real estate. These methods represent the investment community's first attempts at measuring the potential of future cash flows from disposition.

More than 20 percent of the investors surveyed in the evaluation survey (see Figure 5-2) used the first year after-tax cash flow plus the first year amortization (principal) amount to relate to the initial investment. This measurement is sometimes referred to as the "broker's rate." Although this method includes mortgage reduction, it creates another set of problems in that (1) mortgage reduction is not generated until the time of sale and (2) equity build-up assumes the property value will not change during the holding period. Using this criteria as a comparative measure, one wonders if an interest-only loan (no principal reduction) would ever be advantageous.

Using the property from the cash on cash after tax example, an investor might consider:

Purchase Price	$900,000	
Down Payment	250,000	
Mortgage	$650,000	13.5%, 25-year amortization

Checkbook		Tax World	
NOI	$100,000	NOI	$100,000
−Debt Service	90,920	−Interest	87,546
CFBT	$ 9,080	−Cost Recovery	45,000
Tax Savings	$ 16,273	Taxable Income	($ 32,546)
		Tax Bracket	50%
		Tax Savings	$ 16,273
CFAT	$ 25,353		
Plus Principal Reduction	3,374		
	$ 28,727		

$$\frac{\$\ 28{,}727}{\$250{,}000} = 11.5\%\text{ Broker's Rate}$$

Equity Rate of Return

Another procedure is similar to the broker's rate except that it requires the investor to project a future sale price and the loan balance at the end of the holding period. By calculating the first year's Cash Flow After Tax, adding equity build-up and total change in value, the investor might relate the total amount back to the initial investment, hoping to come up with a percentage that can be compared to alternative investment opportunities.

The obvious flaw in this calculation is that after-tax cash flows from future years in the holding period are disregarded and no adjustment is made for the element of time. Also, no allocation has been given to dollars received early in the holding period. It is an accepted theory that there is a time value to having dollars today as opposed to some time in the future.

In this calculation, dollars received at the end of the holding period are weighted as if they were received today.

Although this method begins to consider after-tax effects by using the first year's after-tax cash flow, it proceeds to add a before-tax increase in value and principal reduction. This mixture leads to high percentages but not much consistency or comparative ability. Using our same example:

Purchase Price	$900,000	
Down Payment	250,000	
Mortgage	$650,000	13.5%, 25-year amortization

Assume Value, End of 1st Year: $955,000

Checkbook		**Tax World**	
NOI	$100,000	NOI	$100,000
–Debt Service	90,920	–Interest	87,546
CFBT	$ 9,080	–Cost Recovery	45,000
		Taxable Income	($ 32,546)
		Tax Bracket	50%
		Tax Savings	$ 16,273
CFAT	$ 25,353		
Appreciation	55,000		
Principal Reduction	3,374		
Total	$ 83,727		

$$\frac{\$\ 83{,}727}{\$250{,}000} = 33.5\%\ \text{Equity Rate of Return}$$

Accounting Rate of Return

A method of analysis used by many sophisticated investors, the accounting rate of return makes an attempt to measure all the benefits during the entire ownership period including any after-tax proceeds from an eventual sale.

To compute the accounting rate of return:

1 Subtract the initial cash investment from the total annual benefits (after tax) to get a net dollar return.

2 Divide the net dollar return by the investment holding period.

3 Divide the dollar return by initial cash investment to get the average annual percentage return.

Or:

$$\frac{\text{Total Annual Benefits - Initial Investment} \div \text{Years}}{\text{Initial Investment}} = \underline{\qquad}\%$$

Assume the following after-tax cash flows of an investment:

Initial Investment	($15,000)
First Year Cash Flow	1,600
Second Year Cash Flow	1,745
Third Year Cash Flow	1,534
Fourth Year Cash Flow	1,645
Fifth Year Cash Flow	1,800 + 15,389 from sale
Total Annual Benefits	$23,713

$$\frac{\$23{,}713 - 15{,}000 \div 5}{\$15{,}000} \quad \text{or} \quad \frac{1{,}742}{\$15{,}000} = 11.6\%$$

Although this method does take into consideration the benefits of tax savings and sale proceeds from the investment, it *fails to take into account the time value of money*. That is, all the dollars Years One through Five are given equal value. Again, a dollar to be received in the future is not worth as much as a dollar in hand because the dollar's value presumably is eroded by time and loss of opportunity either for reinvestment or squandering.

The accounting rate of return comes close to being a complete comparative analysis and has been used for years by many investors.

Discounted Cash Flow Methods

All the previous methods of analysis are concerned with only the amounts of cash flows. The sophisticated investor is not only concerned with the *amount* of the cash flow but he is also concerned about the *timing* of said cash flows. Most of the methods we have discussed either ignore future cash flows or treat future flows as having the same purchasing power as those dollars of the present.

Most investors are aware that dollars received today are worth more than dollars received in the future. The logic is that if one were to receive dollars today one would invest them or at least be exposed to the opportunity to do so. If, on the other hand, one is offered cash in the future, one would not have that money to invest for the intervening time period. Because of the loss of opportunity to invest the funds today, the money in the future is worth less than the face amount to be received. Simply put, $1000 to be received one year from today is worth something less than $1000 today. If one had the $1000 today, it could at least be placed in a passbook account and earn over five percent for the one-year period.

This concept is the reason the timing of cash flows is so important to the investment community. Real estate cash flows often take the form of a series of cash flows plus a larger sum when the property is sold. Regardless of this irregular "shape" of cash flows, a discounted cash flow analysis can give the value of an investment today based on the investor's other opportunities in the marketplace. These opportunities are expressed as a "discount rate."

The discounted cash flow method is growing in popularity with many analysts because it is so all-inclusive, reflecting the quantity and timing of all after-tax cash flow benefits returned to the equity owner.

The advantages of discounted cash flow analysis are:

- Takes into account financing on project
- Takes into account tax impact of cash flows
- Treats time value of money
- Provides a convenient measure against alternative investments
- Measures return on owner's investment rather than on entire project's cost

If an investor had an opportunity to put his funds in an 11 percent (after-tax) account, his opportunity cost would be 11 percent (sometimes called 11 percent discount rate). Many sophisticated investors add 2 percent to 4 percent to their discount rates to help account for risk factors involved in real estate. In the following example, a 14 percent discount rate is used to find the present worth of the future cash flows from the investment. By using a 14 percent discount rate, the investor can determine exactly how many dollars can be invested today to receive a 14 percent return in the form of the future benefits as projected.

The Ellwood tables[1] were first published in 1959 and have been widely

1. For complete tables see L. W. Ellwood, *Ellwood Tables for Real Estate Appraising and Financing*, 4th edition (Chicago: American Institute of Real Estate Appraisers, 1981).

used by appraisers and lenders. An experienced user of the tables can easily discount future cash flows and find today's value. Today, the financial calculator makes easy work of what was once a long process.

Assume the following after-tax cash flows:

Year 1	$2700
Year 2	2645
Year 3	2537
Year 4	2417 + 22,000

Discounted at 14 percent in a financial calculator, the cash flows are worth $20,573 to the investor today. (The $22,000 might be from sale proceeds.)

This means that the most an investor can pay for the equity position and still receive a 14 percent annual return is $20,573. If the investor pays more than the $20,573 for the ownership position, the rate of return earned on each dollar during the holding period will be less than 14 percent. Conversely, if the investor could purchase the position for less than $20,573, his rate of return would be higher than 14 percent.

This technique is an ideal way for investors, given other valid rate of return alternatives in the marketplace, to determine exactly what the value of the equity position is to them at that point in time.

Another way to use this discounted cash flow technique is to analyze the cash flows using the investor's return criteria and add any mortgage sum available to total what many analysts call the "investment value" of the property. Because the after-tax yield demands are unique to each investor, the investment value of the property is also unique to that investor.

Assume Cash Flows After Tax:

Year 1	$2700
Year 2	2645
Year 3	2537
Year 4	2417 + 22,000

Investor's return requirement: 15%

Available mortgage: $90,000

Discounted at 15 percent, these cash flows are worth $19,976 to the investor today. Add the $90,000 lender's position in the investment, and the total "investment value" of the project is $109,976. Based on the 15 percent rate of return requirement, the most the investor could pay for the project (considering $90,000 mortgage) would be $109,976.

It is important to note that although this method can be used to determine an owner's equity investment, it can be misleading when there is an extremely high loan-to-value ratio and the owner's initial investment is a nominal amount. In fact, the return on the owner's equity position approaches infinity as the owner's equity investment approaches zero. At times, mortgage financing has even exceeded 100 percent of the project cost, resulting in a negative owner's investment.

Internal Rate of Return

As investors accepted the validity of the discounted cash flow technique, the Internal Rate of Return (IRR) evolved. The IRR is nothing more than the rate that each and every dollar in the investment earns per period. In theory it is the discount rate which reduces all future cash flows to the amount of the original investment. By far the measurement most used by the investment community, IRR is not easy to explain in layman's terms. A simplistic attitude toward IRR is needed to explain the concept to clientele. The easiest way to define it is to compare it to the common denominator of investment measurement—a savings account or a tax-free bond.

In the following example, it should be readily apparent that the rate of return is what each and every dollar earns in the investment.

Initial Investment	($10,000)
Returns	
Year 1	1,000
Year 2	1,000
Year 3	1,000 + 10,000

IRR = 10%

Note that 10 percent is earned on each dollar in the investment and then the return of the original $10,000 is made at the end of the earning period.

Utilizing the financial calculator, we find that the discounted value at 10 percent of the future cash flows is in fact $10,000. If only $9500 was returned at the end of the holding period, it follows that the IRR would be *less* than 10 percent since the original $10,000 was not returned. If, on the other hand, more than the original investment of $10,000 was returned at the end of the holding period, the IRR would be something more than 10 percent. If the $10,000 was returned but the annual cash flows were only $900, the IRR would also be less than 10 percent.

Using Discounted Cash Flows

The same discounted cash flow concept utilized to find the investment value or present value of a series of cash flows is used to find the IRR. The difference, and sometimes the confusing issue, seems to arise when we know the initial investment requirement and project the cash flows into the future considering the timing of those cash flows. What is the rate of return that we discount *all* future cash flows to equal the *same* amount as the initial investment? Using the discounted cash flow technique, the IRR *is* that required or discount rate. When solving for IRR, the discount rate becomes the unknown.

IRR can be used for a projection or to look back at the performance and measure the return of a particular investment. Here is how it can provide useful insights: For years, an investor had bragged about his "100 percent" return on a parcel of raw land. The property was purchased for $50,000 and had been leased for crops for the annual real estate taxes. Four years after the purchase, the property was sold for net proceeds after tax of $100,000. The investor was confident, because he had doubled his investment, that his return had been 100 percent. Showing him the IRR concept helped destroy his enthusiasm for his "100 percent" performance. Failure to take into account time was the reason for the fallacious calculation. Using the financial calculator and a four-year holding period, the investor's return is found to be close to 19 percent. To prove the point, a $50,000 investment earning an after-tax annual return of 19 percent compounded for a four-year period was compared to the land investment and found to grow to $100,000 plus. (Certainly not discouraged by a 19 percent after-tax return, the investor admitted satisfaction with the growth factor.)

Most real estate investments are not as simple as this because they usually include cash flows from operations received annually plus proceeds from a refinance and/or sale. To be compared directly to a savings account or a bond account, the IRR should be calculated on after-tax dollars, making sure that the comparative investment is also calculated *after tax*. (As shown in some of the preceding measurements, tax implications are many times ignored in the measurement of cash flows.)

Property Profile

Trace the following property scenario through the holding period. In this case, the IRR was calculated "after the fact" to verify the investment decisions made.

Property	8-unit apartment project
Purchase Price	$180,000
Initial Investment	$ 30,000
Holding Period	5 years
Sales Price EOY 5	$215,000

After-Tax Cash Flows:

Year 1	Operations	$ 4,710
Year 2	Operations	4,956
Year 3	Operations	5,220
Year 4	Operations	5,501
Year 4	Refinance Proceeds	10,500
Year 5	Operations	1,561
Year 5	Sale Proceeds	16,023

The preceding after tax cash flows can be outlined vertically as follows:

Initial Investment	($30,000)
Year 1	4,710
Year 2	4,956
Year 3	5,220
Year 4	16,001
Year 5	17,584

The question now becomes: what is the rate of return each dollar earns per period? Unlike our last example of a $10,000 investment, this illustration is not so easy to "eyeball" and determine a rate. Using the financial calculator and entering the data per period, we find that the rate which discounts the future cash flows to the $30,000 initial investment is 14.08 percent, the Internal Rate of Return. This return is certainly better than what could have been earned even with an 11 percent (IRR) treasury note.

Wealth Accumulation (FMRR)

As investors analyzed properties and comparative investments using the IRR technique, a variety of problems were discovered.[2] An overview of these problems include:

- IRR is a fine tool when there is one initial investment; however, when future outlays are needed, multiple mathematical solutions exist.
- Many times development projects need additional future cash outlays which, using the discounted cash flow technique, means negative cash flows are discounted along with the positive cash flows. A tool was needed to analyze unique investments which might require additional outlays of cash during the holding period.
- The IRR makes the implicit assumption that all funds are reinvested at the same rate as the IRR. Many times this is not possible, thus creating a situation in which the investor must look not only at the IRR as a comparative measure but also at the *total dollar accumulation* at the end of the expected holding period.
- The IRR assumes any size cash flow can be reinvested at the same rate as the IRR when many times this is simply not possible in the investment world. When opportunities are presented which have different size initial investments, careful analysis is imperative to determine the maximum yield. The lower yield on the disparity amount could create less accumulation of dollars from the investment.

The IRR technique needed to be expanded to be effective in measuring the many unique opportunities within the field of real estate.

The basic premise of the Financial Management Rate of Return (FMRR)[3] is that although investors are concerned with percentage yields as a measurement tool, the ultimate goal of investing is the accumulation of

---

2. A complete discussion of the problems and advantages of IRR can be found in Stephen D. Messner, Irving Schreiber, Victor L. Lyon, and Robert L. Ward, *Marketing Investment Real Estate*, 2nd edition (Chicago: REALTORS NATIONAL MARKETING INSTITUTE®), Chapter 4

3. The FMRR was developed by M. Chapman Findlay and Stephen D. Messner of the School of Business Administration, the University of Connecticut, Storrs, Connecticut, in 1973. J. W. Levine, working with Realtron Corporation, assisted the originators to relate and adapt their model to problems found in the real estate investment market. An explanation of this model was first published as *Determination and Usage of FM Rate of Return*, 1973, by Realtron Corporation, Detroit. An expanded version was presented by Findlay and Messner at the Eastern Finance Association meetings in April 1975, at the University of South Carolina.

cash. The use of FMRR as a valid measurement tool depends on the investor making the following assumptions:

- Only after-tax cash flows from the property under evaluation are considered even though cash from other sources might be available.
- Funds can be invested at any time, in any amount, in "safe" investments, i.e., a savings account with instant liquidity.
- Funds not needed to be as liquid as others can be reinvested at a higher yield than the "safe rate." By definition, this rate becomes a reinvestment rate. Many investors consider only a "reinvestment rate" and do not divide funds into reinvestment and safe funds as suggested in the development of FMRR. The reinvestment rate used is usually a yield available on short-term deposit accounts. Other investors, with the assistance of computers and software, "reinvest" all cash at say a 10 percent yield, comparing after-tax total dollar accumulation with other investments.

The FMRR concept can be simplified if one accepts two facts:

1 Any negative cash flow coming due in the future must be accounted for today. Discounting these anticipated negative cash flows at a safe rate is the same as determining how many dollars will be needed for the investment. Negative dollar requirements are treated as an initial investment requirement.

2 All positive cash flows will be reinvested to grow to one lump sum at the end of the holding period.

By adjusting cash flows in this manner, any investment can be evaluated by comparing the amount of dollars put into the investment and the amount of dollars eventually received.

Property Profile

The following example of after-tax cash flows is typical of raw land development. Note how the adjustment of cash flows works toward an initial investment and total dollars received, enabling comparisons to be made to other opportunities. Assumptions:

- Four-year holding period
- 7 percent after-tax reinvestment rate
- 7 percent after-tax "safe rate"
- $600,000 purchase price
- Phased in sales strategy

Cash Flows

Purchase Price	($ 600,000)
First Year (taxes, roads, sewer Phase I)	(300,000)
Second Year (land sales Phase I)	950,000
Third Year (taxes, roads Phase II)	(275,000)
Fourth Year (land sales Phase II)	$1,100,000

Projecting the above cash flows would in itself be a task, but assuming the projections prove true one must now proceed to adjust cash flows for timing, using the assumed safe or reinvestment rate.

Using a vertical chart, the cash flows appear:

Years	$'s	
0	($ 600,000)	
1	($ 300,000)	
2	950,000	↑
3	($ 275,000)	7%
4	$1,100,000	

Offset $275,000 with $257,009 which will grow to $275,000 when invested at 7% for one year. (7% is safe rate).

Step 1: Adjusting as many negative cash flows as possible using any available positive flows, the adjusted cash flows become:

Years	$'s
0	($ 600,000)
1	($ 300,000)
2	692,990
3	-0-
4	$1,100,000

Remember, $257,009 was used to offset $275,000 in Year 3.

Step 2: Account for any future negative cash flows by discounting them back to initial investment:

Years	$'s	
0	($ 600,000) + (280,373)	↑
1	($ 300,000)	7%
2	692,990	
3	-0-	
4	$1,100,000	

How much would be needed today to grow to $300,000 one year from now at 7%?—$280,373.

Cash flows now appear:

Years	$'s
0	($ 880,373)
1	-0-
2	692,990
3	-0-
4	$1,100,000

Step 3: Now that all negative cash flows have been treated, positive cash flows can be "reinvested." Compound all positive cash flows forward at reinvestment rate:

Years	$'s	
0	($ 880,373)	
1	-0-	
2	$ 692,990 —— 7% ↓	Reinvest $692,990
3	-0-	to end of holding period (2 years).
4	$1,100,000 + $793,404	(7% is also the reinvestment rate)

Adjusted cash flows:

Years	$'s
0	($ 880,373)
1	-0-
2	-0-
3	-0-
4	$1,893,404

The result is an investment requiring $880,373 initial investment and accumulating to a total of $1,893,404.

For many investors, decisions can be made at this point without calculating the actual Financial Management Rate of Return. For those investors who view FMRR as a fine-tuned IRR, the actual yield on the above financial arrangement is 21.08%.

Many computer companies are now producing software which asks early in the program for a reinvestment rate. At the end of each year's after-tax calculation an IRR is determined, making sales timing a matter of sensitivity, not just a whim.

Figure 5-4
Measurement Techniques Overview

	BENEFITS					
METHOD	CFBT	CFAT	Appreciation	Mortgage Reduction	Time	Wealth Accumulation
Payback	X					
Gross Rent Multiplier						
Capitalization Rate						
Cash On Cash	X					
Cash On Cash After Tax	X	X				
Broker's Rate	X	X		X		
Equity Rate Of Return	X	X	X	X		
Accounting Rate Of Return	X	X	X	X		
IRR	X	X	X	X	X	
FMRR	X	X	X	X	X	X

An overview of the measurement techniques utilized in the real estate investment field.

Figure 5–4

Know which measurement criteria the investor is using.

6 MEASUREMENT TECHNIQUES AS SALES TOOLS

Academic Hogwash?

After reading the last chapter, you might be thinking, "All this hogwash is great for the classroom but my investors buy investment property based solely on gut feelings. Done it for years. Why, my best and wealthiest client never heard of IRR and could not spell equity if he had to. It has just been the past few years that he has started to use cash on cash as a measurement. Before that, it was the old 'times gross method.' "

It's easy to live in the past on this subject. However, as the competition for quality properties increases, investors are becoming more aware of sensitive measurement tools. The formal quantitative analyses preached by academia during the past ten years are now needed to compete in the sophisticated investment market.

A 1981 survey at the University of Detroit was conducted to compare what is being taught and what is being applied in the field.[1] Data for the survey were obtained from responses to a questionnaire mailed to 920 real estate firms which were (1) of large size, (2) equity investors and (3) involved in income-producing real estate. Responding to the survey, 354 firms indicated results which are reason enough for the active investment broker to grab a financial calculator and head toward the nearest course teaching discounted cash flow analysis. The respondents were categorized as follows:

Average Project Size			No. of Respondents	
Less than		$ 2,500,000	154	(43%)
$ 2,500,000	–	5,999,000	90	(25%)
$ 6,000,000	–	9,999,000	42	(12%)
$10,000,000	–	14,999,000	34	(10%)
$15,000,000	–	and above	34	(10%)
			354	100%

1. Dr. E. J. Farragher, Associate Professor of Finance, DePaul University, Chicago, conducted the survey.

Type Of Firm	No. of Respondents	
Life Insurance Company	66	(19%)
Real Estate Investment Trust	26	(7%)
Pension Fund	12	(3%)
Syndicator	128	(36%)
Private Developer	102	(29%)
Public Developer	20	(6%)

No attempt will be made to interpret the results other than to say that the discounted cash flow method is being used by sophisticated investors active in the marketplace (See Figure 6-1). As active practitioners we need to be able to interpret with the client what benefits these measurement techniques address. Armed with this knowledge, we can discuss the attributes and benefits of the investment as the client measures them against other investment opportunities regardless of the criteria.

It has been said that there is no such thing as absolute value; value is relative. There is no value to real estate fixed by nature; every value determination is intrinsically subjective to the investor. Bear this in mind if investors place values on investment properties somewhat differently than you would.

Using Measurement Techniques To List and Sell

One problem facing the commercial-investment broker today is the control of property in the form of exclusive listings. Sellers have become extremely sensitive to the market and many times expect the broker to "bid" a property to a listing price which the seller feels is justified. Many a broker has worked on properties in his listing portfolio which are either not marketable or priced over and above any reasonable economic practicality. Usually, the broker ends up with nothing to show for his efforts other than advertising bills, an expired listing and a dissatisfied client.

It is common knowledge that the hardest part of the brokerage business is finding quality product. Buyers seem to be available at every turn, but quality real estate at a price and terms which make economic sense to the buyer (remember, value is subjective) is difficult to find. It is true that every day there are transactions involving millions of dollars of real estate which make no economic sense at all, but generally the buying

Figure 6-1

Primary Evaluation Techniques

Technique	Payback	Internal Rate of Return	Present Value of Cash Flows (specific desired yield)	Financial Management Rate of Return	Gross Rent Multiplier	Net Income Multiplier (Cap Rate)	Before Tax Cash/Equity	After Tax Cash/Equity	After Tax Cash & Amortz./Equity	After Tax Cash & Amortz & Apprec./Equity
Average Project Size (in millions)										
Less than $2.5	16%	16%	22%	22%	7%	13%	35%	48%	23%	29%
$ 2.5 – $ 5.999	20%	62%	29%	9%	7%	20%	53%	47%	13%	22%
$ 6.0 – $ 9.999	14%	62%	24%	19%	14%	24%	81%	38%	24%	24%
$10.0 – $14.999	18%	71%	24%	18%	–	6%	77%	49%	24%	24%
$15.0 and above	18%	29%	35%	24%	–	18%	49%	35%	24%	6%
Type of Firm										
Life Insurance	15%	75%	24%	9%	6%	15%	73%	49%	21%	18%
REIT	15%	54%	8%	15%	8%	23%	77%	39%	8%	8%
Pension Fund Advisor	17%	83%	17%	33%	–	17%	83%	50%	33%	33%
Syndicator	19%	48%	28%	16%	5%	13%	36%	52%	20%	30%
Private Devel. Firm	20%	55%	29%	24%	9%	20%	47%	43%	20%	24%
Public Devel. Firm	–	80%	10%	30%	10%	10%	50%	30%	40%	20%
Overall	17%	62%	25%	18%	6%	16%	51%	46%	21%	24%
Fortune 1000	12%	49%	19%	N.A.	N.A.	N.A.	N.A.	N.A.	N.A.	N.A.

From a survey conducted by Dr. E.J. Farragher, Associate Professor of Finance, DePaul University, Chicago.

market uses the criteria explained in the preceding chapter to evaluate real estate investments.

Cash on Cash as a Listing Tool

Since cash on cash (see Chapter 5) is such a popularly used measurement, the fact that it fails to measure all the benefits of real estate ownership is certainly important when discussing an investment with a purchaser. However, let's see if we can use the technique to help the unrealistic seller come to grips with the facts of life relative to an investment property.

The following scenario depicts a broker's encounter with an owner who has a "pie in the sky" price in mind. The broker's understanding of owner financing and cash on cash returns enables him to obtain the listing at a marketable price.

We pick up the action on the second appointment.

BROKER:
Mr. Jones, I certainly appreciate the opportunity to meet with you again to discuss your Maple Street Shopping Center project. I have taken a close look at the numbers we discussed at our last meeting and I have been down to the tax department. I found that the property was just reassessed for ad valorum tax and the value that the appraisers have placed on the property does not appear to be changing. I think the work we did in projecting expenses will probably remain accurate.

JONES:
As I told you before, young man, this property has been very good to me. I have owned it for over ten years now and I have had no maintenance problems at all. I have written the leases in such a way that the tenants take care of all of the repairs, so for expenses all you have to worry about is the insurance and taxes. Everything else is taken care of by the lessee. What amount have you projected for the expenses?

BROKER:
Sir, I have used $10,000 per year as expenses for the center. If you notice, I have listed a number of considerations on the Maple Street Center, one of which is the fact that expenses will run approximately $10,000. What I would like to do this afternoon is take a look at the cash flow a potential purchaser might have if he purchased the center under the terms you mentioned to me at our last meeting.

(See Figure 6-2, page 163)

JONES:
I told you I am not opposed to financing the center. In fact, my accountant says I should finance it for someone which would give me an installment sale and I would have to pay less money in taxes. I am willing to finance the center for someone with strong economic worth, at 13 percent interest.

As you and I both know, that is substantially less than what is available at the banks today. Twenty-five year amortization is fine with me. I've got my amortization book here and have looked up the payments on $300,000. That would be at the $375,000 purchase price I told you I wanted for the center at the last meeting.

BROKER:
Mr. Jones, let me continue with the considerations. I have just made a sketch outline of items we might want to talk about in reference to the center. As you know it is a 10,200 square foot center, approximately 16 years old. One of the items that you mentioned to me is the fact that you just signed five-year leases with your three tenants.

JONES:
That's right. I have just renegotiated all of the leases. I have all the leases signed and recorded. They are five-year leases. I have the rent schedules here. All of these people are tied into a five-year lease so that ought to make the property more marketable, don't you agree?

BROKER:
I do have a concern in that area, Mr. Jones, and that is the fact that although you have five-year leases, as I look down your tenant list I notice that those leases are tied into the same rent for the next five years. If you will permit me to mention, those tenants are not expected to pay any more than what you are currently receiving today.

JONES:
Well let me tell you young man, my philosophy has always been that if I can have security in those rents, that's certainly worth something. Sure I've got three tenants signed up for five years, same rent each and every year; but I am never going to have to worry about renting out this space. No worries about having vacancies. That's why someone can come in here, pay me $375,000 for the center and they've got five years worth of leases. They know they have $40,000 income; they pay $10,000 in expenses, and they have $30,000 in their pocket.

BROKER:
Well, I agree with you as far as the numbers go, Mr. Jones, but let's continue on my outline with some other items that I wanted to cover with you. As you mentioned, we do have $40,000 annual gross income

coming out of the tenants. After we pay the $10,000 worth of expenses, we've got approximately $30,000 left. Now, most of the marketplace calls that the Net Operating Income of the property.

Salesperson maintains positive attitude even though the seller is somewhat forceful with his comments.

JONES:
This Net Operating Income of $30,000 is what I refer to as NOI. Do you use that same terminology?

BROKER:
As a matter of fact we do, Mr. Jones. I'm glad to hear that you use that language.

Let's continue here, Mr. Jones. We've discussed owner financing. You mentioned the fact that your accountant wants you to carry financing for the buyer. You and I know that money is very expensive at the lending institutions today. Your ability to carry financing will help the marketability of the project.

JONES:
As far as I'm concerned, if I carry someone at say 13 percent, I'm doing them a favor and that's one of the reasons I think the property is going to sell even before the ink on the listing agreement is dry. That is, of course, *if* I sign a listing agreement.

BROKER:
I have also mentioned in this outline, Mr. Jones, that the down payment requirement is $75,000.

JONES:
That is correct. I can live with $75,000 down and still pay your fee out of that cash down payment. What that does is make the property very easy to get into because $75,000 is about 20 percent of the purchase price.

BROKER:
The last item I have marked down here, Mr. Jones, is the asking price of $375,000.

JONES:
It looks like you have all the information there. Do you have any buyers?

BROKER:
Mr. Jones, let's take a look at the economics for just a moment. Let's look at what a $375,000 purchase price might look like to a potential purchaser. Let's base this on the assumption that we've got a buyer who

will pay $375,000 and put $75,000 cash down. You are going to finance the balance, which will be $300,000 at 13 percent for 25 years.

Let's take a look at the income and expenses. The gross income is $40,000 minus the $10,000 in expenses. This leaves our potential purchaser with $30,000 in NOI. If he pays you debt service at 13 percent interest for 25 years on $300,000, his payment to you for the whole year will be $40,602. That gives a potential purchaser a Cash Flow Before Tax of $10,602, but notice, Mr. Jones, that this is a negative cash flow. In other words this is out of his pocket. That doesn't look too good for a purchaser, does it?

"Let's look at it from the buyer's point of view."

JONES:
Well, I don't understand what you're saying to me. What are you trying to show me?

BROKER:
One of the things that I think we should consider, Mr. Jones, is that, based on the income and expenses of this property, a purchaser may not be willing to pay $375,000.

JONES:
Look, let me show you something. We've got 10,200 square feet in this center. If we get a sale price of $375,000, that comes out to about $37 a square foot. You could not replace the building today for $37 a square foot. And I'm talking about that $37 a square foot including land!

BROKER:
I understand that and you are absolutely right. We could not replace this center today with 10,200 square feet of space sitting on this piece of land for $375,000. There is no question in my mind that it would cost us more than that.

JONES:
Let me tell you one other thing. Over the weekend I was with my son-in-law. We were working through some numbers and we noticed that I bought this center for $200,000. If it's worth $375,000 now, it's almost doubled in price. Right?

BROKER:
Well, I'm not sure if it has doubled in price, Mr. Jones. What we have to do is look to the income to see exactly what an investor might be willing to pay for the center.

JONES:
Follow me through on this. A good rule of thumb is that if the property doubled in price and it took about ten years to do so, then that is about

a 6.5 percent increase per year. Inflation was certainly more than 6.5 percent. Inflation was 10 percent or more on the average for the past ten years. I'm asking only to realize a 6.5 percent appreciation factor on my center. Certainly inflation should have taken care of that.

BROKER:
Mr. Jones, the investment community looks at property, looks at investment in fact, not just real estate. They look at the stock market. They look at the commodity market. They look at gold. They discover that when they buy an investment, there are certain advantages to each one. One of the advantages of real estate is that value is usually tied to the income which that investment produces. This shopping center has a net income of $30,000 today and for the next five years will not increase. Here's another way to think about that. Let's say that there wasn't any financing available and someone wants to walk in and pay you all cash for the center.

JONES:
In other words, no financing.

BROKER:
That's right, no financing. They walk in the door and pay you $375,000 cash for the center.

JONES:
Is there someone out there willing to pay $375,000 in cash for this center?

BROKER:
Probably not. But for the sake of this discussion, let's say that there was. If they pay $375,000 for the center in cash, they will have no debt service. Is that correct?

JONES:
That is right. They would have no payment whatsoever to worry about.

BROKER:
How much cash would they have in their pocket at the end of the year?

JONES:
They would have $30,000.

BROKER:
If they had $30,000 and they had paid $375,000 for the center, what rate of return would that be?

JONES:
$30,000 divided by $375,000 equals 8 percent.

BROKER:
Do you think we could find a client in the marketplace who would be willing to pay $375,000 cash for an 8 percent return.

JONES:
Probably not. Especially since that is before tax. That means that money is going to be taxed.

BROKER:
That's right. There are some tax benefits, but stay with me on this. Let's not get discouraged. Let's assume for a moment—by the way, Mr. Jones, that 8 percent we just calculated—have you ever heard the appraisers talk about capitalization rate?

Look who's suddenly taken charge of the meeting!

JONES:
I had an appraisal done on another piece of property I own and the appraiser used a capitalization rate to arrive at the value of the property.

BROKER:
Well, this is the capitalization rate that is used by appraisers when they use what we call the income approach to value. It's made up of a couple of items, but many times an investor will look at property as if there were no financing.

Since we both agree an all cash sale is not probable, let's see what kind of a cash flow position a buyer would be in if he accepts the 13 percent financing and agrees to operate the property on a break-even basis.

JONES:
You mean to say that at the end of the year after he pays all the expenses that he wouldn't have any cash flow left.

BROKER:
That's right. Let's say that we could find a purchaser who is willing to settle for zero Cash Flow Before Taxes.

JONES:
Good luck! I don't know of many investors out there who would be willing to settle for zero cash flow.

BROKER:
Again, for the sake of our discussion, let's say that we have a purchaser who, when he got his $30,000 net income, left us the same $30,000 to

utilize for financing. In other words, use all the net income to service the debt (the payments will be coming to you, you know). Working this on my financial calculator on a monthly basis I find that $30,000 at 13 percent interest for 25 years will support about $221,000 of mortgage. Now if you add that $221,000 that you're financing for the client to the $75,000 in cash that we receive as a down payment, you come up with a total price of $296,000.

(See Figure 6-2a, page 164)

JONES:
Are you saying that a purchaser could pay $296,000 for the property and not have any cash flow at all?

BROKER:
That's exactly right.

JONES:
I wonder if we could find a purchaser who would settle for a zero cash flow.

BROKER:
Well, let's not get too discouraged, Mr. Jones. There are other benefits to real estate than cash flows. I do think with this center, because of the way you have the leases structured, that many of our investors are going to be looking at this investment on a cash on cash basis.

JONES:
Cash on cash; I use that technique myself. That is where you simply take the amount of money you put down and you divide that into the amount of cash you get back. Right?

BROKER:
That's what we call cash on cash in our industry. Many investors use this technique. I'm sure you've read ads in the *Wall Street Journal* where potential purchasers have run a statement that says they require a 7 percent or 8 percent cash on cash return.

JONES:
Cash on cash works very well. In my mind, I don't know that we could find anybody that would settle for much less than a 7 percent return in today's market.

BROKER:
It's interesting you say that, Mr. Jones, because you took the words right out of my mouth. Most of the people we are dealing with in this price range will want to see a positive cash flow. This is the size of an invest-

ment many investors can afford to get into. We work with many investors who have between $50,000 to $100,000 cash and have trouble finding a quality piece of real estate. You have good tenants, you've got a fairly decent location, you're offering financing—the one item we've got to take a look at is that cash on cash return.

Here's an outline I have prepared to give us an idea of how much somebody could pay for the property if they required a 7 percent cash on cash return on their $75,000 down payment. Notice that we are still using the $30,000 Net Operating Income. Let's give a 7 percent return to our investor; 7 percent of the $75,000 is $5250. That leaves us $24,750 for debt service. Working it backwards again with our 13 percent for 25 years, I find that $24,750 will finance $182,872. Add our $75,000 and we come up with a total purchase price of $257,872.

(See Figure 6-3, page 164)

JONES:
I must admit, young man, that $257,000 is certainly a far cry from my $375,000 asking price. Are you sure this is correct?

BROKER:
Mr. Jones, if we're dealing with the client who uses the cash on cash technique, this is exactly the way he will analyze the property. Now, there are a number of items we could change which would enable us to sell the property for more money.

JONES:
I told you before that I bought this property for $200,000 ten years ago and now what you're telling me is that you want me to sell it for $257,000.

BROKER:
One of the items we could change, Mr. Jones, is the amount of down payment.

JONES:
Are you going to be able to get somebody to put more than $75,000 down. I've talked to my accountant and I really don't want any more cash down.

BROKER:
I must admit, one of my concerns would be getting more than $75,000 down on his property. Taking a look at this analysis, I think what we're starting to see, Mr. Jones, is a price hovering somewhere around the $300,000 mark. I question whether we could get anyone to put $100,000 down, since that represents one-third of the purchase price.

The numbers tell the story convincingly.

The investors we deal with, just as yourself, are very knowledgeable and like to utilize leverage. They like to buy as much property as they can for as little money down as possible.

JONES:
Let's rule out the increase in the down payment. I don't think we're going to get anybody to spend more than $75,000 as a down payment. Quite frankly, I don't know what I would do with the cash other than to pay taxes on it.

BROKER:
Let me suggest another idea to you. Let's take a look at this $24,750 available for debt service. What if we, instead of carrying the debt service at 13 percent, carry it for 10 percent.

JONES:
What do you mean?—I only charge 10 percent interest?

BROKER:
I'm suggesting that if we could finance this purchase for the purchaser at 10 percent interest, we might be able to sell the property for more money.

JONES:
Show me what you mean.

BROKER:
Let's take a look at this example. $30,000 net income, $5250 cash flow; that gives our investor 7 percent return and leaves $24,750 available for debt service. That's about $2000 per month; $2062 per month at 10% interest for 25 years will finance $226,972. Add that to the $75,000 and that equals $301,972 value.

(See Figure 6-4, page 164)

JONES:
Well, that does make a difference, doesn't it? In fact, that increased the "value" about $43,000 by lowering the interest rate 3 percent. Do I still get the same amount of money for debt service?

BROKER:
That's right. You're financing the purchase; you still get $24,750.

JONES:
I was thinking about that. I'm going to be carrying the financing and I'll be receiving $24,750 from the sale each and every year, right?

BROKER:
Yes, you'll be getting $2062 per month in payment. What's your mortgage payment?

JONES:
I pay about $15,000 per year in mortgage payments, so I'm going to have about $9750 left over.

"Financing" and "Value": Use each of them to create the other.

BROKER:
Mr. Jones, that's another situation that is sometimes referred to as wraparound financing. We could calculate a yield on that situation. The nice thing about this in reference to our sale is you're going to be receiving $24,750. In addition, you've got $9750 left over. We haven't changed that $24,750 payment to you. The only thing we've done by lowering the interest rate is increase the value.

Don't forget we need to sit down with your CPA and present this program to him. The sale itself is a taxable event, plus the interest you earn will trigger some taxes each and every year.

Let's not forget the after-tax implications.

JONES:
I think you've done something else other than give me $9750 cash per year.

BROKER:
What's that?

JONES:
If I lower the interest rate from 13 percent to 10 percent, we ought to get more people interested because 10 percent is almost unheard of in the marketplace today.

BROKER:
Let me show you one other thing. What if, instead of carrying it for 25 years, we said to the purchaser that you'll carry it for interest only. Watch what happens. If you carry it interest-only at 10 percent, how much could we finance out of that $24,750?

JONES:
Well, that's easy. $24,750 will service $247,500 of the mortgage.

BROKER:
Exactly right! Add $75,000 to that and you've increased the value of the property to $322,500.

JONES:
You've just increased the purchase price $20,000 simply by carrying it interest only?

BROKER:
Correct! In fact, at 10 percent interest only, you can sell the property for $322,000 and offer a client 7 percent cash on cash return, plus an unheard of interest rate of 10 percent on the mortgage.

JONES:
Well, that's better, but I've got to say to you that I'm going to stand firm on my $375,000 purchase price.

BROKER:
I thought you might say that so let's go one step further. Here is the problem we have and this is the bottom line, Mr. Jones. The bottom line, or if you will, the problem with this property, and I know you're not going to like this, is that you signed five-year leases. A prospective purchaser does not have the opportunity to increase the rents. He is locked in at the rents you have written into the leases.

Go easy now, Salesperson, you were doing so well. . . .

JONES:
I see what you're saying, and you're right—I don't like it. What I thought was a good deal and was going to help sell the property is actually going to hinder the sale—the leases.

BROKER:
I've got one other idea I'd like to share with you, Mr. Jones. By now we know that the center is going to throw off $30,000 net income; we give the investor $5275 cash flow or a 7 percent cash on cash return; we've got $24,750 to service debt. If you carried the purchase at 9 percent, that purchaser could afford to finance $275,000. If they gave you $75,000 in cash, you now have a sales price of $350,000.

JONES:
You mean I could sell the property for $350,000 with $75,000 down and still get my $24,750 per year in payments?

(See Figure 6-5, page 165)

BROKER:
That's exactly right.

JONES:
You know, I've got to think about this, young man, but I see what you've

done. In essence, you've created value by lowering the interest rate on the outstanding mortgage haven't you?

BROKER:
Well, I think we've done more than that. I have shown that the property is marketable at the $350,000 price.

You and I both know what the marketplace likes to do. I would suggest to you that we put the property on the market at a price of $375,000. That will give us a little bit of room to negotiate since we don't know who the buyers are at this point. I suggest that we carry the financing at 9 percent interest only and sell at a 7 percent cash on cash return with $75,000 down. I also must caution you at this point that we really need to sit down with your CPA since this entire arrangement has some tax implications we must investigate. The 1984 Tax Reform Act carries a provision to penalize owner financing that is less than 110% of the current treasury rate. Although this discussion is a sound concept, full investigation must be carried out to analyze all tax implications to the seller.

JONES:
I did discuss some strategy with my accountant and he said to go forward as long as I did not sell for all cash in this tax year. You think we can get close to $375,000 with $75,000 down if I carry the financing?

BROKER:
Yes, sir, I do. We would like to go to work for you immediately. We typically use a nine-month exclusive marketing agreement. I feel that, based upon the price and terms we have discussed today, the shopping center is a marketable product even with the five-year level rent leases. I am very excited about working on the project with you.

(See Figure 6-5a, page 165)

JONES:
Well, what are we waiting for? Let's get going!

Teamwork wins again! Nothing was shoved down the client's throat. A case for terms was developed slowly and deliberately with the client sharing in the total thought process. (Although advantageous in this situation, an interest-only loan will not solve the problem in all cases.)

The salesperson recognized the fallacy of the cash on cash measurement, but he used the measurement to his advantage when pricing the property. Knowing that much of the marketplace values property using this type of measurement, the active practitioner can show a prospective seller how far out of line the asking price may be. By stressing the income and expenses and the debt service cost, the salesperson was able to take the client from a 13 percent financing situation to 9 percent interest-only financing, thus creating the value the client thought he had in the first place. The imputed interest rule[2] comes into play, but with the accountant's help the after-tax posture can be analyzed.

If the salesperson had simply forced the issue and told Mr. Jones that his property was not worth more than $300,000, he probably would have walked out without a signed listing agreement and Mr. Jones would have looked elsewhere for real estate services.

This is just one example of how knowledge of measurement tools and financing can create value in real estate. This knowledge helped the salesperson persuade a prospective client to market the property at an economic level which the marketplace could accept.

Figure 6-2

Maple Street Center Considerations

- 10,200 square foot center
- 16 years old
- 5 year leases, just executed
- $40,000 annual gross
- Net Operating Income of $30,000 appears secure
- Owner financing available (necessary in fact)
- Down payment requirement $75,000
- Asking price of $375,000

At $375,000 purchase price, purchaser would review the economics as follows:

$40,000	Gross Income
10,000	Operating expenses
$30,000	Net Operating Income
40,602	Debt Service $300,000 at 13%, 25 years
($10,602)	Cash Flow Before Tax

2. See Messner, Schreiber, Lyon and Ward, *Marketing Investment Real Estate*, 3rd edition (Chicago: REALTORS NATIONAL MARKETING INSTITUTE®, 1985), for explanation of the imputed interest rule.

Figure 6-2a

What if we could get purchaser to agree to still put down $75,000 and settle for zero cash flow?

$30,000	Net Operating Income (NOI)
30,000	Debt Service (will support $221,663 of loan at 13%, 25 yrs,)
-0-	Cash Flow Before Tax

Total purchase price $221,663 + $75,000 = $296,663

Figure 6-3

What if we found a purchaser who not settle for less than a 7% cash return on the $75,000?

$ 30,000	Net Operating Income
5,250	Cash Flow Before Tax
$ 24,750	Available for debt service; at 13%, 25 yrs. will service $182,872
$182,872	+ $75,000 = $257,872 value

$$\frac{\$\ 5{,}250}{\$75{,}000} = 7\%\ \text{cash on cash}$$

Figure 6-4

What if we lowered the interest rate to 10% for 25 years? What could a purchaser afford to pay and still receive a cash on cash return of 7%?

$ 30,000	Net Operating Income
5,250	Cash Flow Before Tax
$ 24,750	Available for debt service; will service $226,972 at 10% for 25 years
$226,972	+ $75,000 = $301,972

10% interest-only would mean $247,500 + $75,000, or $322,500 value

$$\frac{\$\ 5{,}250}{\$75{,}000} = 7\%\ \text{cash on cash}$$

Figure 6-5

Suggested Marketing Approach

Let's go one step further:

$ 30,000	Net Operating Income	
5,250	Cash Flow Before Tax	(7% on $75,000)
$ 24,750	9% interest-only for debt service will service $275,000	
$275,000	+ $75,000 = $350,000	

Figure 6-5a

- Suggested market asking price: $375,000
- Nine-month marketing period
- Seven percent total sales costs
- Property brochure cost to be split 50/50 with owner

Selling Real Estate Using the IRR

Many students of investment analysis find the discounted cash flow concept the most interesting and fascinating philosophy that has yet to hit the real estate industry. A trap that many of us fall into, however, is not being able to relate an after-tax projection utilizing IRR to our clientele.

We might spend 40 to 80 hours studying a sophisticated technique and cannot wait for the first opportunity to demonstrate it to an unsuspecting client. Since our clientele are people, they usually react as human nature directs and that is to avoid the unknown for fear of displaying lack of knowledge. Many clients will steer clear of an investment broker who forces "three pages of numbers, computer printouts and tax computations" on them. Rather than being overwhelmed by the concept, a client may decide to avoid it completely and fall back on a less sophisticated manner of analysis. Not only is this a disservice to the client, but it also forces the client to transact business with your competition.

A simplistic approach to IRR is needed if the broker expects to use the technique as a sales tool. In the hands of a skillful practitioner the IRR is a powerful tool. A fellow broker phrases it best: "The IRR is like a scalpel which, in the hands of a skilled technician, can work miracles. In the hands of the unskilled and reckless, it can do much damage."

To help the client build a foundation of understanding the IRR, try the following steps:

1 Discuss with the client the four benefits of real estate:

(a) Cash Flow Before Tax; (b) tax savings; (c) appreciation; (d) mortgage reduction.

2 Agree that all investments should be viewed on an after-tax basis.

3 Discuss that typically real estate produces cash flow from both operations and disposition.

4 Review the need to measure *all* cash flows of a real estate investment (See No. 1 above), plus consider the timing of the cash flows.

5 Use yield on a savings account as a comparison to the IRR.

Investment clients can easily relate to the savings account. Lenders spend huge sums of money advertising high yields in newspapers and periodicals. Use these ads as a comparison to the IRR. Show how a vertical chart, i.e., "t-chart" (see Figure 6-8), can diagram the initial investment requirement, the expected cash flows and the timing of these cash flows.

A fatal mistake many of us make is showing the client everything we know in the first two minutes of our presentation. Permit the client to enjoy the presentation as he might savor a good meal, piece by piece. If at any time the potential purchaser wants to stop and enjoy the last bite, do not rush him on to the next course.

The following dialogue was overheard when a successful salesperson met with Mr. Rogers who had the purchasing power and need for the small strip center located on Maple Street owned by Mr. Jones. Recall that the property is listed at $375,000 with owner financing available; down payment requirement is $75,000.

BROKER:
Good morning, Mr. Rogers. I appreciate the opportunity to sit down with you and discuss the project I mentioned to you on the telephone this morning.

ROGERS:
I have to admit that when you telephoned me this morning and wanted one hour of my time, I was a little bit baffled. You know I'm a very busy individual and my schedule doesn't warrant long meetings, so I hope we can get right to this.

BROKER:
I understand your time bind, Mr. Rogers, but I believe there are a

certain number of areas we should cover before we get into the project I would like to discuss today.

If we can, let's just sit back and reflect on our first meeting. Let's review the objectives we discussed at the time. I'd like to do this to make sure that, as we discuss this particular property today, I have in mind the objectives you mentioned.

ROGERS:
The last time we met, I told you I wanted a piece of real estate that didn't have much risk. I told you I had $100,000 I could invest if needed. I said I wanted some upside potential, and I also said I wanted to save some money in taxes.

BROKER:
Mr. Rogers, I have each of those areas marked down plus a couple of others. One of the items you mentioned to me was that you weren't interested in nor did you have the time for any management involvement.

ROGERS:
I almost forgot. Management is something that I absolutely do not want to get involved with at this point. I could do some management on weekends. In fact, I prefer to do that rather than turn it over to some real estate management company. Someone told me that real estate property managers have a tendency to spend the client's money whenever they feel it's necessary. What I'd really like to do is to get into a piece of real estate that has a net lease. In other words, they just pay me the rent and I don't have to worry about management.

Re-established objectives and stressed importance of teamwork with client.

BROKER:
As we discussed in our last meeting, I contacted Jim Miller, your CPA. I can't thank you enough for giving me permission to call Mr. Miller because we had a very interesting conversation. Mr Miller is certainly doing a fine job for you in the area of your tax considerations. We discussed this property at length, and Jim gave me some guidelines he wants to be sure we follow.

After our discussion the other day, I went back to the office and talked to my sales associates about our meeting. I mentioned your investment parameters—the $100,000 cash availability and the fact that you want to save some taxes. I confirmed that with Mr. Miller and he suggested that when we do our projections we use a 50 percent tax bracket. The current structuring of your corporation and your salary indicates that 50 percent of your income has been paid to Uncle Sam.

As I talked to the associates, I told them we were looking for a project that offered some potential; potential being that we could increase the rents. I believe we called it upside potential. One of the associates got very excited and said that he had a property that he would like to present to us because he felt it might help us meet your investment objectives.

ROGERS:
What kind of a property is it? Did you bring the information with you?

BROKER:
Yes sir, I brought the information packet with me. Here is a brief outline of some of the attributes of the property. As you can see, it is located here at the corner of Maple and Portage Streets. It's a small strip shopping center of 10,200 square feet. There are three tenants. The current owner has owned the property for 10 years. It's built out of brick and cedar. It was remodeled just a few years ago. The tenants have paid for all their improvements inside. They have completely remodeled the interior. There are new leases that have been signed and the tenants take care of their own maintenance. There is no maintenance concern, the tenants take care of it all. The tenants also have a clause in their leases that any tax or insurance increases you might encounter can be passed on to them.

In other words, Mr. Rogers, it's an investment in which the income is going to stay the same for a period of time because most costs are passed on to the tenant.

ROGERS:
How much is the asking price of the property?

BROKER:
The asking price is $375,000.

ROGERS:
You've got to be out of your mind! $375,000 for a shopping center that's only 10,200 square feet. How much is that per square foot. Wait one moment, I can do that in my head. That's close to $37 a square foot. I can build a brand new property for that. I just had a warehouse built and we only paid about $27 per square foot for that. This property is way overpriced. I can't believe that you even brought it in here to my office and are wasting my time showing it to me.

Client immediately zeros in on reproduction costs.

BROKER:
One of the interesting things about real estate, Mr. Rogers, is that so

many times, at first blush, we only see the total purchase price and we relate that to what it might cost to reproduce. I agree with you that $37 a square foot is a pretty high cost today, but I think that there are some other factors we ought to consider.

Nice, easy consideration of other benefits.

ROGERS:
One thing I'd like to know about this property is how much are the rents.

BROKER:
Mr. Rogers, I've got a before-tax analysis on the property. It outlines the asking price of the property, the down payment, the financing, and the Cash Flow Before Taxes. The owner is asking $75,000 down.

(See Figure 6-6, page 182)

ROGERS:
I can afford $75,000. In fact, I told you that I had $100,000 to invest.

BROKER:
One of my thoughts was that I don't believe we should invest all of your liquid cash into your real estate portfolio at this time, even though I know you have a substantial salary coming in and that you are very comfortable. I thought you might use $75,000 of your available $100,000 and keep the $25,000 in a savings account as liquid assets. Emergencies may arise and I'm aware that your spouse is somewhat sensitive to the fact that you're spending all of your savings at this point for a piece of real estate.

ROGERS:
I see here you show the gross income as $40,000.

BROKER:
That's right. Currently there are three leases on the property. I'll provide them later so you can review them if you have an interest in the property. The $40,000 is made up of three tenants who pay approximately $4 a square foot in rental cost. The leases have just been signed and are five-year leases.

ROGERS:
Five-year leases! You mean I'm tied into this rent schedule for the next five years?

BROKER:
One of the things that the current owner has done, and I have to admit

it affects the value of the property, is that he has written leases for a five-year period with these tenants giving them an advantage of staying in the property at fairly low rental.

ROGERS:
Do you know how much I'm paying in my store here?

BROKER:
I would imagine that you're paying somewhere between $6 and $7 per square foot.

ROGERS:
In this space that we're sitting in right now, I'm paying $6.50 a square foot and the landlord is talking about raising the rent another 50 cents.

BROKER:
What you're suggesting to me, Mr. Rogers, is that maybe this rental schedule with these brand new leases on the center is fairly low?

Building a case for the rents by making the client get involved in the discussion.

ROGERS:
Under no uncertain terms, I think this rent schedule is way out of line. I can't believe the owner of the property signed five-year leases for $4 a square foot! Brand new centers are charging $10 a square foot.

BROKER:
I think we may find that the fact that these leases are signed with low rents could work to our advantage. Let's go a little further here. There are some other very interesting variables that I'd like to show you concerning this property.

Take a look at the Net Operating Income. This is the number we talked about the other day: the cash flow a property throws off before any debt service.

ROGERS:
It says here that's $30,000. You've allowed $10,000 for expenses.

BROKER:
That's correct. I talked with the County Assessor about property taxes and I've got a quote from an insurance agency. In fact, it's the insurance agency that you told me you utilize for your business insurance. They've given me quotes on those items and it appears as though $10,000 is more than going to cover your expenses on the property. As I mentioned, the leases have written into them tax and insurance stops so that any increase in those costs would be passed on to the tenants. The tenants also pay all maintenance costs. So what we have is a situation in which your

expenses are going to be $10,000 per year for the next five years. Or at least for as long as you have those current tenants in place. Take a look at the debt service, or mortgage payment.

ROGERS:
I see you show $24,750 a year as debt service. What is this 9 percent interest only on $275,000? Are you suggesting a sales price of $350,000 with $75,000 down? Where am I going to get 9 percent money?

BROKER:
The owner has agreed to carry financing for a new buyer at 9 percent interest. Not only that, he will carry it at 9 percent interest only.

ROGERS:
This is the first thing about the property that I like so far other than the leases having tax and insurance stops written into them.

BROKER:
Interestingly enough, Mr. Rogers, we've got a $30,000 Net Operating Income and we only have to spend $24,750 in debt service, so it leaves $5250 on an annual basis for a cash flow.

ROGERS:
Let's take a look; $5250 divided by $75,000 down payment equals a 7 percent return.

BROKER:
Yes, 7 percent return on a before-tax basis the first year you own the property. Let's reflect a moment to our previous meeting when we talked about the benefits of real estate. Remember we said real estate has benefits in four areas. One of the benefits that may or may not come from real estate is Cash Flow Before Taxes. We said that, hopefully, after you paid all of your expenses, you'd have some money left over. That money stays in the checkbook. At the end of the year you can spend it if you want to. Remember I showed you some apartments, projects that didn't have any Cash Flow Before Taxes. In other words, the debt service was so high that it ate up all the cash flow.

ROGERS:
Yes, a couple of my friends have those kinds of properties. They call them alligators. In fact, some of the fellows have to pay a couple hundred dollars a month just to own the property. I'm not interested in those types of property. I'm glad to see that you didn't bring me that kind of a dog.

It appears that Mr. Rogers is Cash Flow Before Taxes-oriented.

BROKER:

Let's talk about a couple of other benefits of real estate. We mentioned one of the things that you can look forward to is some tax savings. The reason you can look forward to tax savings is that the Internal Revenue Service uses real estate as a capital asset. Because of that, the asset is a depreciable item. We are able to recover the cost of that asset. A combination of cost recovery and interest deductions can help you save taxes in other areas. In other words, tax savings on the money you earn by the sweat of your brow. Some people call that tax shelter. We have to be very careful with the words tax shelter because interest in itself is not tax shelter; it is only a deduction. Suffice to say, there are some tax benefits to owning real estate.

I'd like to show you a page where I've sketched out the tax benefits of this particular property. I think you'll be favorably impressed with the way the property could perform.

(See Figure 6-7, page 183)

ROGERS:

Let's talk about that right now. What are the tax savings?

BROKER:

Here's an after-tax analysis for your 50 percent bracket. It's done on a first-year basis. Here's the Net Operating Income of $30,000. Remember, we said interest is a deductible item. We said the interest paid was $24,750. This is all done on an annual basis. The depreciation or cost recovery we've taken on the property is $14,583 per year. Here is an interesting point. Interest and depreciation are deductible from our net income. This is what we call the "tax world." This is not a checking account and has nothing to do with the $5250 still in your checking account. This is only how the IRS views the taxation of the property.

Simple overview of the tax benefits of ownership.

Mr. Miller and I talked about the cost recovery amount. He agrees that we can justify that the land is worth approximately 25 percent of the total price.

The 75 percent improvement value, or $262,500, is available for 18-year straight line cost recovery. That amounts to $14,583 per year. The NOI minus interest minus cost recovery equals $9333 negative income. This negative income will be dumped right in with your other personal income, reducing your overall taxable income. In a 50 percent bracket that relates to $4666 in tax savings.

ROGERS:

That negative taxable income is the amount that some people call tax shelter, isn't it?

BROKER:
Yes, I want to remind you that we have to be careful with the words tax shelter; let's just call it negative taxable income. Remember that whenever you see negative taxable income on a real estate project you can relate that to tax savings. In your 50 percent tax bracket, that $9333 is worth about $4666 in tax savings to you. Come April 15, next year, you are going to be, in essence, relieved of $4666 in tax liability. Because you own the property, you save $4666 in taxes.

Let's look at the overall result.

ROGERS:
I can look at the overall result myself. I've got $5250 in the checkbook. I've got $4660 that I've saved in taxes, so I've got total cash that first year of $9916 right?

BROKER:
Like I said, Mr. Rogers, I'm only going to need an hour of your time. You're right on target. That $9916 is actually the total benefit the first year from the real estate. If you take a look at the $75,000 down payment that you made, the first year after-tax return is actually around 13.2 percent. You can compare that to a tax-free bond or a savings account. Remember that savings accounts are on a before-tax basis. You would have to earn about 26.4 percent in a savings account before tax for it to become equivalent to this 13.2 percent after-tax yield.

ROGERS:
I think I'm beginning to like the looks of this property. You tell me that I'm going to get $5250 in the checkbook and I'm going to save about $4666 in taxes. So far, so good. What else can you tell me?

BROKER:
I can tell you this. The two other benefits of real estate we haven't discussed are appreciation, in other words the building goes up in value, and any mortgage reduction that might take place over the time that you own the property.

In the area of mortgage reduction, we discussed the fact that the owner was going to carry financing of $275,000 interest only. So there is no mortgage reduction. However, in the area of appreciation, there are some interesting things that could happen. This is where we need to put our thinking caps on.

If we increase the rents on the property, the value of the property is going to increase also.

ROGERS:
I thought you told me that we have five-year leases. We can't change the income or raise the rents.

BROKER:
That's correct. We can't raise the rents during the five-year period. But at the end of the five years, we could raise the rents. I have a habit of doing projections on properties for five years. It tends to be a magic number. One of the reasons is that throughout the holding period of a piece of real estate, the mortgage amount is reduced, which means the interest amount goes down and sometimes cost recovery changes, and the whole stream of things leads us to a point where five or seven years down the road some of the tax benefits of the property start to diminish and people start to think about selling.

ROGERS:
I've heard that you should only hold a property for around seven years.

BROKER:
Some investors have come up with that number. However, this investment has some very interesting things happening inside of it.

Here's a worksheet to use. Let me show you the bottom line. What I do is take a look at this property on an after-tax basis. Here's what I like to call a "T." It accounts not only for the after-tax cash flow but it also accounts for how much money you put into the investment and when the cash flows occur.

(See Figure 6-8, page 183).

Because we have an interest amount, cost recovery and lease income that is the same every year, the income from this property doesn't change. In other words, the tax benefits stay the same and the Cash Flow Before Taxes stays the same, so each year that you own this property, whether it be two years or five years, the after-tax cash flow will be $9333. Notice what I did here. I drew a "T" on this paper and labeled time down the left-hand column and dollars on the right column. I've shown here in the Year Zero that you make a $75,000 initial investment. Year One you receive $9333, Year Two you receive the same amount all the way down to Year Five. This other number is what I like to call sales proceeds. In other words, let's say we sold the property at the end of the fifth year, this is what your after tax-cash flows would look like. The reason I put them vertically is because the timing of the cash flows is very important in investment real estate.

(See Figure 6-9, page 184) Here the salesperson goes into an explanation of the timing of cash flows. This should be interesting!

ROGERS:
I'm with you so far. I understand the $75,000 initial investment. I understand all of these $9333 amounts. I see what you've done. There's

Year One, Year Two, Year Three, Year Four and Year Five. I don't quite understand why you've laid them out this way.

BROKER:
The reason I've laid these cash flows out in a vertical position is so that we could talk about a concept that is being utilized in the investment marketplace over and over again. The concept I'd like to discuss with you is a rate of return based on something called discounted cash flows. Don't let that throw you. All that means is we are going to look at these cash flows and account for the fact that you don't receive all of the cash flows at the same time. In other words, you get some one year and some more the next year, and some of that money you don't get until five years down the road. One of the things we must consider is that when you sell the property, you don't get any of that money until the end of the holding period. The concept that I want to share with you enables us to measure *all* of the benefits of real estate: Cash Flow Before Taxes, tax benefits, any mortgage reduction and appreciation. The reason it measures appreciation is that this sales proceeds amount in Year Five is after-tax sales proceeds based on selling the property at the end of the holding period. In other words, we've accounted for all of the cash that is going to come in during the time you own the property.

Let me show you one other item. Let's say you took the $75,000 and put it into a savings account or a tax-free bond. Let's say the tax-free bond yields 11 percent. If you put $75,000 in the bank today, Year Zero on our vertical scale, you would have at the end of the first year $8250 paid in interest, right?

(See Figure 6-10, page 184)

ROGERS:
Well, I suppose that 11 percent of $75,000, yes, $8250 in interest. Is that taxable?

BROKER:
No, this is a tax-free bond. Let's assume for a moment that it's a tax-free bond and this is on an after-tax basis. What we're going to do is compare putting your money in a tax-free bond situation instead of this piece of real estate. The reason we're making this comparison is so you can compare the 11 percent yield with the yield we're going to get on the real estate.

ROGERS:
All right, go ahead. I'm with you so far, I think.

BROKER:
Let's start at the beginning again. You put $75,000 in a tax-free bond and

receive $8250 each and every year for, let's say five years. At the end of your time period, you get your $75,000 back, right?

ROGERS:

All right, I'm with you. That's an 11 percent yield, big deal!

Client is actually helping with development of IRR.

BROKER:

It's an 11 percent yield, but it's also called something else. The 11 percent yield is called an Internal Rate of Return. The reason that it is called an Internal Rate of Return is that each and every one of the dollars in the investment is earning 11 percent during the holding period. The Internal Rate of Return is nothing more than the interest rate received on a savings account. It's viewed on an after tax basis so that we can compare a piece of real estate to a savings account or a tax-free bond. The reason we use the words "tax-free" bond is because it's after tax. If we were to use 16 percent on a savings account before tax, then the after-tax yield would only be 8 percent if we assume the same 50 percent tax bracket.

ROGERS:

Oh yes, I've seen the demonstration where you put $10,000 in the bank, take the interest that you might earn on it, pay the taxes because of the interest and you end up with a pretty small yield. But the one thing you haven't addressed is the risk factor. If I put $75,000 in the bank, I might only earn 11 percent on it, but I don't have any risk. If you're telling me I'm going to earn 11 percent on a piece of real estate, I'm going to have more risk than in the bond market or the bank.

BROKER:

Let me show you the after-tax cash flows if we work them through on the Maple Street property. Initial investment of $75,000. We agree that $9333 comes out every year for the next five years. At this point, I'm projecting a sale price of $485,000. I talked to Mr. Miller about how to calculate what he felt would be happening five years from now in the area of real estate taxation. Mr. Miller's response was, 'Your guess is as good as mine.' As close as he could figure, we should make our projection based on the tax laws today, and although there might be some extra taxes to pay on capital gains depending on the preferential income, he suggested that we use the maximum amount of tax that would have to be paid on the sale because anything better than that is money in your pocket. I've used a worksheet and projected a sale of $485,000; Mr. Miller suggests that we should use a 50 percent tax on the capital gain.

(See Figure 6-11, page 185)

ROGERS:
Wait a moment. You can't tax capital gain at 50 percent; the most capital gains can be taxed is 20 percent.

BROKER:
That's correct. Let me show you why we say that capital gain can only be taxed at a maximum 20 percent. Only 40 percent of the capital gain is recognized, right Mr. Rogers?

He's not an accountant, but at least he has some knowledge of the tax law.

ROGERS:
Yes, 60 percent is totally forgotten as far as the IRS is concerned. You only have to report 40 percent of the gain.

BROKER:
What's the maximum tax bracket on the tax schedules, Mr. Rogers?

ROGERS:
Well, it's 50 percent.

BROKER:
That's right. Now watch what the investment community does. Take the 40 percent times the 50 percent, and that equals a 20 percent maximum.

(See Figure 6-12, page 186)

ROGERS:
So that's how the 20 percent is calculated. That makes sense.

BROKER:
Let's get back to our $485,000 sales price.

ROGERS:
Wait a moment. I'm going to buy a property for $350,000; five years from now, I'm going to sell it for $485,000. Where did you get the $485,000 number?

BROKER:
I was hoping you'd ask me that question. Mr. Rogers, five years from now, what do you think the rents in the shopping center will be?

ROGERS:
You're the one in the real estate business, you tell me.

BROKER:
No, I'd like to do this together. What do you think the rents in the shopping center are going to be five years from now?

ROGERS:
Well, they should be $6 a square foot right now; there's no doubt that they're low at $4. I'll take a wild guess; I think the rents should be $8 or $9 a square foot minimum. Who knows? The way our economy has been lately, I can't make a projection like that.

BROKER:
I have the same problem making projections, Mr. Rogers, but would you not agree that a projection that used a $7 per square foot cost might be somewhat conservative?

ROGERS:
I think we could easily rent that space out for $7 a square foot in five years. But wait a minute—that's a 75 percent increase over today's rent. You're never going to get that. Nobody's going to pay 75 percent more in rent than what they're paying now.

BROKER:
Mr. Rogers, remember that we're talking about 75 percent over a five-year period. You know, it's a compounding effect. Let me show you my financial calculator. It's pretty handy tool. Take the $4 a square foot right now and 'tell' the calculator that five years from now the rents are going to be $7 a square foot. 'Ask' the calculator to find us the compound rate at which that rent went up. The calculator tells us that it only went up about 12 percent per year. The tenants have had an advantage of being in there for five years at $4 a square foot. When we go to the marketplace five years from now, we can go to those tenants, explain to them that the rents have increased at a rate of 12 percent per year or approximately what inflation might be, in fact a little bit less than what the inflation rate has been in the past and that the new rents will be $7 a square foot. If the tenants don't like it, then we go to the marketplace and find a tenant who will pay $7 a square foot. You and I both agree that the rents probably should be close to $7 per square foot now. I think we've approached this in a conservative manner.

ROGERS:
So we charge $7 a square foot. What does that have to do with the value of the building? You told me you were going to sell it for $485,000. How do you get to that price?

BROKER:
If we keep the clauses in the lease in reference to tax stops and insurance stops, I think we can keep our expenses approximately the same. Let's say we rewrite the leases and we add another $2500 to our expenses just for a cushion. Maybe we have to rewrite the leases with a little bit different tax stop. Let's assume for a moment that the expenses are $12,-500. If we write the same type of leases that we have now, that's very realistic, don't you agree?

ROGERS:
We shouldn't have any expenses because, as you say, the tenants do pay all the maintenance.

BROKER:
If we have an income of $71,400 and the operating expenses are $12,500, we have a Net Operating Income of some $58,900. If we were to take that $58,900 and give an investor say $10,000 in Cash Flow Before Tax, leaving us some $48,900 to use for debt service, he would pay $4075 per month in debt service. If we took that $4075 and amortized it at a 13 percent rate for 25 years, we find that it will finance about $360,000. If we've given the investor a $10,000 cash flow, he probably will be able to see his way clear to still put $125,000 down on the building. If the investor finances $360,000 and puts $125,000 down, the total value ends up at $485,000. That's how I got to $485,000, Mr. Rogers.

(See Figure 6-13, page 186.) Projected income and expenses are done by both *client and salesperson—the creation of a future sales price is done in a cooperative manner.*

ROGERS:
Well, that's a very interesting process, but I see some items that could be a problem.

BROKER:
I won't disagree with you on that, Mr. Rogers. Anytime we look to the future, we have only one thing to base our projections on and that's what's happened in the past. What items do you see that concern you?

ROGERS:
I think we can charge $7 a square foot in rental and I think we can keep the expenses at $12,500. I'm not sure money will be available at 13 percent interest five years from now.

BROKER:
Mr. Rogers, I don't know the answer to that question. There comes a

point in time where we have to make a projection based on something. I think the only thing we have to look forward to is what the rates have been in the past. With your projected purchase price, we're talking about 9 percent financing. Maybe we can work a situation out down the road where we can offer it to somebody else for 13 percent. That's an installment sale situation and when it's time to sell the property, maybe we could talk about that. Today, I don't know that we can be concerned with that. What we might ask ourselves is if a buyer pays $350,000 today and sells the project for $485,000 five years from now, what is the annual percentage increase in value? Using the calculator I find that it's less than a 7 percent increase per year.

Even if the purchaser were the type of investor that didn't look at properties from the standpoint of value being tied to income, this is still a fairly conservative projection. In other words, the $350,000 increasing at a 7 percent compounded rate for the next five years is going to come to about $485,000. Here's my worksheet on a $485,000 sales price. Pay off the mortgage which is still $275,000 because of being interest-only. The sales costs will be legal fees, broker fees, and any other costs of sale. You come away from the closing with about $175,000 in hand. There are going to be some taxes to pay. Again, being very aggressive like Mr. Miller suggested, I think the most you're going to have to pay in taxes is going to be approximately $34,583. The way I see it is you're going to end up with approximately $140,147 in your pocket after you sell the property. The reason that amount is so important is because it completes our cash flow chart. On our vertical chart we said the time period is five years, the initial investment is $75,000, cash flows were $9333, and at the end of the time period, or holding period, you sell the property and come out with $140,147. If I go to the calculator and I ask the calculator to help me determine what the rate of return is that you earned on that $75,000 initial investment, the calculator will determine an Internal Rate of Return, or it will calculate a return for us on each and every one of those dollars earned during the holding period. Here's how we put it in the calculator; $75,000 initial investment, $9333 as a payment for five years that you receive, plus you're going to receive $140,147 in the future. We tell the calculator that it is over a five-year period and ask the calculator to find that Internal Rate of Return. Mr. Rogers, the IRR for the property, or if you'll permit me to say, the yield that you will be receiving on your $75,000 investment is over 23 percent. That 23 percent we can compare directly to the 11 percent tax-free bond we were talking about earlier.

(See Figure 6-11, page 185, and see Figure 6-9 vs. Figure 6-10, page 184)

ROGERS:

Well, I was concerned about the risk of investing in real estate, but if I could earn more than double on my money than what I could earn in a savings account, I think I'd be willing to take the risk. I think I understand what you've gone through here with me, but let me just review here with you one more time so that I'm sure to understand it. You're suggesting that if I buy the shopping center for $350,000 with $75,000 down payment, because of the 9 percent loan, my cash flow is going to be about $5250 before tax. I'm going to save some money in taxes. About $4600 a year. My total cash flow after tax each and every year is going to be about $9300. Five years from now, I sell the property for $485,000 and I put another $140,417 in my pocket. So really what you're saying to me is if I make an investment of $75,000, I get back five years worth of cash flows at $9333 plus more than what I put in.

BROKER:
You've got the concept, Mr. Rogers. The reason the concept came about is because investors realize that if they have to wait on their money as we have to wait on this $140,417 in sales proceeds, that it's really not $140,417. It's worth something less. What investors used to do is add up all of these cash flows and say that's how much money they got out of the investment. That's really not so because we have to discount the $140,417 that you're going to receive in five years plus all of the other cash flows that you're going to receive depending on how long you're going to have to wait on them.

Some client education is taking place, but in a nonthreatening manner.

Mr. Rogers, I find it rather ironic that the investment community is talking about this Internal Rate of Return as a sophisticated analysis. For years, we've been looking at savings accounts. We've just never called the interest rate on a savings account an Internal Rate of Return. But we do understand yields on savings accounts, and that's all that the IRR is. The reason we calculate the IRR in real estate after tax is to take into account and measure those four benefits of real estate: tax benefits, appreciation, Cash Flow Before Tax and mortgage reduction. IRR takes into consideration all of those benefits; it measures them and gives us a tool that we can compare apples to apples with. The one thing it cannot measure is risk. And that is why I was interested in your comment of the 11 percent money return, 11 percent yield from the bank as opposed to the 23 percent yield from real estate. There is more risk involved in the real estate. The liquidity is not like a savings account. The one thing that the real estate does have is a return that's twice as strong as the one you would receive if your money sits in the bank. I hope you also understand that we've used a conservative approach and a team effort with your accountant. We've used his suggestions to come up with these projections.

Are there any other areas, Mr. Rogers, that we should review and take a look at before we write our first proposal to the owner?

In the preceding dialogue, the broker was able to take a relatively novice investor and explain to him the analysis of cash flow as it relates to the benefits of real estate. The attributes of the building itself could be determined upon physical inspection; inspection of the leases could be made a contingency in any proposal that is written.

The point of studying this dialogue between the broker and buyer was to view the broker's effort to have the buyer understand the cash flows and how they relate to a return. In this sales situation, there is no question that the broker was selling rate of return to the buyer. He was not interested in the amenities of the real estate, and management was not a particular concern.

Mr. Rogers had suggested a list of objectives in the first meeting. The parcel of real estate that was presented met those objectives. The broker realized early in the conversation that the buyer was mathematically oriented, interested in the after-tax calculations. Had Mr. Rogers not seemed interested in those calculations, the broker may have brushed them aside and gone on to an area in which Mr. Rogers had interest. Possibly such an area could have been the stability of the tenants, legality of the leases, questions about strategy should one of the tenants break a lease or questions of management concern. In every sales situation, a broker has to have a sense of what the client or prospect feels is important. The ability to meet the objectives of a buyer can only be achieved by a thorough understanding of the inherent benefits of real estate and the measurement of those benefits.

Figure 6-6

Before-Tax Analysis

Asking Price	$375,000	
Down Payment	75,000	
Suggested Offer:	$350,000	
Gross Income	$ 40,000	
–Expenses	10,000	
NOI	$ 30,000	
–Debt Service	$ 24,750	9% interest only
Cash Flow Before Tax	$ 5,250	

$$\frac{\$\ 5{,}250}{\$75{,}000} = 7\% \text{ cash on cash return; 1st year}$$

Figure 6-7

After-Tax Analysis
50% Tax Bracket
"Tax World," First Year Only

NOI	$30,000
— Interest	24,750
— Cost Recovery*	14,583
Taxable Income	9,333
Tax Bracket	50%
Tax Savings	$ 4,666
Cash Flow Before Tax	$ 5,250
Tax Savings	$ 4,666
Cash Flow After Tax	$ 9,916

$9,916 return on $75,000 first year equals $\frac{\$\ 9,916}{\$75,000}$

or 13.2% after tax

This would be equivalent to a tax-free bond yielding 13.2% or a savings account that was yielding 26.4% before tax—first year only!

*Cost recovery, 75% improvement value to total using straight line 18-year term.

Figure 6-8

Time (Year)	$'s	
0	($$$$$)	
1	$	operations
2	$	operations
3	$	operations
4	$	operations plus $$$$ disposition

Figure 6-9

After-Tax Cash Flow (50% Tax Bracket)

Time	$'s
0	(75,000)
1	9,916
2	9,916
3	9,916
4	9,916
5	9,916

IRR = 23.4%

Same as investing in a tax-free bond that would pay 23.4%.
A savings account would have to pay over 46% to be comparable.

Figure 6-10

Savings Account or Tax-Free Bond

$75,000 deposit

11% Yield

Time	$'s
0	(75,000)
1	8,250
2	8,250
3	8,250
4	8,250
5	8,250 + 75,000

IRR = 11%

Figure 6–11

Cash Flow Analysis

For Mr. Rogers

Purpose Worksheet for New Purchaser

o 5 year Projection
o Outright Sale
o 50% Tax Bracket

Date

Purchase Price 350,000

Encumbrances 275,000

Investment 75,000

Mortgage Data

	Encumbrances	Beginning Balance	Remaining Term	Number of Payments Per Year	Interest Rate	Payment	Annual Debt Service	Remarks
1	1st Mortgage	275,000	25 yrs.	12	9	2062.50	24,750	Interest Only
2	2nd Mortgage							
3	3rd Mortgage							

Taxable Income

	Ownership Analysis of Property Income:	Year:	Year:	Year:	Year:	Year:
4	Gross Scheduled Income	40000				
5	Less: Vcy & Credit Losses					
6	Gross Operating Income	40000	40000	40000	40000	40000
7	- Operating Expenses	10000	10000	10000	10000	10000
8	Net Operating Income	30000	30000	30000	30000	30000
9	- Non-Operating Expense					
10	- Interest – 1st Mortgage	24750	24750	24750	24750	24750
11	- Interest – 2nd Mortgage					
12	- Interest – 3rd Mortgage					
13	– Cost Recovery	14583	14583	14583	14583	14583
14	Real Est. Taxable Income	(9333)	(9333)	(9333)	(9333)	(9333)

Cash Flows

		Year:	Year:	Year:	Year:	Year:
15	Net Operating Income	30000	30000	30000	30000	30000
16	- Annual Debt Service	24750	24750	24750	24750	24750
17	- Funded Reserves					
18	- Capital Additions					
19	Cash Flow before Taxes	5250	5250	5250	5250	5250
20	– Minimum Tax					
21	- Tax Liability on Real Est.	(4666)	(4666)	(4666)	(4666)	(4666)
22	Cash Flow after Taxes	9916	9916	9916	9916	9916

EOY	Mortgage Balance
1st Mortgage	275 000
2nd Mortgage	
3rd Mortgage	

Analysis of Sale Proceeds

Year:

	Adjusted Basis	
23	Original Basis	350000
24	+ Capital Improvements	
25	– Cost Recovery	72915
26	Partial Sales	
27	AB	277085
28		

Excess Cost Recovery (CR)	
Total CR	93750
S/L CR	93750
Excess CR*	0
Exc. CR Carryover	

Gain	
Sale Price	485 000
– Cost of Sale	35 000
– AB	277 085
Gain	172 915
– Excess CR	-0-
Capital Gain	172 915

Tax Liability on Sale	
Excess Recapture Tax	
Capital Gain Tax	
Tax Liability on Sale	34583

Sale Proceeds	
Sale Price	485 000
– Costs of Sale	35 000
– Mortgage	275 000
Proceeds before Taxes	175 000
– Tax Liability on Sale	34 583
Proceeds after Taxes	140 417

*NOTE: On non-residential property, if accelerated CR system is elected, all CR claimed is recaptured as ordinary income in the year of sale.

*Sale Price Based on year 6 NOI "CAP" of 12.1%
Increase in value represents a 7% increase per year

Prepared by

Figure 6-12

Capital Gains
Maximum Tax

40%	
x50%	
20%	Maximum

Figure 6-13

Center Value EOY 5
$485,000 Sale Price

- Raise rents to $7
- Expense stops in leases
- $71,400 gross income
- $12,500 expenses
- NOI of $58,900
- Offer CFBT of $10,000 (8% cash on cash)
- Down payment of $125,000
- $485,000 sale price
- $360,000 financed at 13%, 25 years
- New buyer gets (1) 8% cash on cash
  (2) 12.1% CAP rate
  (3) rents still below market, offering new buyer "upside potential"

Section III
PRACTICAL APPLICATIONS

Chapter 7

Presenting the Package

What data are important in a sales package? What kind of information does an investor need to know about a property? How do I target the market for a particular project? What are the four steps of marketing an investment property? Can I present a property without using IRR? Is there a way to get investors interested without sending them a full package of information?

Chapter 8

People—the Magic Ingredient

OK, so I'm educated—now what? What kind of real estate does a young single person need? How about an executive with a rising income? A doctor? What should I show the professional syndicator? How can an owner turn equity into a monthly income for retirement? In the last analysis, aren't we as real estate practitioners really problem solvers?

Chapter 9

Finding and Servicing Clientele

Where can I find active buyers? How can I establish myself as "the expert" on investment real estate in my community? Is direct mail effective for the real estate business? Is there a way to determine if a prospect is a ready, willing and able buyer? What are the traits and techniques of successful investment brokers? Is it possible to work constructively with attorneys, accountants and other brokers?

7
PRESENTING THE PACKAGE

The Investment Project

When an investment broker secures a marketable investment project on an exclusive basis, he undertakes a marketing task that can range anywhere from making one phone call to blanketing the nation with elaborate brochures. The two packages illustrated in this chapter offer a potential investor important data on the geographic region as well as the financial attributes of the properties. The assumption is that a buyer may be found outside the local market because of the size, attributes and benefits of the real estate project.

One possible marketing approach centers around a four-step process:

"Control" the Property

If there were a list of commandments for the real estate business, surely one should be "Thou shall not work on properties without a signed exclusive agreement." And if there is one creed that novice and experienced salespeople alike violate, this is it. No matter how many times we remind ourselves of disappointing experiences, we still jump head first into a marketing task without any control of our destiny.

It is important to obtain exclusive listings on properties, or to have signed cooperative agreements with other brokers. Some brokers protect themselves to the extent of requiring signed agreements from other brokers even if the intent is only to pass on information to clients, not to show property. This ensures compensation if the property is sold. In short, no type of marketing campaign should be executed without control by the broker over the listing.

Target the Market

This is a trite phrase that usually means "Who should be interested in the property, anyhow?" Past clientele, syndicators, and higher income professionals are excellent targets for the larger investment packages. Knowing the criteria of each potential investor will help determine the target market for an investment package. A presentation on a six-unit apartment building, for example, would not be sent to large syndicators who structure tax-oriented transactions. On the other hand, a four million dollar shopping center package would probably not just be sent to IBM salespeople. There are a number of national investor directories and mailing lists that are useful to the broker searching for an investor marketplace for specific properties.

The easiest way to target a market is to consider the attributes and financial arrangement of the offering. A number of questions should be considered:

- What is the price range of the project? Is it within range of a single investor? Is it better suited for a partnership?
- What is the risk factor? Is the project a typical investment vehicle such as a shopping center, or is it a golf course just "perfect" for an exclusive residential development?
- Does the property produce cash flow as well as tax benefits? Will the project make economic sense without inflating a future sales price?
- Is the apartment complex priced so only a condominium conversion specialist could make sense of the "numbers." Does the financial structuring make the property attractive?
- Is the project management requirement intensive, as it might be with a racquetball court club, for example? Can property management be secured for an out-of-town buyer?
- Can the down payment be spread over more than one tax year? Syndicators typically need this split down payment system and "soft costs" up front which can be capitalized. (Soft costs are items that can be expensed or capitalized on a short-term basis.)
- What is the leverage position? Does the project need to be purchased with all cash because of short-term financing? Is a joint venture possible?
- What kind of entities own similar properties in the adjacent areas? How about the adjacent property owner as a possible buyer?
- Is the equity requirement over the "magic" number of $1,000,000? Many investment groups restrict themselves to this figure as a minimum down payment.
- Are the tax benefits so plentiful that one or two individuals would have difficulty using the shelter?
- Who owns similar projects around the country?

Gain Attention

The third step in marketing a project is to get the attention of the potential purchaser before you drown him in a sea of facts and details. Newspaper advertising is sometimes effective, especially in the investment section of the *Wall Street Journal*.

An excellent media for the attention-getter is direct mail. For the price of a few inches of newspaper space, a direct mail program can be tailor-made for a specific market. There are many theories on just how much information to give in a mailer, but it usually works best as a colorful piece with pictures, price, and most important, the broker's name and phone number. You want to encourage prospects to call you for the details, so don't try to put too many details in the mailer. What you want is a phone call.

One technique that often works to get attention is to send a colorful poster with some pictures and a little general information. A large poster is unique, expensive looking and almost impossible to throw away. Investors have been known to comment on a poster mailed to them even a year after the property in question went on the market—"Your poster looks so expensive I can't bring myself to throw it away, so I thought I'd call just to check on the project's status."

Although Robert Ringer in *Winning Through Intimidation*[1] made some startling comments about the real estate industry, he did offer us his unusual idea of a five dollar calling card. An expensive mailer is often the key to an effective direct mail program. Although color printing can cost considerably more than most offices are accustomed to spending on a property brochure, when compared to the costs of repeated newspaper advertising, the cost may seem within the marketing budget of a particular project.

A detailed investment package should so satisfy the client that all that would remain in the decision-making process might be a physical inspection and verification of the facts.[2]

Present the Package

The fourth and final step in marketing a real estate project is the actual package of material, giving all the details in a logical, detailed manner.

---

1. Robert J. Ringer, *Winning Through Intimidation* (Greenwich, CT: Fawcett Publications, Inc., 1974)
2. Bruce W. Marcus, *Marketing Professional Services in Real Estate* (Chicago: REALTORS NATIONAL MARKETING INSTITUTE®) offers an excellent source on advertising and promoting real estate and real estate services.

When a prospective purchaser requests an information packet, three positive events are taking place. First, personal contact has been made, giving you an opportunity to expose the property to a potential purchaser. Second, you have a chance to demonstrate your professional expertise and knowledge. Last, another valuable prospect has been added to your mailing list.

The two information packages presented in this chapter were used to present potential buyers with the details of two different investment opportunities under exclusive listings. Notice that the shopping center package *does not* include a discounted cash flow analysis. Yes, brokerage without IRR does exist: There's a time and a place for everything.

What To Include in a Presentation Package

There are a number of important variables that should be included in every property presentation. This is not to say that every item listed below needs to be in every presentation. Apartment projects, for example, would require different information than shopping centers. A smaller project being marketed on a local basis might not require the same kind of demographic information a larger project might. Some of this information can be secured from the owner of the property, but much of it will have to come from the broker's own investigation of the property and the factors that influence its value.

Primary Information

- Asking price
- Down payment required, split funding availability
- Financing: availability, underlying notes, terms, prepayment, transfer provisions
- Pictures (in color if possible, with descriptions)
- Aerial photos
- Seller's motivation for selling
- General information: overview of improvements, age, construction, utility metering, gross and net rentable space, amenities
- Size of total project (number of units, square footage)
- Location maps
- Utilities provided at site
- Land size and topography

- Parking spaces and/or garages
- Income and expenses (actual and projected), history of vacancies, expenses per square foot, expenses as percentage of income
- Rent per square foot
- Rent roll
- Lease information: expiration dates, options, overages, years at location
- Capitalization rate
- Cash on cash before tax
- Cash on cash after tax

Secondary Information

- IRR over different holding periods
- Population trends of the Standard Metropolitan Statistical Area (SMSA)
- Households' effective buying incomes
- New construction activity in area
- Age groups within population
- Median age of population
- Retail sales (total and by store group) of SMSA
- Sales volumes of tenants, on square-foot basis
- Dwelling units in the area
- Building permits history
- Employment statistics
- Land use totals in county
- Floor space square footage by category in SMSA
- Sales of comparable properties
- Comparable properties for sale but not sold
- Location of competitive projects
- Efficiency of building
- Traffic counts
- Copies of lease documents

- Chattel to be transferred with property
- Blueprints of buildings
- Reproduction cost
- Original cost

As you read through the following presentations, note that most, although not all, of the above items are represented in each. Concentrate more on the format, method of presentation and the variables featured than on the particular numbers involved in each of these projects.

Investment Opportunity
West Gate Shopping Center
Enterprise, Alabama

William Williams, CCIM
Williams Real Estate
1234 Williams Dr.
Williams 99999
213-111-1111

INVESTMENT BRIEF INDEX

Westgate Shopping Center

I Description of Property

II Investment Overview

III Photos

IV Financial Information
Rental income & expenses

1) Base Rents
2) Overages
3) Square Foot Cost
4) Lease Rates

V Plot Plan

VI Demographics (Coffee County)

1) Population Trends
2) Sales By Categories
3) Income Statistics
4) Retail Sales
5) Tenant Sales Volumes (1978 & 1979)
6) Traffic Counts (1977, 1978, & 1979)

VII Miscellaneous Data

1) Typical Lease
2) News Articles (Fort Rucker Economic Impact)
3) Chamber of Commerce Remarks

Property Information

West Gate Shopping Center

Enterprise, Alabama

West Gate Shopping Center is a locally owned and operated 135,000 square foot center located in southeast Alabama. The owner developed Phase I in 1967 and has expanded the project to its current size spreading over 18 plus acres. West Gate is located at the intersection of Route 84 By Pass and Rucker Rd. (Rt. 248) in Enterprise just 25 miles northwest of Dothan, Alabama.

The adjacent commercial area has shown steady growth in recent years with traffic counts reaching over 15,000 cars daily on Rt. 248. According to the State of Alabama's 1979 Traffic Flow map, the Dothan interchange circle is the only route to show a higher count in lower Alabama.

Located in Coffee County, West Gate Center enjoys the economic support of strong agriculture plus the annual expenditures of approximately $362 million from adjacent Fort Rucker. Fort Rucker has been the sole U.S. Army Aviation Training Center since 1973 and supports a daily population of 19,500. The economic impact of Fort Rucker in fiscal year 1981 is projected to increase an additional 80 million dollars.

West Gate has enjoyed tenant stability over the years as 80% of the tenants have been in business at West Gate longer than five years. Although this stability is attractive, it also causes square foot rental to be substantially lower than competitive space. Square foot rental across the street is double the cost of West Gate. This factor alone gives West Gate owners an opportunity to increase rental income immediately upon acquisition. The owner's philosophy on tenant improvements has been unique in that tenants provide all interior improvements upon rental. The Lessor provides only bare walls, floors, and ceilings. The quality of the interior stores is far above what one might expect in a ten year old center.

Since the center was built originally to hold for long term income, the quality of construction is superior to a similar investment built strictly for resale.

The owners do not have a mortgage on the property and desire an outright cash sale if possible. The property owners are anxious to pursue other interests in retirement and are willing to cooperate in any manner to make the acquisition/management change as smooth and effortless as possible.

1

Originally could not get owner to agree to financing.

INVESTMENT OVERVIEW

West Gate Shopping Center

Enterprise, Alabama

135,000 square foot shopping center (oldest phase built 1967)

Southeastern Alabama 25 miles northwest of Dothan, Alabama

$267,609 annual Net Income 1981

Asking price: $3,000,000 (owner financing not provided)
($22 per square foot)

18 plus acres

Outlot potential, October 1980 sale to bank
250 feet at $1000 per front foot

80% of tenants have been at West Gate 5 years or longer

Original developer/owner; now retired

2

A quick overview of the facts. (It is important to include a color photo of the project at this point in the presentation.)

Financial Information

This property offering is designed to provide authoritative information regarding the subject property. In all areas, information and projections used are from reliable sources; however, no guarantee is made to the accuracy of said information.

Since the proposed sale is all cash, no after tax projections have been included utilizing financing. Although we recommend personal legal or accounting advice be sought, Wm. Williams/Realtors will be happy to provide after tax analysis including discounted cash flows and internal rates of return over the intended holding period of the investment.

3

Let them know that the IRR is available if it is not in the package.

West Gate Shopping Center
Before Tax Analysis
1981 Projection
135,000 Square Feet

Gross Income	$338,099.00	
- Vacancy (2%)	6761	
Expenses:	Per Sq. Ft.	Annual Costs
Real Estate Taxes	$.10	$14,139
Insurance	.07	9,739
Utilities	.04	6,000
Parking Lot Cleaning	.03	3,500
Advertising	.04	6,000
Maintenance & Repairs	.07	9,450
Management	.11	15,000
TOTAL EXPENSES		$63,828
Net Operating Income		$267,509

4

If there are major tenants in the center, break them out showing the percentage of income they produce.

WEST GATE SHOPPING CENTER
Enterprise, Alabama
October, 1980

TENANT	SQUARE FEET	GUARANTEED MONTHLY RENT	APPROXIMATE ANNUAL RENT	@ SQUARE FOOT	LEASE EXPIRATION	OVERAGE	YEARS AT WESTGATE
Block 1							
-	15,000	$2815.50	$33,750.00	$2.25	Jan. '91	Yes	New
-	10,800	1800.00	22,000.00	2.00	June '85	Yes	14
-	3,800	360.00	7,200.00	1.14	Dec. '81	Yes	12
-	4,200	900.00	13,000.00	2.57	June '83	Yes	12
-	3,200	400.00	10,000.00	1.50	Aug. '81	Yes	6
-	2,600	100.00	18,000.00	4.62	Oct. '83	Yes	5
-	1,000	Mgt. Off.	----				13
-	1,000	400.00	4,800.00	4.80	June.'81	No	5
-	1,000	200.00	2,400.00	2.40	Apr. '81	No	1
-	1/4 acre lot	200.00	2,400.00		Mar. '87	No	13
TOTAL	42,600	8060.00	113,550.00				
Block 2							
-	5,600	950.00	11,400.00	2.04	Feb. '82	No	5
-	1,100	175.00	2,100.00	1.91	Monthly	No	10
-	800	7%	3,300.00		Monthly	Yes	10
-	2,000	350.00	6,600.00	2.10	Mar. '82	Yes	9
-	2,500	625.00	12,000.00	3.00	Oct. '83	Yes	
-	3,500	875.00	15,000.00	3.00	Oct. '83	Yes	
-	2,750	800.00	13,000.00	3.49	Feb. '82	Yes	5
-	2,000	450.00	5,400.00	2.70	Oct. '81	Yes	10
-	4,400	562.50	6,756.00	1.50	Aug. '82	Yes	10
-	1,200	375.00	4,500.00	3.75	Feb. '82	Yes	6
-	1,000	250.00	3,000.00	3.00		No	3
-	3,200	600.00	7,200.00	2.25	July '81		1
Vacant off.	800	(250.00)	(3,000.00)	3.75		No	
TOTAL	30,850	6263.00	93,256.00				
Block 3							
-	4,400	800.00	9,600.00	2.18	Feb. '82	No	10
-	6,650	1000.00	12,000.00	1.80	Apr. '82	Yes	10
-	3,100	500.00	6,000.00	1.94	June '81	Yes	5
-	2,500	500.00	6,000.00	2.40	Monthly	No	5
-	2,500	350.00	4,200.00	1.68	Monthly	Yes	3
-	21,000	3325.00	39,900.00	1.90	Feb. '87	Yes	8
Vacancy	3,000	937.00	11,250.00	3.75			
TOTAL	43,150	7412.00	88,950.00				
-	8,200	$1320.00	$15,840.00	$1.93	Sept.'82	No	10
-	2,500	500.00	6,000.00	2.40	Oct. '81	No	5
-	2,500	500.00	N/A	2.40	Sept.'81	Yes	New
-	5,000	1400.00	16,800.00	3.36	Oct. '83	No	10
TOTAL	18,200	$3720.00	$38,640.00				
TOTALS	134,800	$305,460.00	$334,396.00				

- 17,000
-
-

} Not included; owned by tenant.

5

Who pays what for how long?

O V E R A G E S

(Based on Annual Sales)

TENANT	AMOUNT
________	3% vs. base
________	4.5% vs. base
________	3% vs. base
________	3% vs. base
________	4% vs. base
________	3% vs. base
________	3% of gross
________	5% up to $100,000.00 3½% over $100,000.00
________	4% above $200,000.00
________	4% above $250,000.00
________	3% above $400,000.00
________	5% vs. base
________	5% vs. base
________	2% over $200,000.00
________	5% over $120,000.00
________	1% over $3,300,000.00 plus tax stop
________	5% over $120,000.00

5a

Annual Projection (Before Tax)

	1982 (1)	1983 (2)	1984	1985
Gross Income	$386,149	$417,040	$450,404	$486,436
-Vacancy (3%)	11,584	12,511	13,512	14,593
-Expenses	74,912	74,912	80,900	80,900
Net Operating Income	$297,335	$329,617	$355,992	$390,942

(1) 1982 rents determined by taking lease ending space to approximately $3.00 per square foot.

(2) 1983 rents determined by 8% increase in gross rents.
1984 rents determined by 8% increase in gross rents.
1985 rents determined by 8% increase in gross rents.

6

"Here's what we think is going to happen in the future, Mr. Investor."

TENANT SALES VOLUME

Tenant	1979	1978
Store A (Supermarket)	$3,187,006	$3,402,887
Store B	834,964	822,002
Store C	359,556	---
Store D	288,643	---
Store E	414,721	446,353
Store F	171,539	134,476
Store G	325,921	334,918
Store H	107,605	---
Store I	201,315	197,337
Store J	39,345	24,167
Store K	2,555 (tax)	2,470 (tax
Store L	---	---
Store M	152,316	155,262
Store N	355,386	441,822
Store O	337,603	300,504
Store P	69,063	65,871
Store Q	127,754	133,686
Store R	---	---
Store S	33,605	19,170
Store T	41,588	120,479
Store U	216,720	187,690
Store V	378,991	332,273
Store W	69,446	58,490
Store X	217,682	158,368
Store Y	55,073	20,637
Store Z	260,534	211,895
Store AA (Supermarket)	1,746,257	2,322,480
Store BB (Catalog Store)	1,449,918	---
Store CC	---	42,348
Store DD (Movie Theatre)	390,002	266,971

INDEX

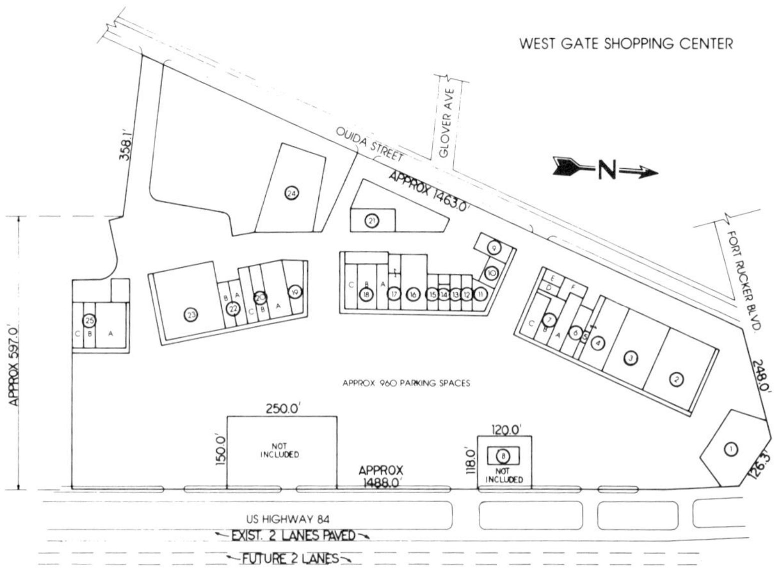

1. Service Station (ground lease)
2. Supermarket (tenant owned)
3. Store
4. Store
5. Store
6. Store
7a. Drug Store
7b. Store
7c. Store
7d. Store
7e. Office
7f. Dance Studio
8. Bank (not included)

9. Store
10. Store
11. Barber Shop
12. Store
13. Store
14. Store
15. Store
16. Theatre (not included)
17. Store
18a. Store
18b. Store
18c. Store
18d. Store
19. Book and Gift Store
20a. Hardware Store
20b. Music Store
20c. Vacant
21. Office
22a. Auto Parts
22b. Store
23. Supermarket
24. Reserve Squad (not included)
25a. Catalog Store
25b. Store
25c. Store

8

COUNTY POPULATION TRENDS

	1940	1950	1960	1970	1976	1980	1985
Barbour	32,720	28,892	24,700	22,543	26,100	26,750	28,000
Coffee	32,000	30,720	30,583	34,872	35,700	37,500	40,750
Covington	42,408	40,373	35,361	34,079	35,100	36,000	37,500
Dale	22,688	20,828	31,066	52,995	41,700	47,000	51,000
Geneva	29,166	25,988	22,310	21,924	23,500	24,000	25,750
Henry	21,918	18,674	15,286	13,254	15,100	16,500	18,250
Houston	45,654	46,522	40,718	56,574	69,700	74,000	82,195
TOTAL	226,534	211,997	210,024	236,241	246,900	261,750	283,445
Percentage Change	NA	-6.4%	-0.9%	+12.5%	+4.5%	+4.5%	+8.3%

MAJOR CITY POPULATION TRENDS

	1940	1950	1960	1970	1976	1980	1985
Eufaula	6,269	6,906	8,357	9,102	11,003	11,954	13,154
Enterprise	4,353	7,288	11,410	15,591	16,056	18,056	19,325
Andalusia	6,886	9,162	10,263	10,092	10,087	10,250	10,995
Ozark	3,601	5,238	9,534	13,555	13,868	14,500	16,000
Geneva	2,803	3,579	3,840	4,398	4,416	4,695	5,000
Abbeville	2,080	2,162	2,524	2,996	3,063	3,490	4,100
Dothan	17,194	21,584	31,440	36,733	44,746	50,345	58,500
TOTAL	43,186	57,869	77,368	92,467	103,239	111,690	125,074
Percentage Change	NA	+34.0%	+33.7%	+19.5%	+11.7%	+8.2%	+12.0%

Source: Bureau of the Census; Center for Business and Economic Research; SEARP&DC.

9

How many people? What is the trend?

COFFEE COUNTY SALES BY CATEGORIES: 1977 & 1978

Category	Amount (1977)	Percent of Total	Amount (1978)	Percent of Total
Lumber/Hardware	$ 6,003,000	5.5	$ 7,409,000	5.8
General Mdse.	4,038,000	3.7	4,727,000	3.7
Food	20,301,000	18.6	23,889,000	18.7
Auto	40,821,000	37.4	47,266,000	37.0
Gasoline	7,531,000	6.9	8,303,000	6.5
Apparel	6,549,000	6.0	7,920,000	6.2
Furniture	9,278,000	8.5	11,497,000	9.0
Eat/Drink	4,257,000	3.9	5,238,000	4.1
Drugs	3,165,000	2.9	3,704,000	2.9
Other	7,204,000	6.6	7,793,000	6.1
TOTAL	$109,147,000	100.0	$127,746,000	100.0

10

INCOME STATISTICS

	PER CAPITA					MEDIAN		
	1969	1972	1974	1975	1976	1970	1976	1977
BARBOUR	$1,792	$2,375	$2,809	$2,920	$3,965	$5,133	$ 8,000	$ 8,400
Eufaula	2,244	2,845	3,424	3,557	4,758	6,795	10,400	11,046
COFFEE	2,264	2,904	3,582	3,796	4,647	6,776	9,900	11,000
Enterprise	2,713	3,475	4,279	4,574	5,595	7,991	11,583	12,905
COVINGTON	1,987	2,540	2,996	3,153	4,457	5,930	8,500	9,700
Andalusia	2,330	3,029	3,514	3,663	5,170	7,047	9,987	11,527
DALE	2,423	3,086	3,714	3,866	4,360	7,402	9,700	12,200
Ozark	2,534	3,172	3,784	3,922	4,534	7,472	9,791	12,316
GENEVA	1,965	2,403	2,924	3,064	4,499	5,787	8,500	9,500
Geneva	2,374	2,953	3,477	3,585	5,263	6,816	10,011	11,219
HENRY	1,663	2,305	2,771	2,949	4,708	5,139	8,000	8,400
Abbeville	2,163	3,058	3,722	4,104	5,461	6,316	9,600	10,256
HOUSTON	2,393	3,058	3,771	4,024	5,203	7,376	11,200	12,100
Dothan	2,696	3,404	4,167	4,433	5,879	8,196	13,001	13,673

SOURCE: Bureau of the Census; HUD; SEARP&DC.

11

How much money do they make?

RETAIL SALES BY COUNTY: 1967; 1970 TO 1979 (In 1000's of $'s)

	1967	1970	1971	1972	1973	1974	1975	1976	1977	1978	First Six Months 1979
Barbour	21,866	26,722	29,885	31,555	33,031	34,180	35,402	48,632	52,971	56,574	29,383
Coffee	43,246	61,979	69,502	68,629	75,400	79,022	77,436	103,767	109,147	127,746	72,193
Covington	46,632	59,063	66,471	72,645	76,449	80,632	84,457	102,636	113,295	125,895	67,603
Dale	29,567	40,499	41,588	39,027	42,998	46,690	50,227	67,384	68,240	75,869	43,865
Geneva	20,979	24,202	27,460	47,504	53,788	67,561	70,233	99,710	90,583	99,129	53,400
Henry	14,316	17,190	20,361	21,675	23,523	29,393	28,929	34,479	38,414	43,841	23,070
Houston	113,626	163,170	189,489	209,217	244,552	270,957	274,748	350,265	380,869	429,803	217,129
Dist. Total	290,232	392,825	444,756	490,252	549,741	608,436	621,432	806,873	853,519	958,857	506,643

AS A PERCENT OF THE DISTRICT TOTAL

	1967	1970	1971	1972	1973	1974	1975	1976	1977	1978	First Months 1979
Barbour	7.5	6.8	6.7	6.4	6.0	5.6	5.7	6.0	6.2	5.9	5.8
Coffee	14.9	15.8	15.6	14.0	13.7	13.0	12.5	12.8	12.8	13.3	14.2
Covington	16.1	15.0	14.9	14.8	13.9	13.3	13.5	12.7	13.3	13.1	13.3
Dale	10.2	10.3	9.4	8.0	7.8	7.7	8.1	8.4	8.0	7.9	8.7
Geneva	7.2	6.2	6.2	9.7	9.8	11.1	11.3	12.4	10.6	10.3	10.5
Henry	4.9	4.4	4.6	4.4	4.3	4.8	4.7	4.3	4.5	4.6	4.6
Houston	39.2	41.5	42.6	42.7	44.5	44.5	44.2	43.4	44.6	44.9	42.9
TOTAL	100.00	100.00	100.00	100.00	100.00	100.00	100.00	100.00	100.00	100.00	100.00

Source: Alabama Department of Revenue; SEARP&DC; Editor and Publishers Market Guide, 1978.

12

How have past retail sales been?

TRAFFIC COUNT OVERVIEW

Average Daily Traffic

	1977	1978	1979
Route 84 by pass	8700	10,140	10,900
Route 248 Rucker Road	13,820	14,290	15,250

13

How many cars pass the center daily?

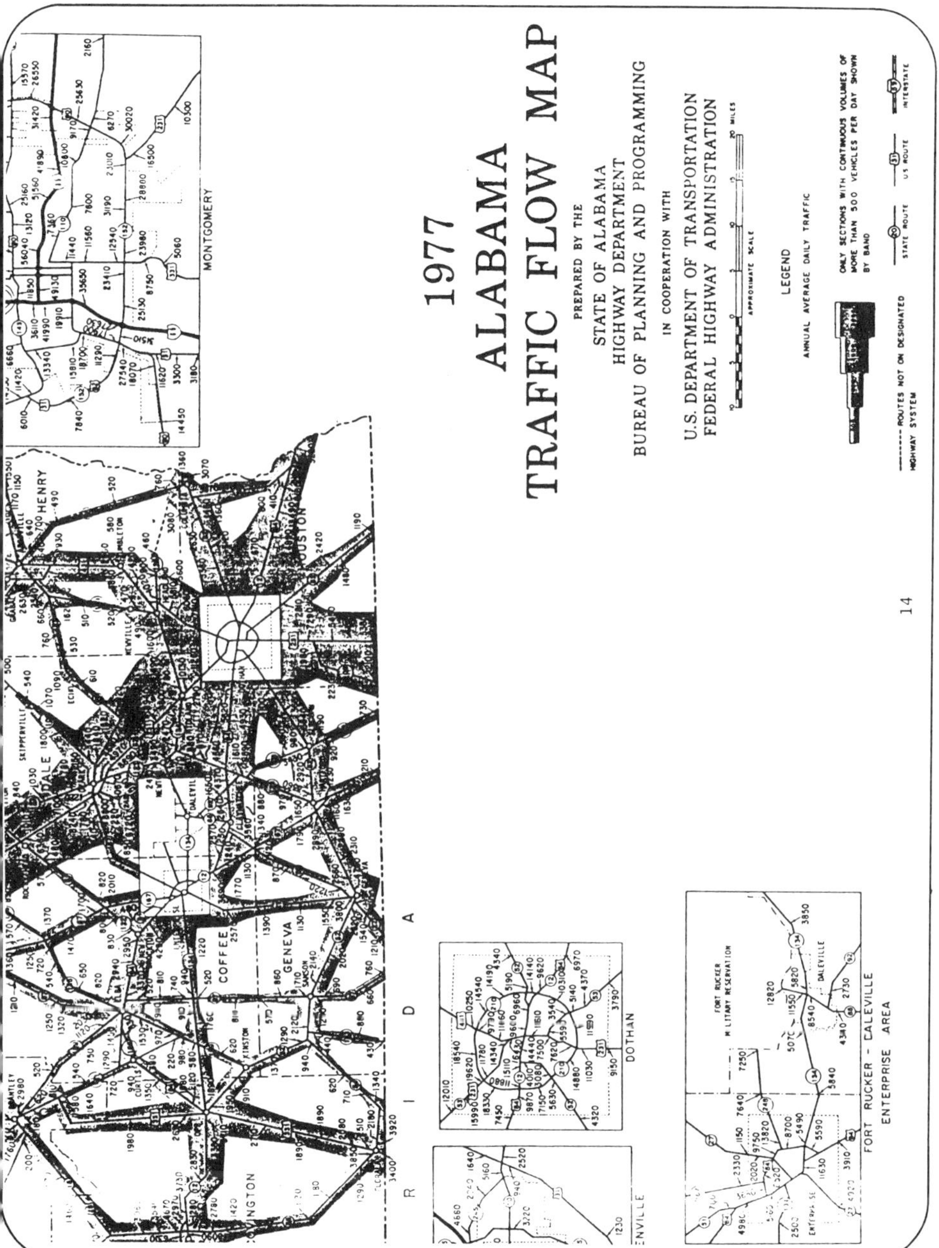
1977
ALABAMA
TRAFFIC FLOW MAP
PREPARED BY THE
STATE OF ALABAMA
HIGHWAY DEPARTMENT
BUREAU OF PLANNING AND PROGRAMMING
IN COOPERATION WITH
U.S. DEPARTMENT OF TRANSPORTATION
FEDERAL HIGHWAY ADMINISTRATION
LEGEND
ANNUAL AVERAGE DAILY TRAFFIC
MONTGOMERY
DOTHAN
FORT RUCKER - DALEVILLE
ENTERPRISE AREA
HENRY
DALE
COFFEE
GENEVA
HOUSTON
F L O R I D A
14

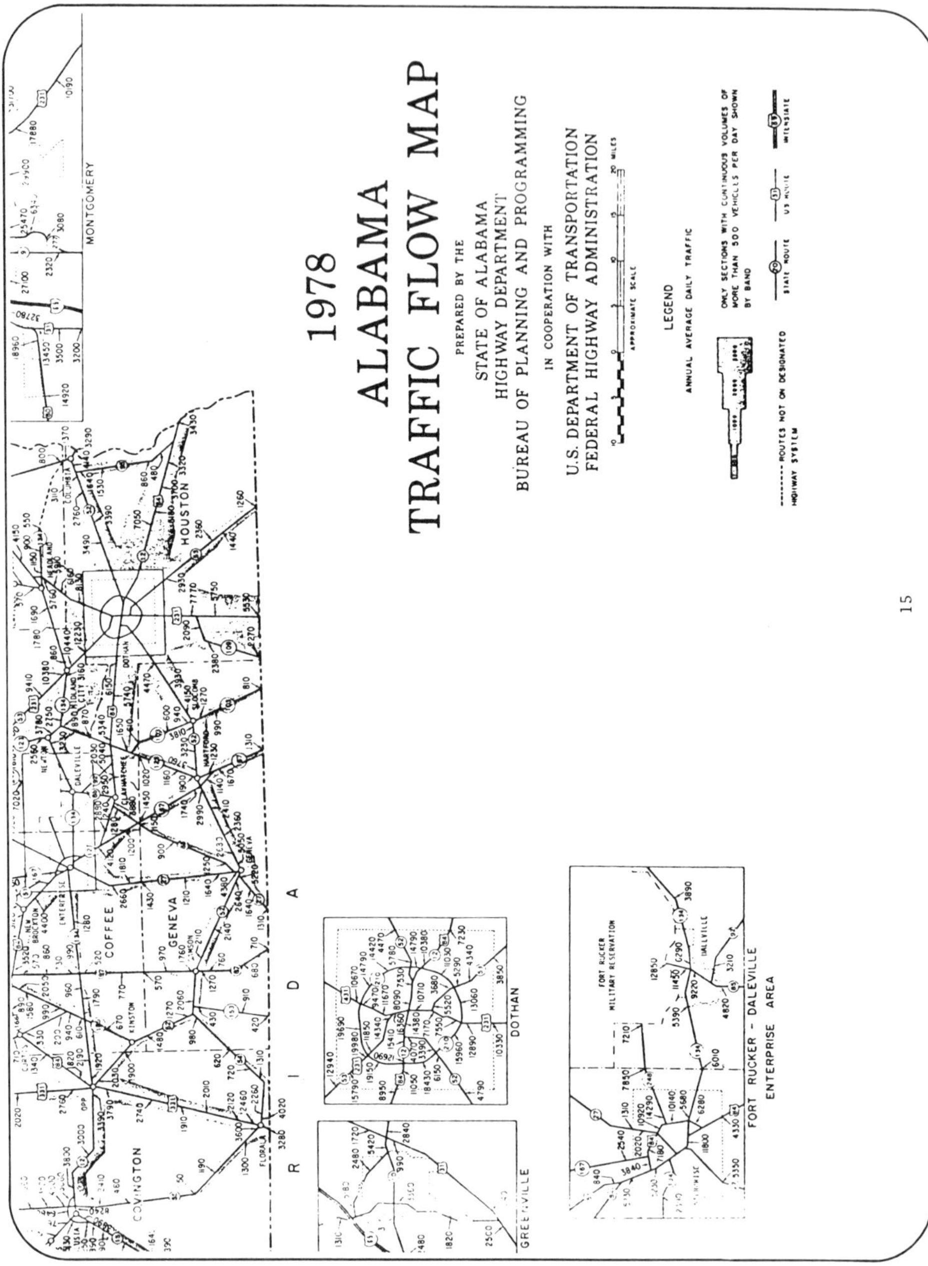
1978
ALABAMA
TRAFFIC FLOW MAP
PREPARED BY THE
STATE OF ALABAMA
HIGHWAY DEPARTMENT
BUREAU OF PLANNING AND PROGRAMMING
IN COOPERATION WITH
U.S. DEPARTMENT OF TRANSPORTATION
FEDERAL HIGHWAY ADMINISTRATION
LEGEND
ANNUAL AVERAGE DAILY TRAFFIC
ONLY SECTIONS WITH CONTINUOUS VOLUMES OF MORE THAN 500 VEHICLES PER DAY SHOWN BY BAND
ROUTES NOT ON DESIGNATED HIGHWAY SYSTEM
STATE ROUTE
U.S. ROUTE
INTERSTATE
MONTGOMERY
HOUSTON
COFFEE
GENEVA
COVINGTON
F L O R I D A
DOTHAN
GREENVILLE
FORT RUCKER - DALEVILLE
ENTERPRISE AREA
FORT RUCKER
MILITARY RESERVATION
15

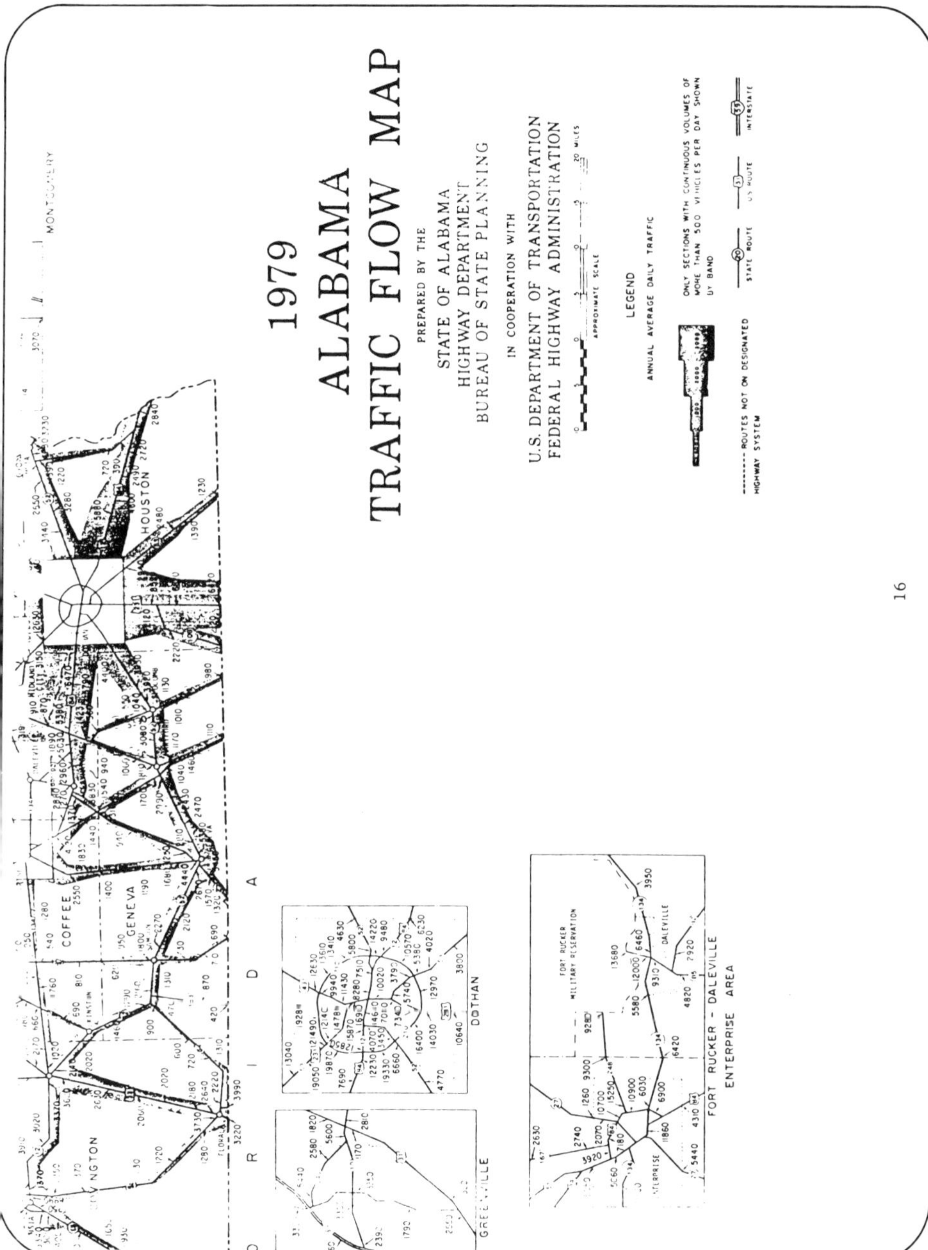
1979
ALABAMA
TRAFFIC FLOW MAP
PREPARED BY THE
STATE OF ALABAMA
HIGHWAY DEPARTMENT
BUREAU OF STATE PLANNING
IN COOPERATION WITH
U.S. DEPARTMENT OF TRANSPORTATION
FEDERAL HIGHWAY ADMINISTRATION
APPROXIMATE SCALE
LEGEND
ANNUAL AVERAGE DAILY TRAFFIC
ROUTES NOT ON DESIGNATED HIGHWAY SYSTEM
STATE ROUTE
INTERSTATE
HOUSTON
GENEVA
COFFEE
DOTHAN
FORT RUCKER - DALEVILLE
ENTERPRISE AREA
16

Rucker Increases Mean
$2.3 Million Area Impact

These remarks are not i
the rule that hypotheses sh
tiplied except as necessary
miliar with Occam's razor
overlook the implications o
The word "razor" correctly
should eliminate unneces
Perhaps, however, we shou
not a razor but a hair-rest
facts are established a hyp
formerly unnecessary may
essary. The original hypot
tended or elaborated or
jected. And sometimes we
razor nor a hair-restorer b
tion or face-saver. The fac
ognition that it is perfectl
without "loss of face," that
to be true but that we are n
to formulate, without furt
a self-consistent theory of
plicity that will embody all
times the best procedure is
unruly new facts clearly be
al nervous system. As a mem
rial board of *Psychosomatic*
ve more than once determine
rticle was appropriate for pub
journal on the basis of whethe
was implicit in it. More br
was that every article shou
cho" aspect and a "somatic" a
could be satisfied by observa.
ed to relate behavior to struct
nality of behavior to patholog
idable objective in research in
nderstand the complexities
mind, the human body, and t

Our pathologic data are
severe damage to the primar
tion pathway bilaterally, w
retrograde degeneration of the
nuclei. We cannot say wheth
amount of residual functiona
tem may account for the subj
capacity to develop speech
seems more likely that the a
afferent systems, has a functi
way in the brain stem and
which is phylogenetically older
situated geniculate-cortical pa
pathway may then be the es
substrate for language develop

Against this hypothesis is th
for conduction of auditory
medial pathway in the adult
hemispheral lesions have been
duce deafness, but these rep
audiometric tests and histolog
ripheral auditory apparatus. F
may indicate only a quantita
degree of compensatory func
lent lesions in infancy and in a

The cerebral lesions in th
limited to the auditory system
picture may be partially relat
of other structures in the syl
ther, it would be gratuitous t
lesions of the geniculate-cortic
ly to be found in most other
aphasia, for a large portion
aphasic population shows no
or laboratory evidence of such

The authors have descri
facts and have accepted th
implications. They have for
ble new hypothesis. They
ever, overstepped the limits
dence by drawing final concl

rtion of the cerebrum was of
configuration. However, pos-
a bilateral loss of cortical sub-
m the inferior and posterior
tral sulci anteriorly and ex-
s along the course of the in-
fissures toward the occipital
. The area of loss on the right
length and about 2 cm. in
ridged by slightly thickened
nilar area on the left had the
xtended 8 cm., almost to the
e gyri of the posterior portion
emporal, and occipital lobes
duced in size. . . .
ions cut coronally through the
wed gross degeneration of the
ula bilaterally. In the brain
ly distinct medial geniculate
related to the lateral genicu-

asteful and often confusin
thesis concerning the relat
t of behavior to structure
by the original observation
ded as established fact, a
d doctrine, with a rigid s
l-body, but sometimes, in
, the tendency to think and
he body, when we logically
think in terms of the mind

Is the area stable? (Include reprint of local news article.)

SAMPLE LEASE

LEASE

Between
________________ INCORPORATED

and

ALABAMA DEPARTMENT OF INDUSTRIAL RELATIONS

This LEASE, made and entered into this 18th day of July in the year one thousand nine hundred and eighty by and between ____________________________ ____________________________, whose address is Enterprise, Alabama, hereinafter called the LESSOR, and the ____, hereinafter called the LESSEE.

WITNESSETH: The parties hereto for the consideration hereinafter mentioned convenant and agree as follows:

1. The LESSOR hereby agrees to lease an air-conditioned, centrally heated, one-story brick and masonry building located at Lot 21, Phase 7, Westgate Shopping Center, recorded in Plat Book 2, Page 103, Probate Office, Enterprise, Coffee County Alabama, in the City of Enterprise, Alabama, to be used for offices including an unemployment compensation office and employment service office, and being the premises now occupied by the LESSEE, and does hereby lease same to the LESSEE for the term herein set out. The dimensions of the said building being 50 feet wide by 100 feet in length for a total of 5,000 square feet gross outside dimensions.

2. The term of this Lease shall be for a period of three (3) years commencing October 1, 198__, and ending September 30, 198__.

3. The LESSEE shall not assign this Lease or any renewal or extension thereof in any event and shall not sublet the demised premises without prior written permission of the LESSOR.

4. The LESSEE shall pay the LESSOR for the premises rent at the following rate: Sixteen Thousand Eight Hundred Dollars ($16,800) per annum payable at the rate of Fourteen Hundred Dollars ($1,400) per

SAMPLE LEASE

Typical lease, included for the investor's edification. (Here we have shown only the first page of the lease.)

MEMO

Re: West Gate Shopping Center

Since you received the presentation on West Gate Shopping Center, the owner has consented to carrying financing. This addendum outlines the economics of the transaction if a purchaser were to take advantage of the terms being offered:

Asking Price	$3,000,000
Down Payment	$ 800,000
Financing	First Mortgage at 9%, interest-only for five years. Year Six: Interest rate to be raised to 11% and balance amortized over 25-year period

19

A good follow-up mailer for this project—here's what happens with a few assumptions.

WestGate Shopping Center
Addendum
First Year only
40% Tax Bracket

Before Tax (Refer to page 4)

Net operating income	$267,509
- Debt Service (9% on 2,200,000)	198,000
Cash flow before tax	$ 69,509

After Tax

Net operating income	$267,509
- interest	198,000
- *cost recovery	150,000
Taxable Income	(80,491)
Tax bracket	40%
Tax Savings	32,196
Total after tax cash flow	$101,705

Cash on Cash return Before Tax $\frac{\$69,509}{\$800,000} = 8.7\%$

Cash on Cash return After Tax $\frac{\$101,705}{\$800,000} = 12.7\%$

* $2,250,000 improvement allocation 15 year straight line

20

Show first year returns as well as five-year projection (see next page).

Sample Holding Period

Years 2 - 5

Assume Outright Sale End of Year 5 at $3,500,000

(Refer to Page 6 of packet for NOI determination)

40% Tax Bracket

	1982	1983	1984	1985
Net operating income	297,335	329,617	355,992	390,942
- interest	198,000	198.000	198,000	198,000
- cost recovery	150,000	150,000	150,000	150,000
Taxable Income	(50,665)	(18,383)	7,992	42,942
Tax bracket	40%	40%	40%	40%
Tax savings (Liability)	20,266	7,353	(3,196)	(17,176)
Cash flow Before Tax	99,335	131,617	157,992	192,942
Tax Savings (Liability)	20,266	7,353	(3,196)	(17,176)
After Tax Cash flow	119,601	138,970	154,796	175,766

Sales Proceeds

Original Basis	$3,000,000
- cost recovery	750,000
Adjusted Basis	$2,250,000
Sale Price	$3,500,000
- sales costs	200,000
- adjusted basis	2,250,000
Gain	$1,050,000
Maximum Tax	20%
Tax on Sale	$ 210,000

Sale Price	$3,500,000
- sales costs	200,000
- mortgage	2,200,000
- Tax	210,000
Sales Proceeds after Tax	$ 890,000

21

Who needs a complicated form? Keep it simple.

Discounted Cash Flow Analysis

Internal Rate of Return

After Tax

Year		Dollars
Acquisition	0	(800,000)
1981	1	101,705
1982	2	119,601
1983	3	138,970
1984	4	154,796
1985 plus sale	5	175,766 + 890,000

IRR = 18%

View the IRR as that rate of return that the dollars invested in the project earn while they are in the investment. A 40% taxpayer would have to invest the $800,000 at over 30% before tax to compare to this investment alternative.

22

Relate IRR to a comparison tool even on a before-tax basis.

The following package demonstrates to the potential investor the competition in the market as well as the economics of the specific project. In this case the apartment project for sale has potential as a condominium conversion. As an apartment project held for rental income only, the apartments appear to be overpriced. Note that the presentation is slanted toward a condominium converter as opposed to a pure investor who might buy based on a strict income approach to value.

PRESIDENTIAL SUITES
80 Residential Units
8274 Traphagen N.W.
Massillon, Ohio

Roberta James, CCIM
XYZ Real Estate
999 Main St.
Hometown, Ohio 99999
222-555-5555

PRESIDENTIAL SUITES

INDEX

PRESIDENTIAL SUITES

8274 Traphagen NW
Massillon, OH

The following information represents the income and expenses for an eighty unit apartment complex located in Jackson Township, Massillon, Ohio.

--16 units are brick Garden style (built 1973)

--64 units are cedar townhouse & flat style

--swimming pool

--tennis court

--putting green

--tenants pay all utilities except sewer

--16 one-bedroom units

--56 two-bedroom units

-- 8 three-bedroom units

--87 garages, plus 70 open parking spaces

-- 8+ acres of land

--originally designed for condominium conversion

--$35,000 @ unit; $7,292 @ room
--67,248 square feet @ $46 per net rentable square foot
--384 rooms plus baths, patios, and carport garages

Asking Price: $2,800,000

Owner Financing Available; Interest Only

Owner Open-Minded To Terms or Joint Venture

Page 1

Just plain facts. (It is important to include a color photo of the project at this point in the presentation.)

PROPERTY INFORMATION

Presidential Suites

In 1973 the owner of Presidential Suites saw the future of condominiums. Incorporating separate design into the project, the developer phased in luxury apartment units with amenities such as a swimming pool, tennis court, putting green, clubhouse, patios, and wide-open grounds.

For the past several years, the developer has operated Presidential Suites as an apartment project. It is recognized as one of the preferred apartment living projects in the area. In 1980, the developer changed the image of Presidential to an all adult community. The change has hurt the occupancy level, but the owner's posturc is one of seeing the quality of tenants improve as families with children were removed.

The owner's tax position now dictates a sale and he is willing to joint venture the project with an individual or group that might have interest in converting Presidential Suites to condominium ownership.

The owner is cognizant of the available financing in today's marketplace and is willing to finance the purchase with necessary releases for condominium conversion. Interest only financing is available for the qualified investor/converter at a rate which offers economic feasibility to the project.

Page 2

What's the history of the property? Why is the seller selling?

Presidential Suites

...in Jackson Township

WE'RE GROWING UP...
to an ALL-ADULT community!

Presidential Suites has begun its conversion to an all-adult community. We are now renting to adults only.

Presidential Suites...Quality, style and value in townhouse or garden apartment living.
One bedroom units at $275.
Two bedroom units at $320.
Three bedroom units at $405.

All apartments have the conveniences...Frost-free Refrigerator. Dishwasher. Oven-range. Garbage Disposal. Washer-dryer hook-ups.

And the luxuries...
Carpeting, Private patio. Carport. And for the total living experience...
Tennis courts. Swimming pool, putting green. Clubhouse.

PRESIDENTIAL SUITES...
A great place to live in a style of your choice!

Two Bedroom Townhouse:

Living Room	12' x 17'4"
Dining Room	10' x 8'
Kitchen	8'3" x 9'2"
Bedroom	12' x 17'4"
Bedroom	9' x 14'
One & one-half baths	

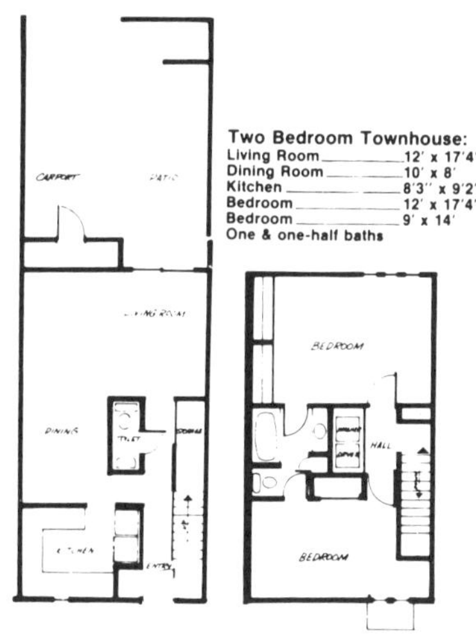

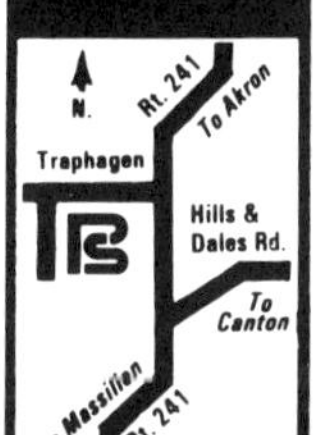

Available for immediate occupancy.

Presidential Suites

Page 3

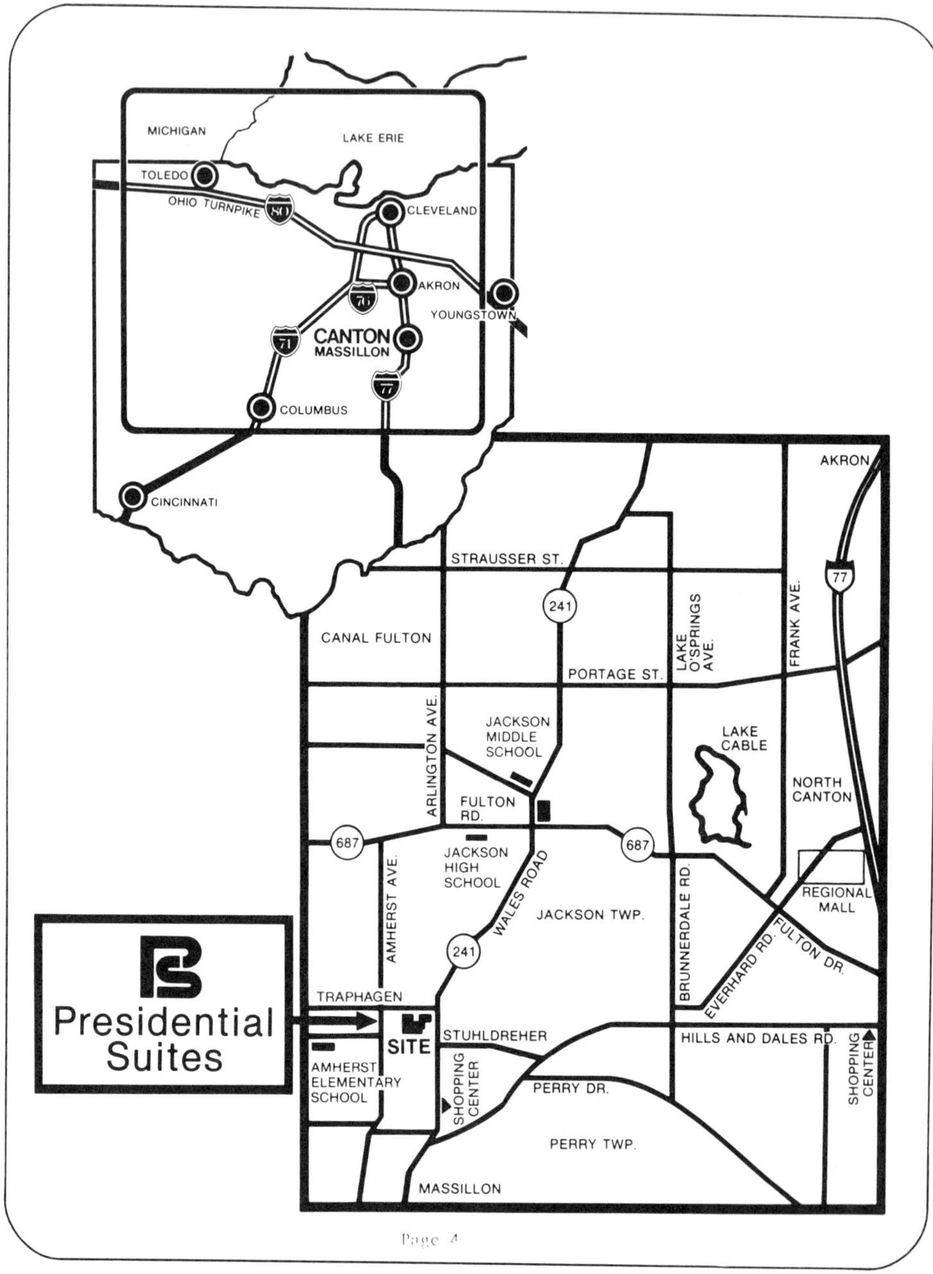
MICHIGAN
LAKE ERIE
TOLEDO
OHIO TURNPIKE
80
CLEVELAND
AKRON
76
YOUNGSTOWN
71
CANTON
MASSILLON
77
COLUMBUS
CINCINNATI
AKRON
77
STRAUSSER ST.
241
CANAL FULTON
LAKE O'SPRINGS AVE.
FRANK AVE.
PORTAGE ST.
ARLINGTON AVE.
JACKSON MIDDLE SCHOOL
LAKE CABLE
NORTH CANTON
FULTON RD.
687
JACKSON HIGH SCHOOL
687
AMHERST AVE.
WALES ROAD
BRUNNERDALE RD.
REGIONAL MALL
JACKSON TWP.
241
FULTON DR.
EVERHARD RD.
Presidential Suites
TRAPHAGEN
SITE
STUHLDREHER
HILLS AND DALES RD.
AMHERST ELEMENTARY SCHOOL
SHOPPING CENTER
PERRY DR.
SHOPPING CENTER
PERRY TWP.
MASSILLON
Page 4

TWO BEDROOM
Monroe & Madison House

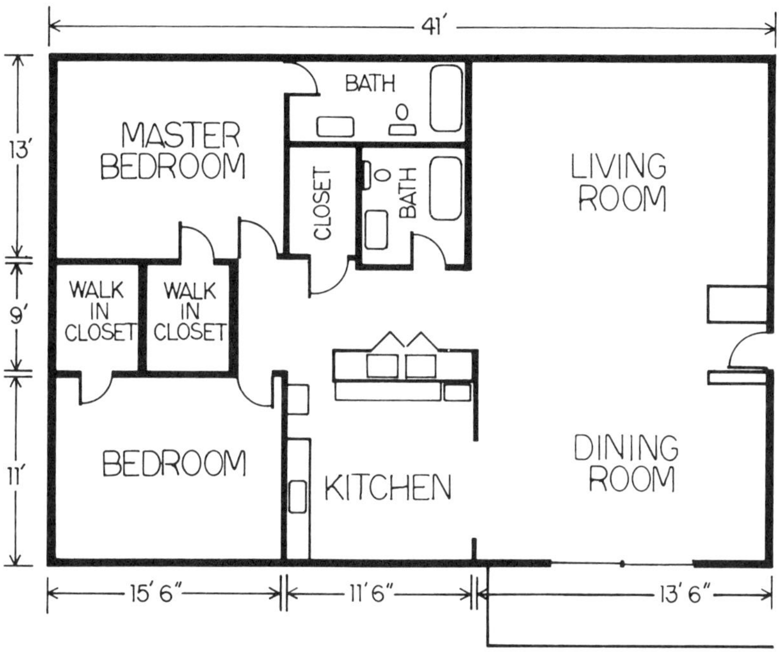

Two Bedroom Apartment

Living Room	13'6" x 17'
Dining Room	13'6" x 12'6'
Kitchen	11'6" x 11'
Master Bedroom	15' x 13'
Bedroom	15'6' x 11'

Two Full Baths
Approximately 1,353 square feet

All units include:
- oven/range
- frost-free refrigerator
- dishwasher
- garbage disposal
- washer/dryer hook-up
- walk-in closets
- air-conditioning
- full carpeting
- balcony
- garage
- gas heating

Page 5

Include all apartment layouts in presentation (we are showing only one layout here).

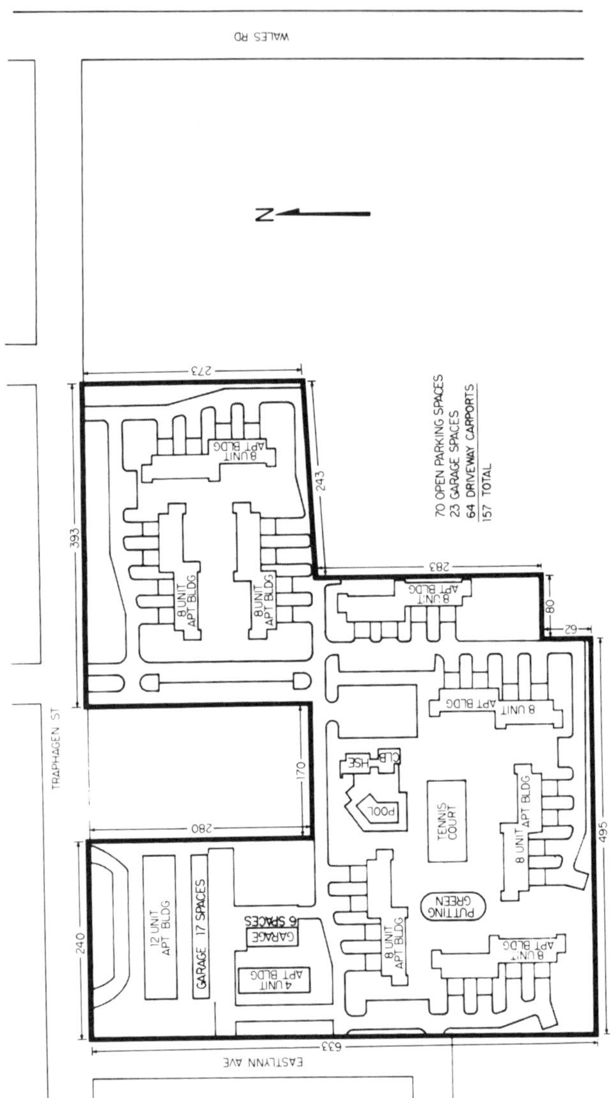
WALES RD
N
70 OPEN PARKING SPACES
23 GARAGE SPACES
64 DRIVEWAY CARPORTS
157 TOTAL
TRAPHAGEN ST
EASTLYNN AVE
8 UNIT APT BLDG
12 UNIT APT BLDG
4 UNIT APT BLDG
GARAGE 17 SPACES
GARAGE 6 SPACES
CLB HSE
POOL
TENNIS COURT
PUTTING GREEN
273
243
393
283
80
62
170
280
240
495
633

Page 6

FINANCIAL INFORMATION

This property offering is designed to provide authoritative information regarding the subject property. In all areas, information and projections used are from reliable sources; however, no guarantee is made to the accuracy of said information.

Since the proposed terms are flexible, no after tax projections have been included utilizing financing. Although we recommend personal legal or accounting advice be sought, XYZ Real Estate will be happy to provide after tax analysis including discounted cash flows and internal rates of return over the intended holding period of the investment.

Page 7

INCOME ANALYSIS (March 1981)

	Month	Year
16 One bedroom ranch style	@$275	$ 52,800
40 Two bedroom townhouses	@ 320	153,600
8 Three bedroom townhouses	@ 405	38,880
4 Two bedroom units	@ 405	19,440
8 Two bedroom units	@ 340	32,640
4 Two bedroom units	@ 350	16,800
TOTAL Gross Scheduled Income		$314,160
Laundromat		2,000
TOTAL		$316,160

Page 8

PRESIDENTIAL SUITES - RENT ROLL - MARCH 1981

Eastlynn: (Monroe House)

3846	2 Bedroom	$ 405.00
3848	2 Bedroom	405.00
3850	2 Bedroom	405.00
3852	2 Bedroom	405.00

Traphagen: (Madison House)

8300	2 Bedroom	$ 340.00
8302	2 Bedroom	340.00
8304	2 Bedroom	340.00
8306	2 Bedroom	340.00
8308	2 Bedroom	365.00
8310	2 Bedroom	350.00
8312	2 Bedroom	350.00
8314	2 Bedroom	350.00
8316	2 Bedroom	340.00
8318	2 Bedroom	350.00
8320	2 Bedroom	355.00
8322	2 Bedroom	355.00

Traphagen:

8220A	1 Bedroom	$ 255.00
8220B	2 Bedroom	320.00
8220C	2 Bedroom	320.00
8220D	3 Bedroom	405.00
8220E	2 Bedroom	320.00
8220F	2 Bedroom	320.00
8220G	2 Bedroom	330.00
8220H	1 Bedroom	275.00
8224A	1 Bedroom	$ 255.00
8224B	2 Bedroom	295.00
8224C	2 Bedroom	320.00
8224D	3 Bedroom	415.00
8224E	2 Bedroom	320.00
8224F	2 Bedroom	320.00
8224G	2 Bedroom	275.00
8224H	1 Bedroom	255.00
8228A	1 Bedroom	$ 275.00
8228B	2 Bedroom	320.00
8228C	2 Bedroom	320.00
8228D	3 Bedroom	395.00
8228E	2 Bedroom	320.00
8228F	2 Bedroom	320.00
8228G	2 Bedroom	295.00
8228H	1 Bedroom	255.00

8252A	1 Bedroom	$ 255.00	
8252B	2 Bedroom	330.00	
8252C	2 Bedroom	330.00	
8252D	2 Bedroom	320.00	
8252E	3 Bedroom	Res.Mgr.	(405.00)
8252F	2 Bedroom	320.00	
8252G	2 Bedroom	320.00	
8252H	1 Bedroom	275.00	
8260A	1 Bedroom	$ 255.00	
8260B	2 Bedroom	320.00	
8260C	2 Bedroom	295.00	
8260D	2 Bedroom	295.00	
8260E	3 Bedroom	350.00	
8260F	2 Bedroom	295.00	
8260G	2 Bedroom	320.00	
8260H	1 Bedroom	275.00	
8264A	1 Bedroom	$ 275.00	
8264B	2 Bedroom	330.00	
8264C	2 Bedroom	295.00	
8264D	2 Bedroom	300.00	
8264E	3 Bedroom	405.00	
8264F	2 Bedroom	330.00	
8264G	2 Bedroom	320.00	
8264H	1 Bedroom	255.00	
8268A	1 Bedroom	$ 285.00	
8268B	2 Bedroom	295.00	
8268C	2 Bedroom	295.00	
8268D	2 Bedroom	320.00	
8268E	3 Bedroom	405.00	
8268F	2 Bedroom	320.00	
8268G	2 Bedroom	320.00	
8268H	1 Bedroom	255.00	
8272A	1 Bedroom	$ 255.00	
8272B	2 Bedroom	330.00	
8272C	2 Bedroom	295.00	
8272D	2 Bedroom	295.00	
8272E	3 Bedroom	405.00	
8272F	2 Bedroom	320.00	
8272G	2 Bedroom	295.00	
8272H	1 Bedroom	275.00	

Page 9

OWNERS RENTAL HISTORY

	1980*	1979	1978
INCOME: (Collected)			
Rental (80 Units)	$223,888	$244,446	$240,411
Laundromat, etc.	1,467	1,773	2,159
TOTAL	$225,355	$246,179	$242,570
OPERATING EXPENSES:			
Real Estate Taxes	$ 15,825	$ 16,669	$ 15,673
Utilities (Gas & Electric)	10,272	10,751	8,254
Sewer & Water	8,097	7,373	6,641
Salaries (Maintenance)	7,175	Below	Below
Salaries (Resident Manager)	5,442	Owner	Owner
Insurance	4,491	6,232	3,965
General Repairs	Above	2,163	2,074
Lawn, Pool & Snow	2,612	4,016	5,225
Refuse	2,440	2,105	2,400
Plumbing Repairs	2,150	584	1,444
Advertising & Promotion	1,813	750	600
Payroll Taxes	1,664	-0-	-0-
Painting	1,363	633	4,212
Supplies	1,126	-0-	-0-
Appliance & Electrical Repair	1,021	1,598	1,536
Cleaning Service	813	977	1,490
Cable TV Fee	622	672	672
Furnace Repairs	224	General Exp.	General Exp.
Pest Control	130	-0-	-0-
TOTAL EXPENSES	$ 67,130	$ 54,523	$ 54,187
% of rent collected	30%	22%	22%
NET Operating Income	$158,225	$191,656	$188,383

*In 1980 owner decided to hire on site management and convert complex to an all adult community. Reduced income reflects increased vacancies due to departure of families with children.

Page 10

Some investors like to see a rental history.

PRESIDENTIAL SUITES
ANNUAL BEFORE TAX PROJECTION
AS APARTMENTS

Gross Potential Income		$ 314,160
Vacancy & Credit Loss	(5%)	15,133
Actual Collected Rents		$ 299,027
Expenses (24%)		70,000
Net Operating Income		$ 229,027

Owner financing available;
Interest only, with terms

Page 11

PRESIDENTIAL SUITES
After Tax Example
First Year Only
As Apartments

Assumptions: Financing - $2,000,000 at 10% only
30% Bracket investor
50% Bracket investor

Net Operating Income	$ 229,027
-Debt Service	200,000
Cash Flow Before Taxes	$ 29,027

Net Operating Income	$ 229,027
-Interest	200,000
-*Depreciation	288,000
Taxable Income	$ (258,973)

	50% Bracket	30% Bracket
Tax Savings	$ 129,486	$ 77,691
Cash Flow Before Taxes	29,027	29,027
Total Cash Flow After Taxes	$ 158,513	$106,718

15-year term, ACRS
$2,400,000 allocation

Page 12

JACKSON TOWNSHIP HOUSING SALES PROFILE

Single Family Homes

	Average List Price	Average Sale Price	Median Price	Sales Price % Increase
1976	$48,963	$47,212	$45,000	
1977	53,924	52,349	49,500	11%
1978	65,072	62,767	57,000	20%
1979	69,399	69,213	68,500	10%
1980	79,187	75,219	72,500	9%

Page 13

Look how sales prices have increased!

CONDOMINIUM COMPARABLES

Stark County

Since condominiums are relatively new to the Stark County area, there are few comparables. Those listed below comprise known market.

SOLD	SQUARE FEET	PRICE
Property A	764	$46,900
Property B		43,500
*Property C	1088	52,500
*Property D	1296	53,000
**Property E	1017	63,900

*Brochures Included

*Brochures Included

*Property C and Property X condominiums are being marketed by developer ranging in price from $47,900 - $60,000. Located in Plain and Perry Townships. No special financing being offered.

**Property E Condominiums are being marketed by _______________ Real Estate and range in price from $63,900 - $74,900. Property E is located in Canton City limits. (Brochure reprinted) No special financing being offered.

14

After showing these comparable prices, it might be a good idea to include copies of promotional brochures of the comparables (not shown here).

CONDOMINIUM CONVERSION OVERVIEW

Twenty-four Months

The following is an example of how the economics might look on a conversion and sale of 80 units known as Presidential Suites on a before tax basis.

	TOTAL	PER UNIT
ORIGINAL COST	$2,800,000	$35,000
Legal	40,000	500
Remodeling & dress-up	160,000	2,000
Total Project Costs	$3,000,000	$37,500

Considering a	$ 7,292	per room cost for purchase
And a	521	per room cost for improvement
	$ 7,813	Total cost per room

TOTAL COST BREAKDOWN:

One bedroom units (4 rooms)	$31,252
Two bedroom units (5 rooms)	39,065
Three bedroom units (6 rooms)	46,878

With the average home in Jackson Township selling for $75,000 in 1980 and projecting (see page 16) 9% increase for 1981 which takes the average sale to $81,750 for the township, the sales price structure might look as follows:

Page 15

Late 1981 and 1982 Condominium Suggested Price Structure

One bedroom	$42,000 - $45,000
Two bedroom	52,000 - 60,000
Three bedroom	62,000 - 65,000

Average home price of $81,750 places condominium sale prices 24% - 48% below housing market prices.

Using conservative sales prices, a sales analysis might look as follows:

16 one bedroom units at	$43,000	$ 688,000
40 two bedroom units at	55,000	2,200,000
16 two bedroom units at	60,000	960,000
8 three bedroom units at	63,000	504,000
Total Gross Sales		$4,352,000
Expenses: Marketing, Administration, Transfer Fee, Legal	8%	$ 348,160
NET SALES		$4,003,840
Original Cost Plus Conversion		3,000,000
Before Tax Net		$1,003,840

Page 16

HUD: Conversions haven't hurt rentals

Sjkdsjkdlsjdklsjkdlsjkdlsjfklsd
jsdkolfjksldfkjsldkfjslkdjfsdlk
jfkdlsklsdjfsldkfdsdkjkllksdfkk
lsdkjfsldkjfslflskdjflsflsdkjfk
fdlskdflskdjflsflskdjflsdkkfdsd
jfkdla;ldksjdfkdsl;adlkfdksljjd
sldkfjsldkfsldkfjslkdjfslkfskjf
fjkdlskdfslflskdflskflsdkfjdklk
sldfjslfsjjssddlkjfsldkfjslfdkj
jflskdjflskdjfslsdksjslfkjlsfjl
Jklsdkfjsldkjfslkdfslfdklsdjf
lskdjflsdkflsdkfjlsdkfjsldkfjsl
lsdfjslkdjflskdjflsdkjflsdkfjld
sdfjsldkfjsldkfjsldkfjsldkjfdff

sjdflsdkjfslkdjflskdjflskdjflsd
klkjkjlkjlkjlkjlkjlsdfsdfsdflkj
lkjdslkjdflksdjlfkjsldjflsdjflk
fjkdslkfdskjdlkkdsdfdfsdsddsdjj
dsdfdsdlkjlkdfsdlkfjsldkjflsdjj
fjkdlksdfslkjfsdkfsldkfjsldkfjf
flksjdlfksjdlfkdjslkdjflskdjfls
lskflskjflskjdflskflskfslksfsdf
jllkkllkkllkkdsdfsdfsdfslkjlkjs
lkjlsdfslkjsdfkjlsdfkjsldkfllkd
fsdfsdfslkjsldkfjslkdfsldkfjsdf
lkjdfslskdjflskdjflsmjflsdkjfjj
slfsdlkfjsldkfsldkfjsldkflsdkfl
fjksdlkfjsldkfjsldkfjsldkfjsldf

How a conversion pro slipped on new turf

urieoweiureweiur
ruieowieeowieure
rueiwoeiuwroiwee
worooiuoiuoiewre
uiroewiueorweiur
woroweiurowieuro
wowowowowowowowo
ieieieieowiewoei
ieoeoweiruwoeiru
rueieoiwueroeiow
woierowieuroweer
owiurowieuroweir
woeroweiuyoeiury
tyuew-ruoieueeui
irewoirowieurwor
uwoeirwoieurowri
wworwoieuwoeruri
wuerowieuryytieo
oiuweoriuwruwiey
tiywiyoiurrwuwie
pqoweiupqwoieqoq
qpopqoiqipqoeiow
qpoweiru-wouruew
qpoiqq-urueiwooo

qpouruewoieuooiw
qporuoweieurwoie
ruiweowieurwoieu
iwuewwiurwo-ruwe
-qwertyuiop©owur
ewrwirowirowiruw
weoruwoiw-rwuowe

ruiewoeiruowieure
qoiuwerowiurwieoi
uweiruwoeiroqpowe
ruiweqpoeurowpoie
ruiqpoiweriuoweir
ruwoeiurwqoirwope
uiopuokwerpoqiwpo

The case for condo conversions

zmxncbvxmnbxcnm
zxnb,xmnbcvmxnc
z,mnbxcvbxzmncv
xmncbvz,mvbx,zm
z,x,zbv,mnbnxmn
xmncbxmcnvbxmcn
xmcnvbxmcnbvxmn
xv-nbxmcnvxmcvm
znxcnbzvxcnbzcn
xcmvbxmcnxmcnvb
xmncvbxmcnvbxmc
zxnvzxnznxbnxbx

zmxzmxnzmnbxnznbx
zznbvcnzbxvcbxznx
cbnxzmxnbcmznxcbn
czxvcnzbxcnzvxzbc
cvzbxcvznxvcznbxn
ncv-znzbxvcnzcnzb
znbxvcnzbxvcnzxvv
zcnzbvxcnzvxcnzvv
vvcbzvxncvznbxcnn
znbxcznbcznbzn;cn
zxncvznxcznbbcvzn
cvcnzbxcvczn.

17

Use reprints of articles from trade magazines to help make your point.

SALE ANALYSIS AS INDIVIDUAL BUILDINGS

Project Layout Makes Individual Sales To Investors Possible

One - 4 unit brick - 2 bedrooms (Monroe House)

One - 12 unit brick - 2 bedrooms (Madison House)

Eight - 8 unit cedar - Two-1 bedrooms, five-2 bedrooms, one-3 bedroom

Suggested Sales Price Say Early 1983

Monroe House (4 units)	$50,000 @ unit	$ 200,000
Madison House (12 units)	50,000 @ unit	600,000
Cedar (8 buildings; 64 units)	45,000 @ unit	2,800,000

Total Gross Sales	$3,680,000
Sales Costs 8%	294,400
	$3,385,600
Original Purchase Price	$2,800,000
Net Cash Before Tax	$ 585,600

Page 18

Condo conversion is only one means of disposition.

In the ten years since the 1970 Census Stark County has experienced solid growth in population as well as in housing. The chart at bottom left indicates the population growth of Stark County over the past decade, from a county population of 372,210 in 1970 to a 1980 population of 395,000. Throughout the decade we see a steady or stable growth pattern, save for 1975. The chart at bottom right indicates the housing growth in Stark County over the past 10 years, from a total of 118,940 in 1970 to 137,641 units in 1980.

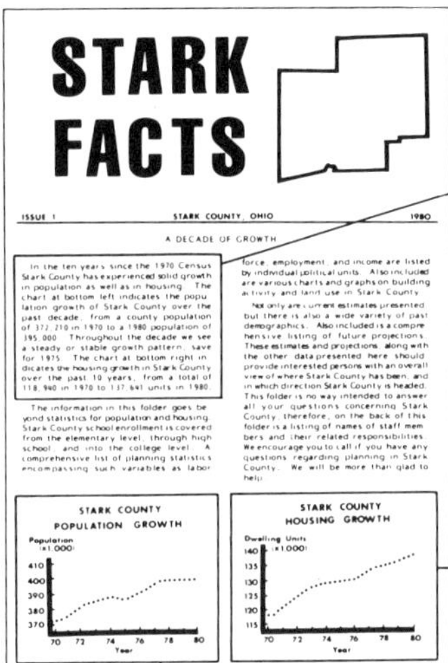

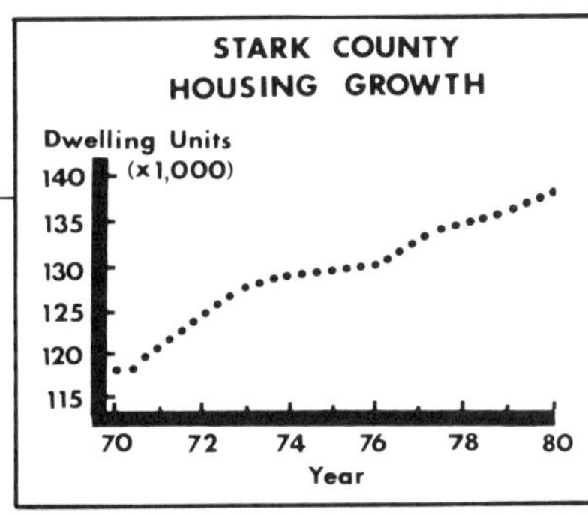

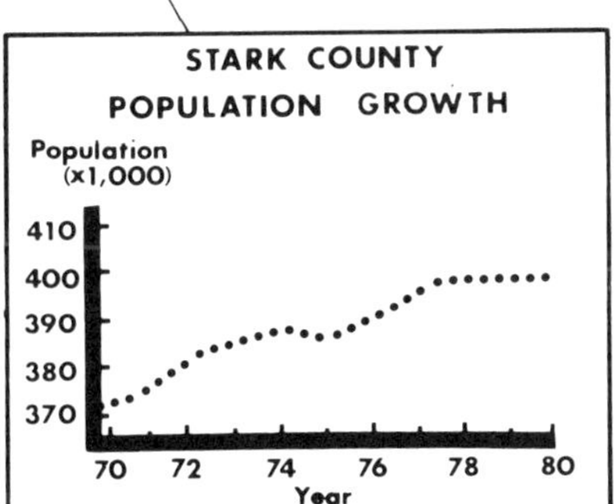

Page 19

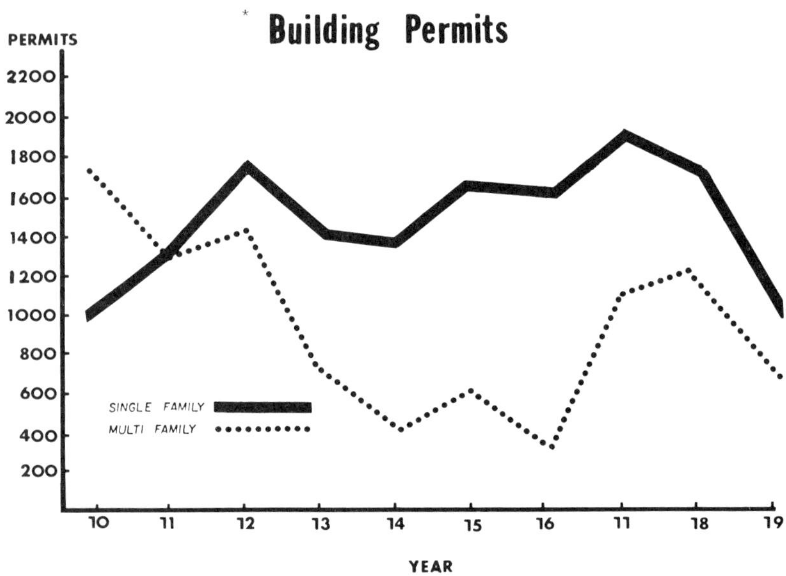

* Stark County

Page 20

POLITICAL UNIT FORECASTS — JACKSON TOWNSHIP

	1970	1975	1980	1985	1990	2000
HOUSEHOLD CHARACTERISTICS						
Population	18,506	23,150	28,930	33,835	38,740	47,470
Dwelling Units	5,457	7,180	9,340	11,170	13,000	16,310
Mean Family Income	$13,426	$16,190	$18,885	$21,621	$24,357	$32,692
Automobile Registration	11,165	13,777	17,071	21,924	24,507	31,500
Autos Available	9,490	11,710	14,510	18,635	20,831	26,775
Labor Force	7,927	9,939	12,587	14,565	16,287	20,192
School Enrollment	5,468	6,006	6,772	7,092	10,549	11,714
EMPLOYMENT						
Industrial	187	1,003	1,137	1,202	1,268	1,503
Commercial	2,494	4,129	4.492	4,801	5,061	5,909
Services	852	1,579	1,981	2,304	2,562	3,516
Other	1,333	1,393	1,564	1,692	1,818	2,357
TOTAL	4,866	8,104	9,174	9,999	10,709	13,285
LAND USE (acres)						
Residential	3,009.1	3,618.6	4,349.0	5,052.4	5,749.9	7,041.6
Industrial	25.7	99.1	106.2	109.7	113.5	126.1
Commercial	193.9	198.0	222.5	242.3	255.8	297.0
Services	247.5	252.8	282.7	309.2	333.9	397.8
Other	1,130.8	1,129.7	1,136.8	1,142.2	1,151.6	1,189.3
Agriculture & Vacant	18,094.0	17,402.8	16,603.8	15,845.2	15,096.3	13,649.2
TOTAL	22,701.0	22,701.0	22,701.0	22,701.0	22,701.0	22,701.0
FLOOR SPACE (sq. ft.)						
Industrial	77,400	377,200	436,440	465,940	495,440	600,700
Commercial	1,494,850	1,697,630	1,921,580	2,089,740	2,250,940	2,622,890
Services	302,780	360,490	491,770	610,150	717,930	1,002,430
TOTAL	1,874,030	2,435,320	2,849,790	3,165,830	3,464,310	4,226,020

NOTE: Forecasts based on 1973 political unit boundaries

Source: Stark County Regional Planning Commission

page 21

PRESIDENTIAL SUITES - UPDATED RENT ROLL - JUNE - 1981
Page One

	Tenant Name	Rent
Eastlynn:		
3846		$ 405.00
3848	vacant	*405.00
3850		405.00
3852		405.00
Traphagen:		
8300		$ 340.00
8302		340.00
8304		340.00
8306		340.00
8308		350.00 + 15.00 garage
8310		350.00
8312	vacant	*380.00
8314		350.00
8316		340.00
8318		340.00 + 10.00 garage
8320		340.00 + 15.00 garage
8322		340.00 + 15.00 garage
Traphagen:		
8220A		$ 275.00
8220B		320.00
8220C		320.00
8220D		405.00 + 10.00 pet
8220E		320.00
8220F		320.00
8220G		320.00 + 10.00 pet
8220H		275.00
8224A		$ 275.00
8224B		320.00
8224C		320.00
8224D		405.00 + 10.00 pet
8224E	vacant	*320.00
8224F		320.00
8224G		275.00
8224H		255.00
8228A		$ 275.00
8228B		320.00
8228C		320.00 + 20.00 pets
8228D		405.00 + 20.00 pets
8228E	vacant	*320.00
8228F	model	450.00 (temporary)
8228G		320.00
8228H		275.00

page 22

Keep the rent roll current with accurate information.

PRESIDENTIAL SUITES - UPDATED RENT ROLL - JUNE - 1981
Page Two

Traphagen

Unit	Tenant	Rent
8252A	vacant	$*295.00
8252B		320.00 + 10.00 pet
8252C		320.00
8252D		320.00
8252E	vacant	*415.00
8252F		320.00
8252G		320.00
8252H		275.00
8260A		$ 275.00
8260B		300.00
8260C		320 00
8260D		320.00
8260E		350.00
8260F		320.00
8260G		320.00
8260H		275.00
8264A		$ 275.00
8264B		320.00 + 10.00 pet
8264C		320.00
8264D		320.00 + 5.00 pet
8264E		405.00
8264F		320.00 + 10.00 pet
8264G	vacant	*320.00
8264H		275.00
8268A		$ 275.00 + 10.00 pet
8268B		320.00
8268C		295.00
8268D		320.00
8268E		405.00 + 10.00 pet
8268F		320.00
8268G	vacant	*320.00
8268H		275.00
8272A		$ 275.00
8272B		320.00 + 10.00 pet
8272C		320.00
8272D		320.00
8272E		405.00
8272F		320.00
8272G		295.00
8272H		275.00

Total rents collected June 1981	$23,405.00
Total additional charges	190.00
TOTAL	$24,595.00
Rents Lost To Vacancies	$ 2,775.00
Gross Schedules Renta	$27,370.00

* Indicates amount of rent if occupied

page 23

June 5, 1981

PRESIDENTIAL VACANCIES

June 1, 1981

ADDRESS		OLD RENT	NEW RENT
3848	East Lynn	$405	$ 405
3812	Traphagen	305	380
8244 E	Traphagen	320	320
8228 E	Traphagen	320	320
8252 A	Traphagen	255	295
8252 E	Traphagen	405	415
8264 C	Traphagen	320	320
8268 G	Traphagen	320	320
Total Monthly Vacancy:			$2,775

1) Bear in mind no children are permitted at Presidential Suites, thus the vacancies in three bedroom units.

2) On an annual basis, rents being collected this month total $295,140 (after vacancy) as opposed to the $299,027 shown in the proforma. (Plus $1700 - $2000 laundry income).

3) Annual gross scheduled rents based on this month's rental would be $328,440 as opposed to the $324,160 shown in the proforma.

page 24

8

PEOPLE— THE MAGIC INGREDIENT

By now you are probably ready to take the first potential investor available and stuff his brain full of rates of return, tax benefits and the wealth potential of real estate. The missing link in everything discussed so far is the fact that none of the investors in the marketplace accept properties, returns and benefits by the book. Although it is fairly easy to say that all investors invest for cash accumulation in the form of growth, income or pure speculation, it is too easy to plug all investors into a set mold.

Investors are people and people have goals, objectives and emotions. They are not always financially prepared, educated or realistic. Their real estate ownership may be one property or a multitude of properties meshed together in the form of an investment portfolio.

One overriding factor needs to be considered when we approach an investor with a piece of real estate. We are not selling bricks and mortar, but we are selling money in the form of present cash flow or future benefits.

Not all investors are at the same point in their life earning curve. They require sensitivity on the part of the broker, and they must have a thorough understanding of the benefits of real estate. An investor close to retirement may not be motivated by the same cash flow schedule as a young couple just starting their working careers. An older investor is probably not moved much by the promise of long-term growth or the tenants paying off the mortgage over the next 15 years. He wants cash flow, a steady, stable income on a monthly basis. He may also want a higher income than he is currently receiving from other forms of investment. Such buyers are looking for income, not long-term growth.

The young couple, on the other hand, may forgo all cash flow and be willing to accept negative Cash Flow Before Tax in exchange for tax benefits and a favorable leverage position in a piece of property.

A pure speculator wants a quick and easy profit. He hopes to buy, at a reduced price, property which is in the right place at the right time. The speculator can play an important role in the marketplace, however, and should not be discarded simply as an opportunist. He may be just the buyer for the property lacking management or financial strength.

A radio real estate "expert" recently told listeners that too many investors emphasize income. His advice was to concentrate on net worth because income frequently is taxed away, thus diluting the overall return. He also advised outlining goals and objectives before investing cash in real estate. All of this is sound advice, but then he started advising listeners of the following:

- Avoid all raw land; too many negative cash flows and zoning headaches.
- Steer clear of all *existing* shopping centers, apartments and office buildings. Cash flow is small compared to the purchase price. Little risk is involved and you will have to pay a premium for the property.
- Be skeptical of all real estate brokers.
- Avoid all government sponsored or guaranteed projects. The government limits your profits.
- Only buy new apartment projects since they can be converted to condominiums.
- Only invest in the Southwest U.S.

It was very frustrating to hear this advice since there was nothing left to buy on the "expert's" list if you do not live or are not interested in the Southwest. The "expert" completely disregarded the fact that some investors happen to like raw land, perhaps just because "father owned raw land and he did very well." Every investment vehicle must be individually structured to meet the wants, needs and objectives of the individual personality involved. Every investor has both financial and psychological limitations.

If an investor could find "the ideal investment," it would by its very nature meet all the objectives of that particular investor. If there were such an investment, it might have the following characteristics:

- Absolute certainty of payback of principal assured within the time frame of the investor's expectations
- Capital appreciation potential with real dollar growth or simply a hedge against the deeply ingrained expectation of probable long-term inflation
- The capability of being liquidated (sold) quickly, easily, and without excessive cost, thus enabling conversion to cash in the event of an

emergency or perhaps to take advantage of a better investment opportunity

- A very high rate of return commensurate with the risk
- Certainty of receipts, which would ensure "return on" as well as "return of" the investment
- Carefree management, requiring little of the investor's time or energy
- Availability as easy collateral for loan purposes
- Income tax shelter with taxes either delayed or deferred or no taxes of any sort, or even the possibility of extra "tax shelter"
- Effective leverage potential requiring a minimum of equity and attractive debt terms, including limited liability
- Pride of ownership

If it were easy to match the perfect investment with the perfect investor, a broker's job would become one that could be performed by a computer. The job is not quite that simple. A broker must listen carefully and interpret what a client means when he describes his objectives and goals for investing. The remainder of this chapter is devoted to profit and investment considerations for particular investors, assuming certain parameters. Each represents only one possible strategy an investor might choose.

The Young Single

Dennis Smith graduated from college last year. While in school he became interested in real estate investing. He is very aggressive and has read every book on real estate imaginable. He cannot wait to "buy something" and says his father is willing to co-sign a note for a down payment of up to $20,000 cash.

Here are the real estate broker's notes from the first interview:

Interview Notes

- New job (fairly secure) at advertising agency, $22,000 per year, 9–5 work
- Up to $20,000 to invest (borrowed)
- Wants to amass a fortune (quickly!)
- Thinks he can buy with "nothing down"
- Renting apartment for $350 per month

- Does not need cash flow for living; would settle for break-even cash flow
- Tax benefits secondary at this point (in his mind)
- Co-owner of remodelng company while in school; very handy mechanically
- Capable of management
- Investment goals: Simply wants to get started. Will buy anything at this point.

Points of Discussion

After talking with Dennis Smith, the broker has the following to consider about his potential client.

- Need to temper enthusiasm to keep from buying properties with unsolvable problems
- $20,000 is borrowed capital; repayment strategy?
- Purchase property in need of minor repair below market value
- Multifamily property with apartment for owner; two units or larger?
- Borrow funds with co-signer to establish credit; partnership with father on larger purchase?
- Deposit some funds in account for liquidity
- Management of property by owner; rent savings to go toward repayment of down payment or savings for next purchase
- Older, run-down residential property with strong cash flow, heavy management and low cost; continue renting apartment for living quarters
- Highly leveraged property might yield enough tax savings to offset entire tax liability from personal income
- No negative cash flow
- A break-even cash flow residential property with appreciation potential might meet Dennis' goals; if he chooses to be an owner occupant so much the better
- Single family home for rental bought under the right terms could be a good start

What Actually Happened

Dennis was very difficult to control since it seemed like he wanted to buy every run-down property in town. After two weeks of intensive searching, the broker found a four-unit apartment house that was in need of repair but was located in an established rental area of town. The apartments had been converted from a large home; all together, there were more than 20 rooms.

The purchase price was $52,000 and only an $8000 down payment was required. The remainder of Dennis' credit line was left open in case cash was needed for remodeling.

Dennis has upgraded one apartment at a time. As each apartment was remodeled, the rents were increased substantially and the overall cash flow is now over $250 per month. Dennis is currently moving into the largest unit, and the broker is looking for another similar project since Dennis has just paid off his original $13,000 note which represented his down payment plus remodeling costs.

Young Rising Executive

Jody McKay is a 30-year-old salesperson with a small corporation involved in retail sales. She had been asked to take a management position, but originally declined because of the independence sales offers her. She is very successful and averages between $50,000 and $60,000 in income per year. The president of her firm has personally asked her to reconsider the management offer and it appears now she will accept. She has $30,000 in savings she could invest in real estate.

Interview Notes

- No real estate other than personal condominium
- Single, no dependents
- Living income is sufficient
- Income has been climbing steadily for last five years
- Management position offers $50,000 salary plus overrides; could approach $75,000 per year
- Usually pays $15,000–$16,000 in income taxes per year
- No retirement fund at company
- Enjoys extensive travel and recreation
- Cash currently in money market fund
- No management experience but willing to try; time somewhat limited
- Sharp individual who will undoubtedly do very well in chosen field
  Note: Talk to her about getting into commercial-investment real estate.

Points of Discussion

- Condominium for rental
- Speculation on house in new subdivision
- Suggest hiring management
- Hold back some of $30,000 for liquidity—i.e., travel, recreation?
- Show after-tax effect of money market fund
- Lean toward professionally managed residential property
- Tax savings needed
- Income appears to be on rise; work through straight line cost recovery as well as accelerated
- Partnership unit of a project?
- Small commercial property for first purchase?
- Future liquidity could be needed for possible purchase of company interest
- Possible ideal partner for investments, depending on personality

Jody is obviously a person on the rise in her organization. Time is her greatest asset. Management-free partnerships might be ideal. The return must be better than the current money market fund and some liquidity should be available for other opportunities that might arise.

What Actually Happened

After physically viewing a couple of condominium projects, Jody decided to invest $20,000 in a limited partnership involved in renovating a small downtown office building. Jody received 10 percent interest in the property for her investment. The first year of ownership will yield $7000 in taxable loss plus over $4000 in investment tax credit. The $7000 taxable loss will continue for a few more years. The Cash Flow Before Tax has been minimal, but the building is still carrying a 20 percent vacancy factor. The partnership projects a sale in Year 10 of ownership.

With this project doing so well, Jody has decided to concentrate on tax-oriented partnerships for her portfolio and to avoid smaller projects that she might own by herself. She now uses IRR as a comparison tool to measure her real estate investments against the current money market rate.

Level Income Couple

Brad and Bonnie Norcia are a 42-year-old couple. He is a blue collar worker and she is a nurse. They have three children, ages 15, 12 and 8. Bonnie is involved in the investment decisions of the family. Brad's job is secure and will probably not change until retirement. His salary is $25,000; Bonnie earns $15,000. They own their home outright, having paid off their mortgage early. They have $20,000 in savings and will receive $75,000 after tax from Brad's father's estate.

Interview Notes

- *No* deductions on tax return
- Have never paid less than $6000 in income tax in last six years
- Concern about college funds for youngsters
- Conservative couple; pride of ownership for sure
- Want real estate to supplement retirement income
- $20,000 is in certificate of deposit; considering putting $75,000 in C.D. also
- Management and maintenance capabilities
- Do not want management "headaches"
- Have been paying taxes of $6000 and saving $9000 per year from Bonnie's income

Mr. and Mrs. Norcia are very conservative and have never in their marriage had as much money as they do now. They do feel they should invest their inheritance so the entire family can benefit from the cash. They are not even considering spending any of it initially on material goods. Pride of ownership is evidenced by the condition of their personal residence. The return on their C.D. will probably be their comparison barometer. Liquidity and tax savings will also be a concern of the Norcias.

Points of Discussion

- Determine cash needed for college fund, including savings for next few years
- Quality real estate even if low cash flow, such as apartment (three or four units)
- Small office building or retail store—permit Norcias to maintain exterior

Figure 8–1

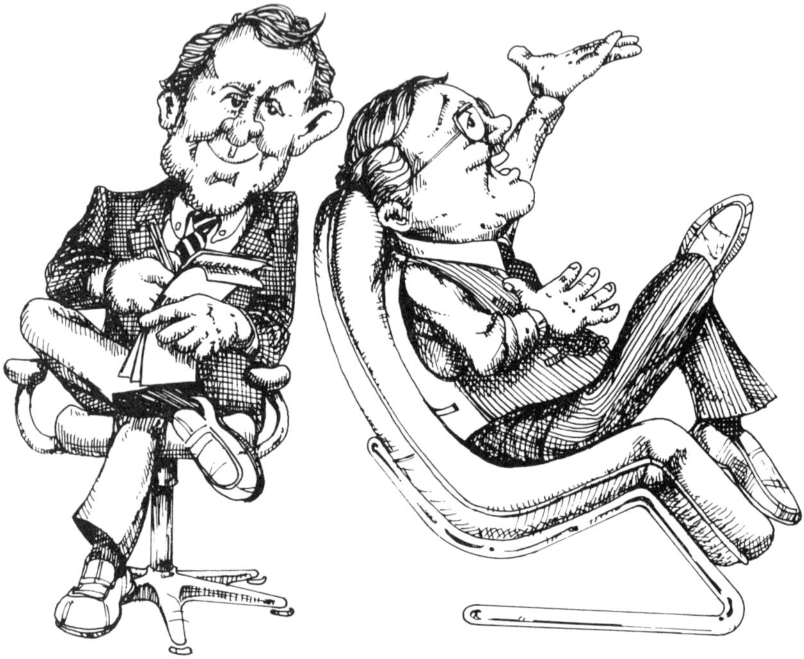

The broker must listen carefully to people's goals and objectives and must be sensitive to their feelings.

- Use IRR as after-tax comparison to savings account
- Low risk investment
- Limit down payment requirement to possibly $50,000
- Could in-laws use apartment housing instead of current single family home?
- Condominium in vacation area for eventual retirement?
- Management and maintenance: a family project!
- Explain capital gain on sale at later date
- Tax savings could enable Norcias to save more of Mrs. Norcia's income
- After mortgage is paid, cash flow will be generated for retirement

What Actually Happened

The Norcias looked for property for over three months before finally deciding on their investment vehicle. They viewed quality apartment units in both large and small projects. They even looked at a condominium on the beach in Florida.

They finally purchased a five-year-old brick building leased to a union's credit union. The union has signed a 20-year lease with increases built in every three years. The Norcias maintain the exterior, parking area and the yard, but the union handles everything inside.

Owner financing was utilized which consequently increased the projected IRR to over 18 percent after tax. The rental increases were projected at 10 percent every three years, and the building was projected to be sold at the same price as it was purchased. The purchase price of the building was $210,000, with a $55,000 down payment required. The mortgage will fully amortize in 15 years.

Middle Management White Collar Worker

Earl Williams is a 50-year-old engineer at an electronics production plant. He and his wife, Carol, have two children, both grown and on their own. Earl does not anticipate retirement until the age of 65 even though he is eligible in seven more years. His income is $55,000 per year plus benefits. The mortgage on the Williams' home was paid off two years ago. The Williams own a duplex (two-units) apartment building worth approximately $80,000. The mortgage is under $30,000 since they have owned the property for nine years. Although the duplex will be paid off in another ten years, Williams is concerned about retirement income. He has plenty of extra time on his hands even now with a part time business of antique furniture dealing.

Interview Notes

- $100,000 certificate of deposit is Williams' entire investment for the future
- Williams enjoys antique furniture business; will be full time after retirement
- Furniture business deductions have kept tax liability to a minimum
- Duplex managed personally, Williams enjoys personal contact with tenants
- Cash flow oriented, not tax benefits
- Would refinance duplex for $25,000–$30,000 extra cash; will not refinance personal residence
- Will not deplete savings below $50,000 unless it's an "exceptional deal"

- Goal is to retire with $25,000 to $30,000 income per year; personal retirement programs will yield $15,000 per year
- Can some of their cash today create $10,000 to $15,000 income per year after retirement?

Williams is too close to retirement to take much risk or to buy with hopes of tremendous appreciation in a selected project. By his nature he is conservative and yet he has seen the benefits of real estate at work in the duplex rental property. The strategy to create retirement income may lie partly in providing a place for his antique business. (Decisions are not always based purely on economics.)

Points of Discussion

- Desired cash flow will require strong down payment
- Cash on cash return after tax to compare to CD rate (after tax)
- Amount of retirement income generated with and without refinance of duplex?
- Small commercial strip with storeroom for antique store?
- Exchange equity in duplex for strip center?
- Refinance or sell duplex for extra cash to buy strip center?
- Owner management for commercial strip center?
- Early retirement to open antique business?
- Keep part of CD for security?

What Actually Happened

Williams found an ideal location for his furniture business in a small strip center. Without the help of a broker, his accountant and attorney structured an exchange of Williams' two-unit building for the strip center. The center's value was set at $365,000 and the two-unit was valued at $75,000. Williams added $55,000 in cash to his equity in the two-unit ($45,000) to provide a total of $100,000 cash down for the center.

The center's mortgage is $265,000, and the lender increased the rate from 10.5 percent to 13.25 percent interest. Williams is now operating his furniture store from his strip center and enjoying a small cash flow because of the amount of cash put into the transaction.

This is an example of lack of follow-up on the part of the broker. It was the broker who had first brought up the idea of an exchange, but he felt that Williams was too conservative to go forward. Once Williams found suitable space for his business, however, he simply asked if the owner would be interested in selling the shopping center. When the owner agreed to sell, the exchange became almost second nature, since Williams now knew (from the real estate broker) that an exchange would reduce his tax liability. This is just one of many examples of a real estate broker educating a client without compensation for his expertise or structuring ability. The broker should have followed up with Williams and discovered his true feelings about an exchange once he understood the advantages.

The Established Physician

Dr. Tom Louis is a 45-year-old cardiologist. He has a well established practice, two children at home, a son in college and an annual income of $200,000 to $300,000. He has a very hectic schedule and refers all investment strategy to his accountant who seemingly makes all investment decisions for him. Dr. Louis' involvement is limited to the initial overview of a potential investment. If the project warrants investigation, the accountant takes control of all decisions. Dr. Louis currently owns a 20-unit apartment project, a partnership unit of a piece of development land and a vacation home on the beach.

Interview Notes

- Dr. Louis is in the 50 percent tax bracket
- Quality projects are a must
- Tax benefits are foremost in accountant's mind
- Accountant does not respect brokers
- No negative cash flow! Land partnership has been a drain on doctor's patience and checkbook; initial wild projections by general partner have led doctor to believe land is too speculative for his portfolio
- Accountant is *very* protective of doctor's financial information
- Professional management needed
- Liquidity of invested capital not important
- Property does not have to be local
- Has owned apartments for seven years; low interest mortgage but has $150,000 to $200,000 equity position in project
- Doctor is opposed to selling; likes to hold real estate, quote, "I do not sell"
- Doctor will judge property on merits of physical attributes and Cash Flow Before Tax

- Has $150,000 cash in CD available for investment; has open credit lines of another $100,000 if needed

Dr. Louis is a client who could easily benefit from the services of a professional investment broker. His income needs to be sheltered from taxes and he has the down payment available for a purchase. The biggest obstacle seems to be that the accountant acts as if all real estate people are sharks ready to attack helpless clients. The land partnership has not worked as represented by the general partner, causing the doctor to be skeptical of all promoters who approach him with investment opportunities. A level of trust needs to be built one step at a time with both the doctor and the accountant.

Points of Discussion

- College fund for children?
- Investment goals, long range, short term
- Ask accountant *his* opinion of ACRS as opposed to straight line cost recovery
- Discuss doctor's posture on risk
- Use IRR as comparative tool
- Income will probably continue at current level or higher
- Refinance, sale or exchange of apartments to utilize additional capital
- Stay with income-producing property
- Limited partnership units?
- Partnership with other doctors to enable exposure to larger properties?
- Constantly ask accountant his opinion of certain tax strategies
- Office building for doctor's practice?
- Apartment units to provide more cost recovery?
- Down payment of $250,000 to enable larger purchase? Line of credit serviced by personal income
- Break-even Cash Flow Before Tax and tax benefits from ACRS if possible seem to fit doctor's needs at the time; appreciation not as important as eliminating high tax liability every year

What Actually Happened

After the broker had two meetings with Dr. Louis, all communication was directed to his accountant.

The owner of the building that houses Dr. Louis' office was approached as to his interest in selling the office building. The accountant helped structure the purchase from the beginning and seemed to be very impressed with the service provided by the real estate broker.

The sale price of the building was $950,000, requiring a $175,000 down payment. The balance was financed by the seller at 12 percent interest. A first-year after-tax return of over 22 percent was projected based on the current rent schedule. Property managers project that a before-tax break-even cash flow will take two years. The property is an attractive building and Dr. Louis seems very satisfied with the benefits it provides at this time.

The accountant and the broker are currently working on a way to help Dr. Louis take advantage of his $200,000 equity position in the apartment project.

It is very difficult to spend time with physicians since their time is valuable. But, since the medical profession is an excellent source of clientele, a job well done for one physician will provide other clients because medical people interact on a daily basis. Income tax is a subject often discussed in medical circles, but many times these professionals are so busy with their patients that they tend not to pay close enough attention to their investment portfolios.

Physicians will often use legal and accounting professionals to structure a portfolio of investments for them. The approach can be particularly challenging to the broker who has never encountered the "team approach" to investment decisions. One needs to proceed with caution, bearing in mind that providing truly professional service to clientele is the fastest and best way to build a foundation of trust and confidence.

The Professional Athlete

Jeffrey Douglas is a 27-year-old professional baseball player. After three years in the minor leagues, he finally broke into the majors with a salary that can support his family in a comfortable style. Having just been traded, he has been blessed with a $200,000 per year salary plus $15,000 playoff pay if the team continues to play at its current pace. His family includes two children, ages two and four. Jeff does not own any real estate since the family has moved many times during his young baseball career. He has no investment program because his salary in the minor leagues was less than $12,000 per year. He is very excited about his contract but, as a catcher, knows that his health and batting average are the keys to his financial well-being.

Jeffrey has deferred $25,000 of his income into a retirement program and has a three-year contract for $200,000 per year. He would like to use some of his new-found wealth as a start into the investment field and hopes that real estate can help him defer the tax bite he anticipates.

Interview Notes

- Three-year contract at $200,000 per year
- Tax problems for the first time—ever
- Anticipates needing $75,000 of first year salary to live a comfortable lifestyle
- Will invest $75,000 first year if needed
- Would like to buy a home for family
- Phone has been ringing constantly with callers offering "investment opportunities"
- Travels eight months out of year
- Wants tax shelter portfolio now, but is concerned about only playing for another six to seven years
- Is enjoying cash almost to the point of being wasteful
- $25,000 contribution per year to a retirement program
- Salary could skyrocket if he continues to perform
- Agent who negotiated contract wants to handle all funds for Jeffrey

Some professional athletes have a very interesting earning curve. While they are rookies their salaries are very low; then suddenly they may sign a six-figure contract for three to five years. The income may then be substantial, but it usually falls dramatically when a career ends at the ripe old age of 35.

Many athletes have devoted their entire energies toward making a "team" and have sacrificed all finances to get there. When a contract is signed the money is sometimes like a pot of gold. One ballplayer signed a $125,000 per year contract, went out and bought matching Mercedes for himself and his wife and then had to get a $50,000 loan to pay his monthly living obligations.

The athlete's financial position is very sensitive and must be well planned and somewhat conservative. Many times an agent will handle the entire investment account and will not want his client to "risk" investing in anything other than certificates. Since most agents are paid on a percentage of the gross earned, they are not all as cooperative as one might hope. Their job is usually to negotiate contracts—not to be concerned with the long-term strategy. A delicate balance of investments to help defer taxes may be needed now, but the strategy must be considered short term until the time when the athlete retires from his professional career.

Points of Discussion

- Is purchase of a home important?
- Resort condominium for off-season?
- Needs accelerated cost recovery now!
- Recapture implications after retirement not prohibitive *unless* done in year of high salary
- Cash reserves for retirement?
- Delayed salary from club owner?
- Partnership structure with tax benefits going to J. Douglas
- Joint meetings with Jeff's agent if he is involved in decisions
- Property could be located anywhere in United States
- Invest cash now to receive benefits at a later date when taxed at capital gains (converting ordinary income to capital gains through real estate investment)
- Down payment to be funded over a couple of years
- Strong down payment to guard against heavy negative cash flow
- Avoid negative cash flows in case career ends early
- First-year investment could be one that may not totally solve tax problem; it may, however, leave some cash reserves this first year to enjoy (regardless of tax payment)

Jeffrey Douglas can be helped through real estate and will eventually be a good client. The important point at this time is to move slowly in creating his portfolio so that it gives him a chance to enjoy his current income and provide an income for the future. That future income may come from the sale of his portfolio a piece at a time after retirement or from accumulating enough cash-yielding investments to provide cash flow strong enough for living expenses supplemented by a new career.

What Actually Happened

Jeffrey joined the broker in the purchase of a 48-unit apartment project. The purchase price was $1,300,000, with the owners carrying financing for ten years. The owners guaranteed a gross income for the first two years of ownership. The down payment was $130,000 with the broker leaving his fee in the transaction as his cash contribution. Management has been hired and the property is operating as expected.

Jeff has also bought a home for his family and has set a strategy of buying one or two investment properties per year to help build a retirement program for himself. He likes small partnerships because of his travel schedule and he likes the security of having the broker as a partner. In this case the broker has become Jeff's exclusive agent for real estate and is now talking to other ballplayers through Jeff to establish similar relationships.

The Retirees

Karl and Jane Reginald are just two years away from retirement. They are very active both mentally and physically and intend to stay in their home. Karl wants to continue to be productive but hopes to use their $85,000 savings account to buy a piece of property to occupy his time in retirement. They want to travel and enjoy their freedom following retirement but feel real estate could supplement their monthly retirement income.

Interview Notes

- $85,000 cash in short-term deposits
- One child, only heir
- House value: $120,000, no mortgage—large home
- Not comfortable with debt but would accept owner financing
- Want additional $1000 to $1500 per month income after retirement (above retirement income)
- Karl enjoys light maintenance work
- Want to travel, so minimal management needed
- Very security minded, low risk
- Want growth area location
- Not interested in partnership
- Will leave real estate to son

Karl and Jane have done well financially over the years. They live in a comfortable home, have cash in the bank and are simply trying to supplement their income after retirement. Their home is large beyond their needs and represents most of their net worth. Karl would like a piece of real estate to give himself a job more than he wants financial rewards. They do not appear to be interested in long-term growth although quality construction came up in the conversation more than once.

Points of Discussion

- Keep $45,000 in term deposits for security and cash
- Sell home to son for extra cash and pay rent to son to cover mortgage payment
- Contact local lender regarding "reverse amortization" mortgage with Reginalds getting monthly payments from house mortgage
- Residential rentals with $40,000 down, low mortgage will help provide cash flow
- Sell house, buy luxury duplex for live-in plus rental
- Using owner financing, buy two or three single family homes
- Small office building with long-term lease; maintain exterior

What Actually Happened

The Reginalds have yet to buy an investment property. It seems as though they cannot make the decision to purchase a piece of real estate. They have looked at a number of projects, but always seem to shy away when the conversation turns to financing. It may just be that they never will find the right project to motivate them sufficiently to overcome their fear of debt.

The Syndicator

Dick and Norman Worthy have been supplying their clients with real estate products for years. They currently own 27 different projects through limited partnerships. They typically play a general partner role and keep 10 percent ownership. They own their own management company and try to provide professional service to the projects and the investors. They called the broker on an advertised property and do not seem to have an exclusive relationship with any other broker.

Interview Notes

- Dick and Norman are conservative investors
- Typical projects sell to one of two types of investors: tax oriented or cash flow oriented
- No balloon payments closer than ten years

- Tax-oriented transaction must be at least break-even; cash flow must provide cash on cash of at least 5 to 9 percent depending on type of project
- Need Cash Flow After Tax of at least 15 to 17 percent first year
- Apartment projects should be government backed
- Use IRR, but project future sales price same as purchase price
- Like shopping centers
- Maximum down payment typically $600,000 to $700,000; like split funding (two or more payments over a few tax years)
- Like owner to guarantee cash flow for year or so
- Will invest only east of Mississippi and especially in Southeast
- Must include reserves in cash flow projections
- Want detailed information packet on property

Dick and Norman are active buyers who are intelligent, thorough and professional in their approach to buying real estate. They must provide leverage and financing to their clientele. They must also buy just below market conditions so they can afford to keep a portion of the transaction and still pass on favorable benefits to their investors. They use IRR and cash on cash returns to compare the properties to other opportunities available to them. They have not established a broker relationship because most brokers have not understood their buying techniques. Their questions are so detailed that most brokers are intimidated by their knowledge of the product.

Points of Discussion

- Need detailed demographic material on any specific project
- Need past rental history on specific project
- Avoid properties that are not income producing
- Owner financing of split-fund down payment
- Income and expense data must be actual, not projected
- Will ACRS be used?
- Provide IRR projections based on level sale price
- Point out management problems
- Rents must have some "upside potential" (potential for increase)

What Actually Happened

The Worthys bought a 90,000 square-foot shopping center in the Southeast. The purchase price was $4,100,000 with a $1,000,000 down payment. The down payment is scheduled over a three-year period with $500,000 paid at closing. The first year cash on cash is 13 percent with the after-tax cash on cash to a 50-percent-bracket investor being over 24 percent.

A thorough investigation of the income and expenses was done before an initial offer was made on this property. Long-term financing of ten years or more was a major consideration in the transaction. A computer program was used to project a sale from Years 3 to 10 of the ownership period. The after-tax IRR ranged from 19 to 25 percent.

The rental income of the center is at market rates, but the local tenants of the center have short-term leases, so rent increases may be possible. Major tenants account for 45 percent of the gross rental income.

Because of the split funding on the down payment, an FMRR was used to show the true effect of the delayed down payment. Using a safe rate and a reinvestment rate of 6 percent, this analysis showed a slightly lower return than a straight IRR. All projections were done using a future sales price of $4,500,000.

Investor Ingenuity

Try as we may to meet our clients' needs, sometimes they satisfy their own investment objectives without the services of a broker. The following illustrates an interesting problem solved by the ingenuity and creativity of two investors.

Clients

Robert Farnsworth owns four real estate projects which yield inconsistent Cash Flows Before Tax. The properties were terrific as tax-oriented transactions as long as Robert owned a printing company and received a $60,000 per year salary.

In early retirement he sold his company for very little cash down and a monthly payment of $3000 for the next 20 years. His goal was to create $4000 per month in the form of cash payments.

As the owner of a small shopping strip, he had watched his equity position grow to approximately $100,000 and still not yield much besides tax benefits. No longer needing tax benefits, Robert set out to sell the shopping center for $100,000 cash down and assumption of the current note.

This cash would provide Robert and his wife retirement security and could be put in a certificate for at least a 13 percent yield. Robert did not really need the cash, only the return that the $100,000 could produce.

Enter Dick and Janet Shapiro as potential buyers. Dick is making $50,000 per year with a large corporation and is rapidly climbing the corporate ladder. The young Shapiros need the tax benefits the shopping strip can yield, but they do not have $100,000 in cash for the purchase. They could absorb $12,000 per year maximum in negative cash flow if needed.

Problem

How can the tax benefits be transferred from seller to buyer and still meet the objectives of both?

Solution

- Property transfers to buyer without down payment
- Seller holds second mortgage on property as security for $100,000 note (down payment)
- Buyer pays seller interest only on $100,000 at rate of Chase Manhattan prime adjusted every quarter
- Rate cannot go below 11 percent or above 18 percent (protection for both seller and buyer)
- Seller gets cash of $1000 to $1500 per month secured by real estate for tax benefits he no longer can use
- Buyer gets $400,000 center without any upfront cash; negative cash flow easily serviced by personal income, and tax benefits reduce personal tax liability
- $100,000 has no call date, but note could easily be sold if seller needed cash
- Buyer has permanent financing forever if he wants it!

The after-tax implications were certainly ignored in the preceding description, but Farnsworth had his accountant view the transaction before consummation and he found it to be very favorable for his tax posture.

Although this unique situation matched perfectly, we as investment brokers must constantly be aware of the needs of our clientele. Never let it be said that the real estate broker "sells real estate for a living." We are only problem solvers and it so happens that many times real estate provides the solutions to problems.

9

FINDING AND SERVICING CLIENTELE

A fear of salespeople new to the investment field is that they will not be able to find clients qualified to buy or sell investment real estate. A newly trained salesperson comes to his sales manager and asks, "Now that I have all this knowledge, what do I do to get face to face with a client?"

Numerous opportunities are available to the active salesperson or broker to contact clients if he thinks, breathes, eats, sleeps and studies real estate. Buyers and sellers of investment real estate are usually not encountered on a one-time basis. The key is to be in constant contact with people who are involved in the investment field.

Deciding Who To Work With

Once a potential client has been found, the broker must decide if the client has the necessary capital, attitude and motivation to invest. If the client lacks any of these, a broker may find himself educating the client about investment real estate for free. Provide service, certainly, but only if the client is a qualified one, capable of decisive action. There are a number of questions that need to be answered before you can identify a client capable of action:

1. Will the client come to your office to meet with you? If possible, have the client come to your office where you can have his complete attention. A professional atmosphere with prominently displayed photos of past transactions can subtly convince the client that you are an active, successful professional in the real estate business.

2. Is the client cooperative during the interviewing process? Does he understand that the more you know about the situation the easier it will be for you to help him? Probe for objectives, expectations and goals by gathering facts. The client should understand that simply looking at property is like a doctor starting surgery without first asking the patient, "Where does it hurt?"

3. Will the client disclose how much cash he can invest? Avoid the words "cash" or "how much do you have?" Concentrate on talking about "initial investment" or "capital to invest." Make sure you know how much is available and the source of the income.

4. Are the client's expectations of the market realistic? An investor who has been away from market activity for a while may not understand the prices, terms or financing vehicles of the present market.

5. Is the client prepared to inspect property that appears to satisfy his needs? If the investor delays the decision process, you might consider asking a few more questions about the client's capital resources. Many times a client will be embarrassed to tell you his true abilities or needs.

6. After inspecting a number of properties, does the client make an offer? If the client is properly qualified and sincerely motivated, he will probably at least express an interest in negotiating price or terms of a particular property that appears to meet his needs. If no activity is generated, it might be time to ask the client if his objectives have changed since your initial interview. Possibly you have misinterpreted his needs and a realignment is in order.

7. After writing an offer, does he stay interested if a counteroffer is presented? Human nature usually dictates that some negotiating must take place in real estate transactions. Price is not always the object of compromise. Terms or conditions are often more important than the overall price. A client who states his "*first* offer is the *last* offer" may not be as motivated to buy as he might have us believe.

Traits of a Successful Salesperson

The successful real estate salesperson succeeds not because he is a good salesperson, but because he has developed success strategies and habits which help him provide a service in the area of real estate marketing. Typically, in the real estate industry, anyone providing better than mediocre service is looked upon as a superstar. It is easy to rise above competitors when mediocrity is the measure of the day. The following is a compilation of the advice that good salespeople most frequently give when asked what makes them successful in the investment real estate sales field. Not all the salespeople follow all the points listed, but the general advice, principles and observations vary little from one to another. Some points relate directly to attitude and professionalism while others are isolated closing techniques.

Enjoy Selling

If you do not enjoy selling, real estate will be a constant struggle. Good salespeople are constantly selling. When they are not selling real estate, they are selling ideas, hobbies or a new diet. They tend to be enthusiastic about everything they find rewarding. If you do not enjoy the confrontation of sales, you will probably never achieve the success you personally desire.

Gain the Respect of Others Through Professionalism

You do not get a second chance to make a first impression:

- Look and dress like a success. There are successful people who dress like bums, but there are very few bums who dress like successes. Note the dress of the successful people in your community. A professional appearance carries a strong command of presence.
- Be active in community affairs; the contacts are valuable and the exposure is good for leads.
- People judge you by the company you keep. If your friends are successful, it will be assumed you are also.
- Take care of your physical being. Good salespeople often eat, smoke and drink too much and get little sleep because of their high energy levels. For most of us the better physical shape we are in, the sharper we are, the faster we react and the more we enjoy life. If a physical activity is not a part of your life, start one. Prospects prefer to deal with healthy, attractive, successful people.
- Be courteous at all times.
- Never be condescending about anyone—especially a competitor. Either find something complimentary to say or do not comment at all.
- Talk concisely and clearly—eliminate words like "yep," "you know," "OK" from your dialogue. There is no such word as "irregardless." Avoid "let me be honest with you."
- Know your product and its benefits in depth.
- Never lose your cool with a client or his representative.
- Keep current through education, professional designations and investigation of new ideas.
- Always make a quality presentation regardless of your attitude.
- Do not be a comedian. It has no place in business and doesn't impress anyone.
- Be proud of your chosen field of work.

- Never blame a problem on an individual. Always state and isolate the problem with a solution in mind.
- Value your time and your client's time. Be punctual! If you are going to be late, call and advise the client of the delay. If a client keeps you waiting, wait a reasonable time and then excuse yourself. Tell him that another meeting can be arranged when his schedule permits. Maintain a positive attitude in this situation.
- Maintain integrity and unquestionable ethical and moral standards at all costs.
- Develop a high degree of tact and diplomacy.
- Be self confident but not arrogant or overbearing.

Create Successful Personal Sales Techniques

- Be yourself in a sales situation. Use your sales strengths and play down your weaknesses, i.e., phone prospecting versus door knocking, financial presentations versus property showings.
- Make a 9 a.m. appointment every day. It forces you out of the office and into the field.
- Be an action person. Never delay what you need to do today.
- View objections as buying signals and propose solutions to the problems.
- Act successful. Drive an expensive car with a phone if warranted. One transaction will pay the extra cost.
- Present personalized presentations with the client's name in bold print.
- Attempt to close the sale whenever it "feels" right. Do not wait for a special moment.
- Use the word "we" instead of "you" or "I" in sales situations. Make "I" the least important word in your vocabulary.
- Remember that the client is a person with personal likes and dislikes. Show interest in more than just his bank account.
- Be flexible, almost agile, in your sales presentations.
- Guard your time as if it were money, because it is.
- Avoid long coffee breaks and lunch breaks. Have lunch with clients instead of associates. If you do not have an appointment, call a past client and treat him to lunch. This way you can maintain contact without a sales pitch.

- Arrange appointments early in the day before clients' schedules fill.
- Do your bookwork and reading in off hours.
- Don't revel in the last sale. Immediately work on the next one.
- Constantly think about converting wasted time into productive time.
- Use questioning in your presentations to probe for clients' objectives.
- Never use the phrase "I sold them that property." Most clients are uncomfortable with being "sold" something. "I assisted them," "I worked with them," "I was involved in that transaction with them" are much more palatable.
- Regardless of what you may have read, intimidation of the client may end in short-term victory, but very seldom does it provide a lasting business relationship.
- Maintain contact with clients even if the report is "no activity" to report.
- Be persistent in your sales attitude but do not offend the client. Maintain a positive attitude and view a rejection as a running start to an opportunity to prove your ability the next day.
- Take time from the sales schedule to enjoy the fruits of your labor. Family, friends and activities soon pass the workaholic by. Do not be afraid to pursue pleasure in your life.

Working with Other Professionals

Lawyers

One of the most frustrating experiences a broker can encounter is the confrontation with a lawyer over the legal aspects of a transaction. Most lawyers do an excellent job representing their clients legally, but occasionally they have a tendency to get involved in the business decisions after the fact. This tendency is what has prompted many brokers to suggest that lawyers get real estate licenses "so they can blow their own deals."

Most such confrontations are partially the fault of the broker who storms in with a contract from "his" client and wants it approved immediately because the closing is scheduled the day after tomorrow. What's a lawyer to do? After all, he is being paid to protect "his" client. (Whose client is it anyhow?)

Compare the following conversations:

Conversation I

BROKER:
Yeah, Mr. Davis. Are you Dr. Martin's attorney? This is Jim Pushy, Dr. Martin's broker—OK, well we are closing tomorrow afternoon on some apartments I sold Dr. Martin and he wants you to check over the legal work. Why don't you call the seller's attorney and get it worked out for my client Dr. Martin. The closing is scheduled for 3 p.m. so you don't have much time.

ATTORNEY DAVIS:
What apartments did Dr. Martin buy?

BROKER PUSHY:
I sold him a 40-unit on Riverside Drive.

ATTORNEY DAVIS:
That's not a very good location, is it?

BROKER PUSHY:
It's OK considering the price; the location doesn't really matter. Listen, I just need to get that legal work done, OK.

Possibly a bit overdone, but you get the picture. The legal work will never get done. In fact, it's doubtful the transaction will ever close regardless of how much the doctor needs the property. The broker and lawyer are immediately in adversary positions. Let's try again.

Conversation II

BROKER PUSHY:
Mr. Davis? This is Jim Pushy. Dr. Martin suggested I call you. I am a real estate broker and I just met with Dr. Martin who wants us to find him an investment property. He told me that you are his legal counsel so I thought that I might call and ask for your thoughts concerning his investment purchase.

ATTORNEY DAVIS:
I appreciate your calling, but specifically what do you want?

BROKER PUSHY:
Sir, I was hoping you might have time to review the purchase agreement format before Dr. Martin finds a property. We find that clients are much more confortable if their lawyers have reviewed the purchase documents *before* a purchase rather than after the fact. We also hoped you would give some thought to secondary financing documents since just about

every transaction we have been involved in recently has had some form of secondary owner financing. If I dropped a few examples at your office, would you have time in the next week or so to review them for Dr. Martin? That way, if we do find a property, Dr. Martin will at least be protected by your legal review.

ATTORNEY DAVIS:
Drop the documents at my office this afternoon and I'll take a look and call Dr. Martin. By the way, how is the market today? Is it a buyer's market?

BROKER PUSHY:
The market has been very active so it's really necessary to be able to move fast when an opportunity presents itself. If you cannot reach Dr. Martin, feel free to call me with any information. I am looking forward to working with you on this for Dr. Martin. He speaks very highly of your legal expertise. He was well satisfied with your representation on his other investment acquisitions.

ATTORNEY DAVIS:
Yes, we have been working together for a long time. Listen, why don't you stop in when you bring those documents this afternoon and we can chat a moment.

Quite a difference! Jim Pushy realizes in Conversation II that a teamwork approach is necessary to provide a service for Dr. Martin. Many times a lawyer is put in a position of either approving all documents immediately or delaying the transaction. If the client does not complete the transaction, the lawyer cannot go wrong since it's impossible for him to make a mistake. Ask the lawyer for his legal input initially and you will be surprised at how much of a team player he suddenly becomes.

Accountants

Communication with a client's accountant should always be solicitation for help in determining the after-tax benefits for the client. The accountant's guidance should be sought early in the search for the property.

Your knowledge of the tax laws should be used to help ask intelligent questions of the accountant about the client's tax position. These questions will help establish credibility because, rest assured, the accountant is not accustomed to real estate "people" paying any attention to his tax opinion as it pertains to his client. Be sure the accountant knows that your job is to find a piece of property which meets the needs of the client through the guidance of his tax advisor. And be sure the accountant understands that he is in complete control of all tax decisions as far as you are concerned. Avoid giving tax advice at all cost. Look to the client for business decisions, but help coordinate those decisions with his tax advisor. The broker's role becomes one of subtle leadership to guide the efforts of both the attorney and the accountant.

Bankers

The attitude of some brokers when it comes to securing financing for a client is often amazing. It is almost as if the broker and the banker are opponents in a contest. If financing is secured the broker wins, if the loan is rejected the banker wins.

There are a number of thoughts that come to mind whenever this discussion arises:

- Bankers are in the lending business, *not* the rejecting business.
- Loan committees have good days and bad days. Why? Because they are people. They fight with their spouses, get traffic tickets, have car trouble and get chewed out by their bosses, any one of which could ruin your day, too.
- Lenders typically are *not* risk-takers. Don't ask them to be.
- Lenders are like baseball umpires. It is difficult to make a call against a cooperative, friendly ballplayer. Argue constantly on every call, expect the benefit of the doubt on every pitch, and scream violently when a call does go against you, and you will find that if it is even close, a "strike" will be called.
- Make the banker's job easy. Know the information needed to present to loan committees and provide it. Ask for a format that is to the bank's liking. Provide multiple copies with quality bound covers just oozing in professionalism.
- Don't intimidate a banker with your financial calculator technique. Buy him one for Christmas and then invite him to lunch to show him the fantastic capabilities of the machine. While you are at lunch, you might talk about the lending business in general and how your real estate company might help solve some of the bank's property foreclosure problems.
- Realize lending institutions move slowly on decisions. Do not rush the process.
- Keep your bankers abreast of recent sales. They like to know what the current activity is if for no other reason than to be ahead of the real estate gossip column.
- Publish their involvement when you publicize closed transactions.

Include the loan officer's name if permitted. You'll be surprised at the positive results in the community.

- Understand the bank's yield requirements and today's problems with long-term fixed financing.

By associating with bankers other than just from across a loan application, you will begin to see fewer and fewer rejections. Their jobs will become easier as you understand their perspective and requirements.

Other Brokers

Here are a few thoughts that are probably taken for granted by most brokers; nevertheless, they are worth mentioning.

- Treat all other brokers, regardless of their competence, with professional respect.
- Always cooperate with other brokers and outline your fee split in the initial conversation.
- Never withhold another broker's offer until one of your own arrives.
- Work only on properties that have a control factor such as an exclusive listing of your own or one under written agreement with another broker. (See example of cooperating broker agreement, Figure 9-1.)
- Carry your work load in the transaction, if not some of the cooperating broker's as well.

Personal Success Strategies

Action Idea Contact owners of apartment units and collect data for a survey of rents, expenses and tenant turnover in a particular area, township or county. Publish the results in a special newsletter prepared specifically for those owners. Call the owners and review results or ask if they have any questions pertaining to the apartment market survey. As the surveys are completed area by area, provide the owners with additional information concerning the rental market. How can any owner refuse to talk to you when you are simply providing a professional service to him which increases his knowledge of the market? From time to time provide the owners with an investment opportunity or a request from a buyer who needs a property "just like the one you own." Be professional in the survey or your requests, and the owners will eventually seek your services.

Action Idea Along the same lines, gather information on office space vacancies and provide the information in printed form back to the own-

Figure 9–1

TO: Cooperating Brokers

FROM: Fantastic Real Estate, Listing Broker

For Your Protection:

We are pleased to furnish you with information on ______________ ______________________________________. This is copyrighted material and cannot be reproduced without permission. It is given to you with the understanding that you will submit the information to qualified PRINCIPALS only. The fee for the selling office is ___% of the sales price or $___________ at the listed price and terms payable at closing.

This information is given to you with the further understanding that principals you submit the listing to will sign a copy of the form letter provided acknowledging receipt of the information from you. A copy of this receipt will be forwarded to the seller as registration, and IS THE ONLY TYPE OF REGISTRATION ACCEPTABLE.

If you are interested in marketing these properties on the above basis as a cooperating broker, please indicate your agreement by acknowledging same in the space provided below and return one copy of this letter to my office. Third party brokers will not be recognized.

Let us know if we can help you further.

ACCEPTED BY: ____________________
Cooperating Broker

Date ____________________ By ____________________

Return to: Company____________________

Fantastic Real Estate
123 Main Street
Small Town, U.S.A.

Address____________________

Telephone____________________

Figure 9–2

The successful professional recognizes and provides the service that clients need, want and are willing to pay for.

ers. The survey does not have to be a sophisticated computer printout. Personal contact with the owners is the goal.

Action Idea Compile a booklet of the shopping centers (large and small) in your town with the name of the center, location, size, parking spaces, owner's name (if approved), tenants, layout sketch and other comments about the area. Personally deliver the booklets to the Chamber of Commerce, shopping center owners and potential retail tenants. Be sure that your company name and phone number is prominently displayed.

Action Idea Direct mail is the best way to make consistent contact with potential clients. An up-to-date mailing list should be used including attorneys, accountants, bankers, physicians, past investors, specific property owners and anyone who has made contact with you concerning investment real estate. Follow the property transfers (by whatever means you can) and include everyone who is involved in a purchase or a sale. Remember, investors buy more than one property. A direct mail program must be consistent and professional.

An investment newsletter mailed quarterly with recent transactions, pictures of properties and people and an article on some facet of investing can produce unbelievable results. It is a good idea to have a piece of mail (flyer, newsletter or survey) in the hands of potential clients at least once a month. This constant exposure through direct mail has been found to be much more productive and less expensive than classified advertising.

Action Idea Establish yourself in the community as the expert in investment real estate. There are a number of ways to do this, but the following suggestions can be powerful when used together.

1 Get a professional designation such as CCIM, SIR, CPM, MAI, or SRS[1] and publicize it.

2 Teach an investment course at the local college.

3 Publish a free newsletter with an article on investing and other activity in the market.

4 Publish a regular column in the local paper about real estate investing. Call the newspaper publisher; he needs good copy (see the Appendix of this book for list of possible titles).

5 Call the local radio or TV station with the idea for a real estate question and answer show.

6 Publicize transactions with names, pictures and your role (locally and nationally if possible).

---

1. These are designations of REALTORS NATIONAL MARKETING INSTITUTE®, the Society of Industrial REALTORS®, the Institute of Real Estate Management, the American Institute of Real Estate Appraisers, and the Real Estate Securities and Syndication Institute, respectively.

7 Teach the investment course at the local real estate board.

8 Attend state and national meetings and come home to "report" to the press the real estate activity "on a national level."

9 Hold a free investment seminar and present facts about investing. Display pictures and flyers, but never once solicit listings or sales. Make clients want to do business with you instead of you chasing them. Maintain an impeccable professional attitude.

10 Call or write local service clubs and offer to do a half hour speech on real estate investing at their next meeting.

11 Call "for sale by owners" and "for lease by owners" to inquire about the property, price and terms. Make the call an information call and not a solicitation for a listing.

12 Make a presentation to the local builders' association on "Real Estate Cash Flows and New Construction."

13 Make a presentation to the local apartment owners' association on "Buyers' Parameters in Today's Market."

14 Promote yourself as a "problem solver" in the real estate industry. Always talk in terms of creating wealth for clients or building a larger portfolio.

15 Develop a professional brochure telling who you are as a company/individual and what you have done.

Action Idea Buy quality pens with extra thin points and black ink with CONGRATULATIONS and your company name printed on the pens. Send one to each business and community leader whose name appears in the newspaper. Remember how impressed you were the first time somebody sent you a note about an article you wrote or something else you achieved?

The pen must be a quality pen—maybe even $5 to $10 per pen. Send one a week; the exposure will more than pay for the pens. Send a copy of the newspaper article with the pen stating how impressive the article in the paper sounded.

Action Idea Watch TV for advertisers who are spending ad money in your coverage area but who do not currently have a store in the area. One could make a living providing sites for companies who are expanding their TV coverage faster than their site locations.

Action Idea Certainly clients will be generated from personal contacts, newspaper advertising and referrals, but to serve qualified clientele one needs to take consistent action on a daily basis. Keep a personal mailing list of all the clients you have generated through sales and listings. Use the mailing list to keep all your clients abreast of your activity in the business. Announcements of transactions, designations or recognitions should be consistently passed on to the clientele.

Back of an Envelope and a "T"

A Story

Broker Green presented a property to an insurance company last year for its real estate portfolio. The property had passed all checkpoints and had been inspected and analyzed until there was not a stone unturned. Broker Green was called before a three-person committee at the insurance company to answer a few questions before the final contract was drafted. Imagine his excitement; the insurance company had already expressed its approval of the five-page computer projection, the cash flows, the tax benefits, the financing structure, the IRRs, the FMRRs, the cap rates and the quality of the improvements. Broker Green had even provided detailed demographic studies to prove that the area was in a growth pattern just as the buyer's criteria list required.

Green was ecstatic over the fact that this five-million-dollar property was about to be put under contract by a seemingly default-proof purchaser. Just one more short approval meeting and he was home free! It was tempting to mentally start spending the commission!

As he entered the meeting with the acquisition board, little did Broker Green know that the committee had only one question they needed answered.

"Mr. Green, we appreciate the professional presentation you have made to our company regarding this property. It meets all of our qualifications and we are excited about the acquisition. Before we move forward, though, there is one question we need you to answer. In your professional opinion, on a scale of 1 to 10, how does this property rank?"

Broker Green was speechless; he had anticipated questions on IRRs over the holding period or space absorption into the market but not a scale of 1 to 10 rating.

"It's difficult to say, sir, but my opinion of this quality project is that it would certainly rate at least a 9. But, as I say, it's really tough to put a rating of that nature on a piece of real estate."

The committee members simultaneously pushed their chairs away from the table as the chairman explained, "We appreciate your presentations, but under no circumstances will this company buy a piece of property that in the opinion of a professional broker, which you obviously are, is anything less than a 10. We will get back to you. Thank you for your time.

Broker Green did everything right and lost the transaction through no fault of his own. It is important to remember that no matter how sophisticated the buyer may be, there are still emotional implications in buying real estate.

Once we as real estate professionals become educated, we feel we have to cram every client or prospect full of everything we know everytime a question is asked of us. If we want the client or prospect to have information, we could do it as simply as drawing a vertical "t" chart (see Chapter 5) on the back of an envelope and showing him the numbers accordingly. A simple presentation like this has sold many real estate projects over the years. In a sense, it's like a car salesman giving a five-minute speech on the ratios of rack and pinion with ball steering gear segment actuated by power assist, when all we asked was, "How does the car handle?"

If the decision process becomes too difficult, the prospect will seek a broker who makes the decision process easier. Somewhere between "it's a good deal" and ten pages full of computer numbers lies the information a particular prospect needs to make a decision.

We should never try to educate our clients in five minutes with all the information that it has taken a career for us to accumulate. There are times when it pays to be an intellect and there are other situations when we must play the role of a strong salesperson. The successful professional recognizes the difference and provides the service the client needs, wants and is willing to pay for.

Life is precious, so don't tiptoe through it with a lukewarm attitude. Find something you can do with enthusiastic passion . . . and do it.

APPENDIX

What kind of investment topics can I write about? What kind of questions about investing can I use for discussion purposes in our sales meetings? Are there case studies available that can help me understand investment real estate and its benefits? Are there case studies available that can give me ideas to help me generate more commissions?

APPENDIX

Newspaper Column

Following is a list of topics that can be utilized in the preparation of a regular newspaper column to help establish credibility for a local broker in the investment field.

- The condo conversion market
- What's the story on all this owner financing?
- Survey of local financing on past sales
- Is real estate still a good investment vehicle since the enactment of the tax law changes?
- Avoiding the due on sale clause in a mortgage can result in a catastrophe
- Ten mistakes to watch out for when investing in real estate
- How real estate value is diminished or created by financing
- The four benefits of real estate investments
- Five factors to evaluate in "Tax Shelters"
- The current opportunity in investment real estate
- Measuring return on investment
- Tax deferred exchange overview
- Why should I buy real estate when I can get 13 percent tax free in a certificate of deposit?
- The imputed interest law and owner financing
- Installment sale equals tax savings
- What is a lease purchase agreement?
- What is a shared appreciation mortgage?
- Save the sale—impasse over income tax?

- Save the sale—impasse over asking price?
- Save the sale—impasse over balloon payment date?
- Shock waves roll through real estate in the '80s
- Owners suddenly become lenders
- Mortgages in today's investment market
- Obtaining future commitments for development projects
- Condominiums as investments
- Apartments as investments
- Office buildings as investments
- Self-storage warehouses as investments
- Single family homes as investments
- Raw land as an investment
- Shopping centers as investments
- Be a partner with your investment broker
- How will real estate fare in an economic downturn?
- The best way to sell—open versus exclusive listing
- How to persuade owners to take back financing
- How to use the wraparound mortgage
- Does it pay to use accelerated cost recovery?
- The time value of money
- The Internal Rate of Return
- Rules of thumb used in real estate
- Myths about making money in real estate
- Nontraditional ways to raise money for real estate
- Real estate syndications
- Are you really investing for the bottom line?
- Finding a good property management firm
- Should you diversify out of real estate today?
- Why use a real estate broker?
- How long should you keep an investment property?
- Where's real estate headed?

- Why invest in your hometown?
- How to buy real estate at a discount
- How to buy real estate at an auction
- How to get high leverage through "split funding"
- Using the option in real estate
- What is a joint venture?
- Owner financing spurs real estate activity
- Profit in historic structures
- Income property expense checklist
- Vacancy is a blessing compared to a bad tenant
- Computer software and real estate investing
- Group investing—trend for the '80s

(Take special care to suggest that readers consult their attorneys or accountants for specific legal or tax advice.)

Questions and Case Studies in Investment Real Estate

The following case studies and questions can be used in a sales meeting for training or can be used by an individual to stimulate thought processes in the analysis of investment real estate. Case study answers have deliberately not been given so that the cases can provide material for discussion and probing among investment real estate practitioners. The chapter of this book where background information can be found is noted after all questions, and answers for questions 1–20 can be found on page 300.

General Questions

1. Interest and principal deductions provide tax shelter in real estate investment. (*See Chapter* 3)

   (A) True

   (B) False

2. Low risk investments usually yield high returns. (*See Chapter* 2)

   (A) True

   (B) False

3. A real estate investment must show a negative cash flow to offer any tax benefits. *(See Chapter 3)*

   (A) True

   (B) False

4. An amortizing mortgage reduces principal and interest equally over the stated term. *(See Chapter 3)*

   (A) True

   (B) False

5. What is the appropriate monthly rent if the capitalized value (at 10%) of a beauty shop is $144,000? *(See Chapter 5)*

   (A) $1,200

   (B) $1,440

   (C) $1,000

   (D) $14,400

6. One desirable factor in real estate investments seems to be: *(See Chapter 2)*

   (A) Low risk

   (B) Effect of inflation on equity

   (C) Low management

   (D) Rapid liquidity

   (E) Stable interest rates

7. Cost recovery enables the sharp real estate investor to: *(See Chapter 3)*

   (A) Reduce tax liability

   (B) Increase before-tax cash flow

   (C) Improve the quality of the investment

   (D) Avoid all tax liability

   (E) Pyramid his real estate portfolio

8. The proper method to use to arrive at a capitalization rate is: *(See Chapter 5)*

   (A) Capitalization rate divided by income

   (B) Income divided by value

(C) Value divided by income

(D) Capitalization rate divided by value

9. Savings accounts and insurance policies are noted for their ability to appreciate in value. (*See Chapter 1*)

(A) True

(B) False

10. Basis changes during the holding period of a shopping center. (*See Chapter 3*)

(A) True

(B) False

11. In investment property, value is never connected to income. (*See Chapter 5*)

(A) True

(B) False

12. Real estate is easily compared to other investment vehicles. (*See Chapter 1*)

(A) True

(B) False

13. Capital gain treatment is provided for property that: (*See Chapter 3*)

(A) Does not produce income

(B) Is owned by a dealer

(C) Has been held longer than 6 months

(D) Has a 60% exemption clause

14. Rules of thumb are easy to figure but dangerous to use. (*See Chapter 5*)

(A) True

(B) False

15. The maximum amount of leverage available should always be used. (*See Chapter 1*)

(A) True

(B) False

Cost Recovery and Basis Determination Questions

(See Chapter 3 for background information to answer these questions.)

16. A property selling for $95,000 was acquired 12 years ago for $55,000. The cost recovery was based on a 18-year economic life using the straight line method with an improvement allocation of 75 percent. If the present sales costs are $6500, what is the long-term capital gain?

17. A parcel of land was purchased for $14,000 and a building was completed on it on January 1, 1982 at a cost of $100,000. The building was cost recovered on a 18-year economic life using the accelerated cost recovery system. What is the cost recovery amount available for 1982?

Taxable Income and Tax Liability Questions

(See Chapter 3 for background material to answer these questions.)

18. A property having a loan of $120,000 with payments of $1537 per month, including interest at 15 percent, has a net operating income of $15,500. If the annual cost recovery is $6000, what is the taxable income? What are the tax savings for a married, filing jointly taxpayer earning $45,000 taxable income in 1982?

19. What is the tax liability in 1982 on a sale which has a long-term capital gain of $43,000 for a married couple filing jointly who have a taxable income of $45,000 after deductions and exemptions exclusive of the sale?

20. A commercial property was "depreciated" over the past three years using the accelerated cost recovery system. Total cost recovery taken was $31,000; straight line would have been $20,000. New sales price is $200,000 and the adjusted basis at time of sale is $115,000. What is the amount of recapture? What amount of the gain will receive capital gain treatment?

Internal Rate of Return Questions

(See Chapter 5 for discussion material to answer these questions.)

21. What does IRR really measure, tell you and/or show you?

22. What components of the property are included in IRR?

23. Is IRR a return *on capital*, a return *of capital* or a *combination*?

24. Does IRR assume that all intermediate cash flows are reinvested? If so, at what rate of return?

25. How is IRR useful to a commercial–investment broker?

26. What are the advantages and disadvantages of IRR compared to other investment measures?

Financial Management Rate of Return Questions

(*See Chapter 5 for background material to answer these questions.*)

27. What does FMRR really measure, tell you and/or show you?

28. Does FMRR replace IRR, and if so, how? If not, why?

29. Why are additional assumptions added to IRR in order to calculate FMRR?

30. When are IRR and/or FMRR applicable to investor decision making?

31. What are some of the limitations of the FMRR model in investment decision making?

32. How does one determine applicable safe rates and reinvestment rates?

33. How is FMRR useful to a commercial–investment broker?

Financing Variables Questions

(*See Chapter 5 for background material to answer these questions.*)

34. Is it advisable always to borrow as much as possible?

35. How can a decision be made on financing choices?

36. What is negative leverage?

37. Why is participation financing so prevalent today?

38. Why is anticipated holding period of an investment an important consideration in analyzing financing alternatives?

Case Study I
(Fugate Part 1)

You are contacted by Mr. Wilfred Fugate who owns a 17-unit, two-and-one-half story apartment building with one-bedroom units, located at 8317 Easy Street. Each unit has carpeting in the living and dining rooms, a kitchen, a bedroom and a bath. There are three basement units which rent for $95, $100 and $105 respectively. All other rents are $225. Tenants pay their own utilities. Mr. Fugate is willing to sell this property for $295,000 and lists it with you at that price. He assures you that the rents should be raised.

Mr. Fugate gives you the following income and expense information for the previous year.

Rental Income Collected:		$39,460
Expenses:		
Taxes	$ 1,535	
Total loan payment	12,684	
Cost Recovery	3,672	
Insurance (3 yr. prem.)	2,650	
Water	1,150	
Gas	475	
Electricity	250	
Advertising	125	
Occupancy permits	85	
Plumbing	335	
Painting	380	
Maintenance	1,350	
Carpet repair	750	
Automobile	250	
Miscellaneous	75	
Total Expenses		$25,766

Mr. Fugate has a mortgage with an unpaid balance of $102,596 payable at $1057 per month including the interest rate of 11 percent per annum. He purchased the property five years ago for $135,000. He has taken $3672 cost recovery per year. The adjusted basis at the beginning of the sixth year is $116,640.

Lenders in the area have a willingness to lend up to 75 percent of the sales price at an interest rate of 15.5 percent with monthly payments for a 25-year term. Under these loan terms, the monthly payment would be $2919.68 with a 10-year balloon.

As the listing broker, how would you represent the *rate of return* on this property to a potential investor?

Case Study I
(Fugate Part 2)

Having listed Mr. Fugate's property, you list the following variables:

- Rents are currently at market level
- Expenses are 40 percent of scheduled rents (includes vacancy factor)
- Fugate will "carry" a second mortgage of $30,000 maximum at 10 percent interest only for five years
- Loan available of $185,000 at local lender at 15.5 percent for 25 years with a 10-year balloon.
- Assume purchase on January 1
- Land/improvement allocation 20 percent/80 percent
- Accelerated cost recovery system taken
- Assume a 40 percent tax bracket for new owner

Assume the purchaser would buy the property as stated above at a purchase price of $250,000.

- Prepare first year before-tax cash flow
- Prepare first year after-tax cash flow
- What is the capitalization rate?
- What is the cash on cash return?
- What is the cash on cash after-tax return?

Case Study II
Alternative Choices

A purchaser has several choices of financing the investment two-unit you have located for him. The facts are as follows:

- Price: $60,000
- Owner has $13,500 cash to invest
- Net Operating Income after all operating expenses is $6000

- Purchaser wants *maximum before-tax cash return* on his down payment
- Assume $1000 closing costs
- No closing costs on owner financing
- Land/Building ratio: 15/85
- Accelerated Cost Recovery System
- Assume purchase is January 1
- 30 percent tax bracket

Loans Available:

1. $48,000 at 15.5 percent for 25 years with a 10-year balloon

2. $48,000 at 15 percent for 20 years with a 10-year balloon

3. $51,500 at 12 percent for 25 years with a 10-year balloon (owner financing, but price increases to $65,000)

What would you advise your client to do? Be consistent with your client's goals. Be sure that you consider the rest of the investment "picture."

Determine the following returns:

	Before-Tax Cash on Cash Return %	After-Tax Cash on Cash Return %
Loan 1	__________	__________
Loan 2	__________	__________
Loan 3	__________	__________

Discussion: How would a sale in the future affect the client's decision?

Case Study III
Sale Proceeds Analysis

After running an ad on your new apartment house listing, you receive a call from a gentleman who says he has the necessary $72,000 down payment for the purchase. After a few questions, you learn your new client has sold, but not closed, a smaller apartment house deal. He says the sale price is $200,000 and he only owes $110,500. You would like to put your new listing under contract but are skeptical since it's a "hot" listing. Further investigation reveals the following facts about your "buyer's" position in the other property that is being sold:

1 He has *no* funds other than what he will receive from the sale.

2 XXX Realty has a listing and is charging a 7 percent fee of the $200,000 sale price. Additional sale costs total $2000.

3 Purchased property for $140,000 January 1, 1980.

a. Installed a new roof on building—cost: $7385

b. Took total of accelerated cost recovery of $8396, instead of straight line of $6300

4 a. Sale to take place December 31, 1982.

b. Absolutely must have money out of sale to pay taxes on sale.

c. 1982 *taxable* income is $28,000 (married, filing jointly).

d. Mortgage balance is $110,500.

Question: Will your new buyer have the $72,000 coming from the sale in order to warrant you "writing it up" and taking your new listing off the market? In other words: What will the *proceeds after taxes* be on the sale?

Case Study IV

One of your best clients has called you to ask your advice on an opportunity he is evaluating. He has found a net leased restaurant on a commercially zoned piece of land and it looks pretty interesting. He presents the following facts:

- A single-purpose building leased to John's Coffee Shop, Inc.
- Building is 17 years old
- Three years left on the lease

Purchase Price	$120,000	
Mortgage available	96,000	15%, 25 years amortization, 3-year balloon
Down Payment	$ 24,000	
3 Points	2,880	
Total cash needed	$ 26,880	

- Rent is $1500 per month net (tenant pays everything)
- Cost recovery information: land/building 35/65 allocation; 18-year straight line cost recovery
- Client in 50 percent tax bracket
- Taxable income in year of sale (third year) is already in 50 percent bracket
- Sale price (at end of third year) is $120,000 (value in land, not building)
- Costs of sale: 7 percent
- Assume purchase January 1 and sale December 31
- What is gross rent multiplier?
- What is cash on cash?
- What is cash on cash after tax?
- What is cap rate?
- What is the IRR?

Discussion: Should the client consider a 12 percent certificate of deposit as an alternative investment?

Case Study V

Assume your client is considering the purchase of the following property. Your assignment is to project a five-year holding period and sale based on the following information:

- 36-unit apartment complex
- Brick structure
- Six years old
- No extra building land
- All two-bedroom units with appliances and electric heat
- Tenants pay all internal utilities
- Owner provides water, sewer, rubbish and lawn service

Owner financing is available at 10 percent, with 25-year amortization, seven-year balloon. Your investigation of the market indicates a 3 percent vacancy factor and 30 percent expenses (of effective gross income). Rents increase $10 per month per apartment per year (second year rents will be $225, third year, $235).

Owner's expenses last year:		Rents are currently all $215 per month, month/month tenancy,
Taxes	$ 6,300	
Insurance	1,200	
Lawn and snow	1,000	
Rubbish	1,200	
Sewer and water	6,060	
Total expenses	$ 15,760	

Price	$680,000	
Cash Down	100,000	Includes all closing costs
Mortgage	$580,000	

Assumptions for your projection:

- Assessed valuation 85/15 (building/land allocation)
- 18-year table, use maximum cost recovery available
- 50 percent tax bracket, married, filing jointly
- In Year 5, client's taxable income is $110,000.
- Sale price at end of the fifth year is NOI of Year 5 "capped" at 10 percent.
- Assume 8 percent sales costs.
- Reinvestment rate opportunity—6 percent (after tax).
- Work toward after-tax cash flows:

EOY 1 $ ____________

EOY 2 $ ____________

EOY 3 $ ____________

EOY 4 $ ____________

EOY 5 $ ____________ + ____________

- What is gross rent multiplier?
- What is cap rate?
- What is cash on cash?
- What is cash on cash after tax?

- What is IRR?
- What is total wealth accumulated?

Discussion: Should client consider a 12 percent certificate of deposit as an alternative investment?

Case Study VI

The air conditioning equipment in an office building owned by an investor/client of yours has just been struck by lightning and damaged beyond repair. An air conditioning consultant has recommended either a gas or an electric replacement system. The consultant estimates that an energy-saving gas system will cost $50,000 to install, as compared with an electric system for only $35,000. He forecasts that energy costs for the operation of the gas system would be $3600 the first year with 15 percent increases each year thereafter. Electricity would cost $6000 the first year but would increase only 12 percent per year. Further, the consultant estimates higher per-year maintenance costs for the electric system of $1000 versus only $500 per year for the gas system.

The following table provides a summary of the cost estimates described above. In addition to this information, the consultant estimates a ten-year life for either system, and neither system will have a salvage value at the end of the tenth year.

Year	Cost of Alternative Systems Gas System	 Electric System	Cash Difference
0	$50,000	$35,000	(15000)
1	4,100	7,000	2900
2	4,640	7,720	3080
3	5,261	8,526	3265
4	5,975	9,430	3455
5	6,796	10,441	3645
6	7,741	11,574	3833
7	8,827	12,843	4016
8	10,076	14,264	4188
9	11,512	15,856	4334
10	13,164	17,638	4474

Your client is not sure exactly what his yield opportunities are with respect to investing his funds over the next ten years. He is sure only that he must provide air conditioning to the tenants in his office property. He seeks your advice on this "investment" decision. (Disregard tax considerations in this problem.)

1 At what discount rate (opportunity cost of capital) would your client be indifferent between the two systems?

2 Which system would you recommend and why?

Case Study VII

After years of persistence, you *finally* list a "popular" developer's shopping center. The information is as follows on your listing agreement:

Price	$3,000,000
NOI	291,000
Terms	None—all cash!
Current mortgage	$1,764,226 at 8%; payment is $15,436.32 per month.
	Lender will agree to contract sale (wraparound) without changing rate.

You receive an offer of $2,900,000 with $700,000 cash down ($100,000 of which is your fee) if the owner will carry the financing at an 11 percent rate amortized over 20 years to be ballooned at the end of the fifth year.

The seller says, "No deal! I want to buy some long-term certificates of deposit (five years) which pay 13 percent. I'll worry about the taxes, so no after-tax business. Just give me my cash so I can receive 13 percent cash on cash and not just a crummy 11 percent as you are suggesting. I have my tax situation well under control with plenty of write-offs."

It appears your seller's goal is to have $1,000,000 in cash earning 13 percent so as to throw off $130,000 annually.

Consider: You need the fee to buy a new Mercedes. Can you demonstrate to the client:

- What the first year cash will be (as he sees it)
- The actual yield on financing arrangement
- What about accumulation of wealth?
- Compare sale to $130,000 from C.D.

Build a presentation to convince the seller to accept the offer and still meet his goals. Remember that Mercedes!

Answer Key (Questions 1-20)

1. B
2. B
3. B
4. B
5. A
6. B
7. A
8. B
9. B
10. A
11. B
12. B
13. C
14. A
15. B
16. $61,000
17. $9000
18. $3303
19. $7638
20. $11,000, $74,000

BIBLIOGRAPHY

This Bibliography has been compiled especially for this book by the Library of the NATIONAL ASSOCIATION OF REALTORS® (with special assistance by Mabel Wong, Librarian).

Alberts, William W. and Castanias, Richard P., II *The Impact of Changes in Tax Depreciation Rates on Holding Periods for Real Estate Investments*. NATIONAL TAX JOURNAL, Mar. 1982, p. 43–54.

American Society of Real Estate Counselors *Office buildings: development, marketing & leasing*. Chicago, Ill., 1981. 22p.

Andersen (Arthur) & Co. *Federal taxes affecting real estate*. 5th ed. New York, Matthew Bender, 1981. Looseleaf.

Anderson, Jerry D. *A Year's Supply of Commercial Sales Meetings: perk up your meetings (and the sales force) by putting some of these ideas into practice*. REAL ESTATE TODAY, Sept.–Oct. 1981, p. 17–22.

Anderson, Jerry D. *Racquetball Court Club Site Selection*. REAL ESTATE PERSPECTIVES, Vol. 1, No.1, 1979, p. 8–9.

Arnold, Alvin L. REAL ESTATE INVESTOR'S DESKBOOK. Boston, Mass., Warren, Gorham & Lamont, 1982. v.p.

Aronsohn, Alan J. B. *Real Estate Investment and the Economic Recovery Tax Act of 1981*. JOURNAL OF REAL ESTATE TAXATION, Spring 1981, p. 291–300.

Blumberg, Daniel A. *Guides for Determining Return on Investment*. REAL ESTATE REVIEW, Spring 1981, p. 21–23.

Boykin, James H. and Hardwick, James G. *Installment Sales, What Do All These Terms Mean?* REAL ESTATE TODAY, Sept.–Oct. 1981, p. 52–53.

Braitman, Howard L. and Stine, John B., II *New Tax Legislation Benefits Real Estate Investors*. COMMERCIAL INVESTMENT JOURNAL, Winter 1982, p. 4–6.

Brueggeman, William B. and others *Choosing the Optimal Depreciation*

Method Under 1981 Tax Legislation. REAL ESTATE REVIEW, Winter 1982, p. 32–37.

Building Owners and Managers Association International *Downtown and Suburban Office Building Experience Exchange Report*. Washington, D.C. Issued annually.

Curcio, Richard J. and others *Alternatives for Assessing Risk in Real Estate Investment*. REAL ESTATE ISSUES, Fall–Winter 1981, p. 25–32.

Curry, Paul L. *Maximizing Cash Flow May Not Maximize Value*. REAL ESTATE REVIEW, Summer 1981, p. 9–10.

Depreciation Planning—Selection of Optimum Depreciation Method. REAL ESTATE TAX IDEAS, Jan. 1982, p. 4–5.

Dolben, Joseph A. *The New Investment Equation for Real Estate*. REAL ESTATE REVIEW, Spring 1982, p. 18–25.

Edwards, Charles E. and Gaines, James P. *Alternative Accelerated Depreciation Methods and Rates of Return on Real Estate Investments*. REAL ESTATE APPRAISER AND ANALYST, Fall 1981, p. 13–22.

Fisher, Jeffrey D. and Sanders, Anthony B. *Capitalization Rates and Market Information*. APPRAISAL JOURNAL, Apr. 1981, p. 186–198.

Friedman, Edward A. *The Installment Sales Act of 1980; an attractive financing method simplified*. REAL ESTATE TODAY, Sept.–Oct. 1981, p. 51–52.

Friedman, Jack P. and Ordway, Nicholas INCOME PROPERTY APPRAISAL AND ANALYSIS. Reston, Va., Reston, 1981. 490p.

From Baseball Cards to Blue Chips; investors look for new strategies to cope with disinflation. TIME, May 24, 1982, p. 64–65.

Gale, Bradley T. and Branch, Ben *Cash Flow Analysis: More Important than Ever*. HARVARD BUSINESS REVIEW, July–Aug. 1981, p. 131–136.

Gale, Jack L. COMMERCIAL INVESTMENT BROKERAGE: AN INTRODUCTION WITH CASE STUDIES. REALTORS NATIONAL MARKETING INSTITUTE®. Chicago, Ill., 1979. 269p.

Girard, Weldon HOW TO MAKE BIG MONEY SELLING COMMERCIAL and INDUSTRIAL PROPERTY. Englewood Cliffs, N. J., Prentice-Hall, 1977. 252p.

Girard, Weldon PROFIT OPPORTUNITIES IN COMMERCIAL AND INDUSTRIAL REAL ESTATE. Englewood Cliffs, N. J., Prentice-Hall, 1979. 273p.

Golden, Edward John *Office Building Case Study*. COMMERCIAL INVESTMENT JOURNAL, Spring 1982, p. 9–17.

Greenberg, Herbert M. and Greenberg, Jeanne *The Psychology of the Successful Commercial Broker*. REAL ESTATE TODAY, Jan. 1981, p. 21–25.

Hall, Craig CRAIG HALL'S BOOK OF REAL ESTATE INVESTING. New York, Holt, Rinehart and Winston, 1982. 313p.

Hazlinger, Paul M. *Marketing Commercial Property*. REAL ESTATE TODAY, June 1981, p. 12–14.

Higgins, J. Warren *Depreciation of Real Estate and the Economic Recovery Tax Act of 1981*. REAL ESTATE APPRAISER AND ANALYST, Spring 1982, p. 71–75.

Institute of Real Estate Management *Income/Expense Analysis: Apartments*. Chicago, Ill. Issued annually in midyear.

Institute of Real Estate Management *Income/Expense Analysis: Suburban Office Buildings*. Chicago, Ill. Issued annually in midyear.

Institute of Real Estate Management *Expense Analysis: Condominiums, Cooperatives, & Planned Unit Developments*. Chicago, Ill.

Ising, Thomas J. *A Program for Cash Flow Analysis*. COMMERCIAL INVESTMENT JOURNAL, Winter 1982, p. 30–34.

Jaffe, Austin J. and Sirmans, C. F. *Improving Real Estate Investment Analysis*. APPRAISAL JOURNAL, Jan. 1981, p. 85–94.

Jaffe, Austin J. and Sirmans, C. F. REAL ESTATE INVESTMENT DECISION MAKING. Englewood Cliffs, N. J., Prentice-Hall, 1982. 556p.

Katz, Richard J. *To Sell or Not to Sell?* COMMERCIAL INVESTMENT JOURNAL, Winter 1982, p. 19–21.

Kendall, Donald R., Jr. *Give Me Shelter: the Economic Tax Act of 1981*. REAL ESTATE REVIEW, Winter 1982, p. 23–30.

Kesten, Theodore *Realty Investments Outperform Securities*. REAL ESTATE FORUM, Feb. 1981, p. 354.

Kilbourn, Edmond M. *Buying and Selling Investment Real Estate by Objective*. REAL ESTATE TODAY, Jan. 1982, p. 50–56.

Kinnard, William N., Jr. and others INDUSTRIAL REAL ESTATE. 3d ed. Washington, D. C., Society of Industrial REALTORS®, 1979. 750p.

Kurn, Neal and Nutter, Jack O., II *The Installment Sales Revision Act of 1980: in the name of simplification has a measure of complexity been added?* JOURNAL OF REAL ESTATE TAXATION, Spring 1981, p. 195–212.

Levin, Perry Keith *Medical Condominiums: ownership versus leasing cost analysis*. COMMERCIAL INVESTMENT JOURNAL, Spring 1982, p. 6–8.

Lyon, Victor L. *The ABC's of Investment Analysis*. REAL ESTATE TODAY, Feb. 1980, p. 20–25.

Lyon, Victor L. and others *Practical Aspects of Cash Flow Analysis*. COMMERCIAL INVESTMENT JOURNAL, Winter 1982, p. 22–29.

McCoy, Bowen H. *Adventures in Marketing Large Real Estate Portfolios*. REAL ESTATE ISSUES, Spring–Summer 1981, p. 13–18.

McPherson, Douglas K. *Understanding Debt Coverage Ratios; how many of us are familiar with this standard tool of commercial real estate lenders?* REAL ESTATE TODAY, APR. 1981, P. 22–23.

Messner, Stephen D. and others ANALYZING REAL ESTATE OPPORTUNITIES: MARKET AND FEASIBILITY STUDIES. REALTORS NATIONAL MARKETING INSTITUTE®. Chicago, Ill., 1977, 319p.

Messner, Stephen D. and others MARKETING INVESTMENT REAL ESTATE: FINANCE,TAXATION, TECHNIQUES. 2d ed. REALTORS NATIONAL MARKETING INSTITUTE®. Chicago, Ill., 1982. 546p.

Metzger, Jerry SHOWCASING COMMERCIAL PROPERTY. REALTORS NATIONAL MARKETING INSTITUTE®. Chicago, Ill., 1980. 102p.

Montgomery, J. Thomas and Roper, Charles F. *Equity Yields and the Reinvestment Issue*. APPRAISAL JOURNAL, Oct. 1981, p. 509–521.

Osinski, Dora *Do In-Depth Review before Purchasing Income Producing Property*. SHOPPING CENTER WORLD, June 1982, p. 18–19.

Penny, Peter E. *Modern Investment Theory and Real Estate Analysis*. APPRAISAL JOURNAL, Jan. 1982, p. 79–99.

Perry, Tony *Getting Into Commercial Investment*. REAL ESTATE TODAY, Jan. 1981, p. 26–29.

Petersen, Sandy and Ross, Knobby *Working with Attorneys in Commercial and Investment Real Estate*. REAL ESTATE TODAY, Nov.–Dec. 1981, p. 32–35.

Real Estate Education Company SUCCESSFUL INDUSTRIAL REAL ESTATE BROKERAGE. 2d ed. Chicago, Ill., 1980. v.p.

Real Estate Education Company SUCCESSFUL SALES AND LEASING OF OFFICE PROPERTY. Chicago, Ill., 1980. v.p.

Real Estate Education Company SUCCESSFUL SALES AND LEASING OF RETAIL PROPERTY. Chicago, Ill., 1980. v.p.

Sear, Michael *Choosing a Recovery Method for Non-residential Property: an internal rate of return approach*. REAL ESTATE SECURITIES JOURNAL, Fall 1981, p. 38–49.

Sirmans, C. F. and Page, Daniel E. *The Real Estate Investment Decision —a wealth maximization approach*. REAL ESTATE ISSUES, Fall–Winter 1981, p. 33–37.

Steele, Robert A. and White, John R. *Beware the Abusers of IRR Methodology*. APPRAISAL JOURNAL, Apr. 1982, p. 204–211.

Study: Real Estate Has Outperformed Stocks and Bonds. NATIONAL REAL ESTATE INVESTOR, June 1982, p. 18, 20.

Tanzer, Milt COMMERCIAL REAL ESTATE DESK BOOK. Englewood Cliffs, N. J., Institute for Business Planning, 1981, 414p.

Toscano, James R. *New Trends in Office and Warehouse Leasing*. COMMERCIAL INVESTMENT JOURNAL, Spring 1982, p. 37–38.

Urban Land Institute DOLLARS AND CENTS OF SHOPPING CENTERS. Washington, D. C., 1981. 325p.

Valachi, Donald J. *On Interpreting the Internal Rate of Return on a Real Estate Investment*. REAL ESTATE APPRAISER AND ANALYST, First Quarter, 1981, p. 35–42.

Wauterlek, John *Strategies for a Changing Industrial Market*. REAL ESTATE TODAY, June–July 1982, p. 38–39.

Webb, James R. and Sirmans, C. F. *Yields for Selected Types of Real Property vs. the Money and Capital Markets*. APPRAISAL JOURNAL, Apr. 1982, p. 228–242.

When to Accelerate Depreciation for Commercial Real Estate. MORTGAGE AND REAL ESTATE EXECUTIVES REPORT, Feb. 15, 1982, p. 2–3.

Whitmire, Robert L. and Reynolds, Kerry M. *Selecting the Optimum Depreciation Method for Real Estate Under the New ACR System*. JOURNAL OF TAXATION, Dec. 1981, p. 360–363.

Wiedemer, John P. REAL ESTATE INVESTMENT. 2d ed. Reston, Va. Reston, 1982. 304p.

Wyndelts, Robert W. and Davis, Joseph M. REAL ESTATE INVESTMENT DECISIONS: TAXATION AFTER ERTA; ITC, ACRS, AND SIGNIFICANT PROVISIONS AFFECTING INVESTMENTS. Chicago, Ill., Real Estate Education Co., 1982. v.p.

Young, Michael S. *Comparative Investment Performance: common stocks versus real estate—a proposal on methodology*. REAL ESTATE ISSUES, Summer 1977, p. 30–46. Critique and reply appeared in Summer 1978, p. 84–87.

INDEX